women loving

A journey toward becoming
an independent woman

women loving

A journey toward becoming

an independent woman

by

ruth falk

with drawings by the author

a random house • bookworks book

First printing, August 1975:   25,000 copies in paperback

Typeset by Vera Allen Composition Service, Castro Valley, California
    (Special thanks to Dorothy, Karin and Michele)
Printed and bound under the supervision of Dean Ragland, Random House

This book is co-published by Random House Inc.
                             201 East 50th Street
                             New York, N.Y. 10022

                      and   The Bookworks
                             2043 Francisco Street
                             Berkeley, California 94709

Distributed in the United States by Random House, and simultaneously
published in Canada by Random House of Canada Limited, Toronto.

Booksellers please order from Random House.

From *The Diary of Anais Nin, Volume I,* edited by Gunther Stuhlmann,
copyright © 1966 by Harcourt Brace Jovanovich, Inc. and reprinted with
their permission.

Our Bodies, Ourselves, The Boston Women's Health Book Collective,
Simon and Schuster.

From *Pentimento* by Lillian Hellman, by permission of Little, Brown
and Co.

Library of Congress Cataloging in Publication Data
Falk, Ruth, 1942-
    Women loving.

    "A Random House/Bookworks book."
    1. Lesbianism—United States—Addresses, essays, lectures.
2. Women—Sexual behavior—Addresses, essays, lectures.
3. Self-actualization (Psychology)—Addresses, essays, lectures. I. Title.
HQ76.3.U5F34   301.41'2   74-23230
ISBN 0-394-49562-4
ISBN 0-394-73052-6 pbk.

Manufactured in the United States of America

To My Mother

Miriam Peskin Falk

Preface

This book is a woman's experience of love. It speaks the truth of what loving is about: that it is a process, not a state that is attained; that it is frought with uncertainty; that it is bitter as well as sweet; that it involves anger, confusion, and pain as well as joy and peace; that it demands awareness, courage, strength, and hard work; that, like the river continuously seeking its path, the flow is grating and tumultuous as well as smooth.

Love is not easy, with its obstacles, wounds, and bewilderment. There are few maps. So often in fear and pain we seek the way in our heads; but love is a thing of the heart. It is feeling and emotion that must flow. The source of the flow is the self, and the process begins with being in *touch* — with ourselves, with our feelings, with now. This knowing and trusting of ourselves is the first step to touching and loving others. Few of us have learned to trust ourselves and our hearts. We have been taught the story of how love should proceed: that a woman grows up to marry a man and lives happily ever after. The tale ends with the horseback ride into the sunset, and we learn nothing of how the lovers survive on the trail. As we are discovering the myths of love to be incomplete or invalid, we are seeking ways to reconnect with our own experience, our own paths, with each other.

Women Loving speaks Ruth's honest experience of what *is*, not what ought to be. Her investigation of love is refreshingly untouched by the "research seive" that too often screens out subjectivity, spontaneity, emotion. She goes to the source of the subject itself: the lives, hearts, and minds of women experiencing it. Her personal story, the interviews with other women, and her conceptualization of some of the issues involved are open, honest and searching. At many passages of the book I have sighed and said to myself "Yes. That's how I've felt. I'm not alone." Such open sharing of feelings is a support and confirmation that is important in learning to know and trust ourselves. This book has been, to me, a validation, a comfort, a light along the path.

The *form* of the book is unique, and as important as its content. It is the journey, the process, the movement itself, captured in words. It is the sharing of human experience *as it occurs:* with acute sensitivity and awareness; with raw feeling; with intuition, memory, imagery, poetry; with perspective, intellect, integration, and understanding. The form dispels the myth that life and growth proceed linearly and smoothly, from start to finish, without circling and sliding back, re-traveling old territory, seeing again, anew. The form flows as life does: sometimes smoothly, sometimes in spurts, often moving forward, sometimes roving back; at times with pure emotion, often with sharp analysis; questioning and unsure, then strong, focused, clear.

I see this book as an honest, deep revealing of a woman's soul. Such exposure is an act of courage by a woman of great integrity, a sharing that is a gift of love.

April 1975
California

Diane Fabric,
Poet and Therapist

Brief Contents

Contents

Introduction

This is a book about feelings.

One of the essential contributions that women are making in this society is to place human feelings — the world of the subjective, of internal reality — in its rightful place. In this culture which practically worships objective reality and outside authority, women are more in touch with their feelings.

Women Loving is the story of my life in two cities: Washington, D.C. and Berkeley, California. This book is a journey through my feelings and the processes I experienced as I explored my love feelings for other women and for myself.

The book covers the period between 1964 when I graduated from college and began my life in Washington, D.C. through 1974 after I had already lived one year and a half in California. I focus on the last year of my life in D.C. which I call *Isolation in D.C.* and my first year living in California which I call *California*. These two years were for me most difficult; an intense period of isolation and search for community, and then a period of rebirth. It was also the period of growth and resolution in my feelings for women and for myself.

The book is a journey taking some of its form from the diary. People and events are often described in terms of my feelings for them rather than in their outward characteristics.

Through my journey a lot of people flow in and out of my life then disappear from the reader's view.

For me exploring my feelings was an important way to see the world. I began to realize clearly that "rational thinking" is just one way and feelings and other perceptions are another — just as valid if not more so. Through my feelings I was able to see my life more whole.

I wrote of events in my life by topic rather than by their linear occurrence. Often the material is non-linear and follows my feelings and my own growth processes. I would describe events and feelings by trying to feel exactly the way I felt when the events occurred and then express myself in my writings. I tried to portray those feelings and thoughts which at the time in the past I felt were most important and on which I focused. Sometimes I wished that I had not experienced some of these feelings but I did.

Often when I went back to work on a piece (a description of a feeling or event) I would remember other things that happened at that time or the event would seem to have new meaning to me. And I realized that events and feelings meant different things to me at different times.

At the time I decided to write the book five years ago I made the decision that if I could ever work out my love feelings for women I would write a book about the process. I hoped that other women who would share some of my experiences might live their lives less painfully than I had around this issue. In actuality through the process of writing this book I resolved many of my feelings.

Form and Politics

Integrating the
personal and the political
I felt the form of the book in itself was political
I felt showing love feelings
between women was political

My original fantasy was that the book would be romantic and show women sharing and exploring feelings with each other. I once described the book to a friend as a long Salem Ad — two women on horse back galloping across tall grass.

I was angered by the rhetoric which told women to love each other. My book wasn't going to be one of rhetoric. I felt the form of the book in its new thought structures and definitions was going to be my political statement.

However, as I explored deeper into my feelings, peeling layer after layer, I realized further political implications of my feelings. And I saw that my life as a whole did not reflect a romantic story of two women galloping across tall grass.

The relationships I describe in this book reflect a political context. I found that sharing feelings was not sufficient, and that the political meanings of my feelings had to be explored.

I wanted to teach myself to rely on my own experiences and feelings to be my own authority for my life rather than looking to experts and authority models outside myself. I wanted to get a balance in my life of the internal and the external. If I have over-emphasized the internal it is because the external is so over-emphasized in society. We have been indoctrinated always to look outside ourselves.

I had made the decision that if I went deep into my feelings I would touch upon something in everyone.

"Growing up is after all only the understanding that one's unique and incredible experience is what everyone shares." Doris Lessing — *The Golden Notebook* p. XIII.

But sometimes at the point of describing my feelings I would forget that other people experience those very same thoughts and relationships to the world. And then in another split second I realize the power of my writing is to describe things that everyone feels, does and sees which are often not verbalized or written down.

Stretching the Boundaries of What Is

We need to expand the boundaries of who we are. Women's images, feelings and experiences have for the most part been described by men. We need to define and explore our feelings and discover who we are for ourselves. Each of us gives each other courage. Reading the writings of other women, talking with other women and sharing and observing their lives gives me courage to keep on growing and exploring who I am.

I want to emphasize the need to learn from experience; to judge things from the internal; not by outside authorities. To look at someone else's feelings and experiences and take from

them what you want. And then to look at your own experiences and feelings and say: Now what do I feel? How do I
want to live my life?

Anais Nin talks about the form diary or the journal taking
its form from life. Life is not like a novel. There is no finality
in our lives. Friendships wane and then are renewed. The
only finality is death.

Most of the people in my book are part of my on-going life
and we continue to flow in and out of each others lives, as my
journey, of course, continues.

The process of the journey has been both inward and outward. What I have attempted to capture is some of the whole-
ness of human experiences. I found myself using a variety of
modes of expression to describe my journey and have expressed a gamut of feelings. The different writing modes I
have used reflect the different modes of being human — poetry, feeling images, essays, oral language, dialogue, analysis
and rational thought, letters, journal entries, photographs,
and political statements.

Ruth

May 1975

In this book some of the names and places have been
changed because of the sensitivity of some of the issues
covered.

The dialogue of the various people in the book should not
be taken to represent their verbatim statements.

WOMEN LOVING

We don't share each other on a

deeper level.

That's why there is so much loneliness.

Anais Nin at a speech in San Francisco, 1974

THE NARRATIVE

THE death announcement of my mother in the Hartford Times listed a son David from Evanston, Illinois, and a daughter Ruth from Berkeley, California. That was very important to me symbolically — that I lived in Berkeley. Yes, a daughter Ruth Falk who resides in Berkeley. At the time I didn't know how important this symbolism was. I was to learn only later its full meaning which I am sure is still unfolding before me, even today.

I was drowning in Washington, D.C. after eight years — I was suffering a slow insidious death there. Berkeley represented a symbolic place to change my life. I was at a dead end in Washington. My last year there I spent up in the air as much as possible. I traveled and traveled. I hated every moment I was there, every moment waiting to leave. Not really wanting to leave but knowing full well that I had to or I would die. I was so painfully alone.

By all standards of success I had made it in Washington — all that is, except the definite standard which includes having a man to eventually get married to and having a family. I had a good paying job in the government, and considerable freedom to travel and to develop my own programs. I had many good friends, and in the years after living with four women, Anne, Meg, Kate and Pam, at Aberfoyle Street, a lovely apartment in Georgetown. But as I turned thirty I could see no place where I belonged.

My old roommates from Aberfoyle who had become my family and were my closest friends had married and moved to the suburbs. And my last year in Washington, Mandy my best single woman friend and Larry my lover of one year had both left the Washington area. Their absences intensified my feelings of aloneness.

I felt alone because I felt I had feelings no one else had, or feelings which I felt were wrong. I had very strong love feelings for women and though I had love feelings for men, my feelings for women confused me. I did not want to love women because of the strong societal taboo. I wanted to be with a man — I wanted to be married and live out the American Dream. Or at least I had the fantasy about wanting to be married. I felt a man could help me get a great big house filled with art. But mostly I was also afraid to be married. I was very much concerned about my independence and found in my experiences with men that often it was difficult to maintain an equal relationship. My affairs with men often were so tumultuous that the emotions I experienced during and after a liaison wore me down.

I found my relationships with women much more supportive and equitable. And the emotions I experienced often more nurturing and soothing. But yet I still held the hope that if I could just find the right man — Mr. Right — my life would be happy and settled and exciting.

I also wanted to be non-monogamous. There were always many people in my life that I loved. And as my feelings for women intensified I felt such a structure would allow for a woman lover in my life, at the same time that I had a man.

I felt particularly isolated because my closest women friends did not seem to share my feelings for women and because often they were critical of my aggressive behavior at work. They did not share my intense feelings about working nor did they experience conflicts like I found myself in at work with men who were often threatened by me.

In our society one of the ways femaleness is defined is by one's sexual and emotional involvement with men and by one's passivity. I had very strong feelings towards my women friends and I was very aggressive — characteristics ascribed to maleness. Because these feelings and behaviors were not "feminine," I sometimes felt ugly and isolated. Liking women affected my sense of self as a woman and my sense of my own femininity. As I explored my feelings and became closer to women I gained a greater sense of both my femininity and my sense of myself as a woman.

I had always looked for a book which showed women sharing love feelings. I wanted to know that the feelings I experienced existed in the universe and that these feelings were okay.

I remember driving home from work along the Potomac in my little red VW, talking to Sara Hawthorne, a friend that I had met my last year working at NIMH. She was visiting me from Minneapolis. I told her that I planned to write a book one day. I wanted her to ask me what the book was about. I wasn't sure that I had the nerve to tell her, but she did ask. After hemming and hawing a bit I finally got it out that the book would be about love — my love feelings for women. It was one of those excruciating hot summer days in Washington. When we reached my apartment, I showed Sara the latest issue of *Off Our Backs* that I had discovered — the issue on women loving women. There was a poem in it about smelling the lap or skirt of a woman; it particularly struck me as loving and warm.

I remember in D.C. feeling in such a quandry about my strong feelings for my close women friends that I was sometimes unable to be affectionate with them, nor were they able to be affectionate with me.

Anne Touching Eric
Wanting Anne to Touch Me Like That

As I type this, my mind wandered to the time in D.C. when I went out with Anne and Eric on a blind date. Anne was one of my roommates from Aberfoyle. She and Eric had decided that they were going to get married; I remember watching them as we all sat together in an Army bar. They were at a table one down from me and my blind date, facing each other next to the wall. I was sitting against the wall too, my blind date not in view of the camera as I watched Anne grab Eric's arm across the table as she talked to him. It was a wonderful touch. I had always loved it when on those rare occasions she had touched me. Her touching him like that made me weak and I wished she would touch me like that too.

The Contrast

Now in Berkeley I feel very close to my friends and hug and kiss and hold arms. There is none of that painful intensity about being able to touch or to make love. The closeness is inside or inside/outside. Our affection is more an integral part of our relationship and touching is just one way of expressing it.

The contrast is almost inexplicable between the closeness I feel as I write of Anne in D.C. and think about my relationship to Jean, a friend now in California. My feelings keep flipping back to last night and the closeness that I experienced with her. It goes before me like a movie.

Finishing dinner after a long talk and going out into the night air, a little spaced, wanting to touch her but feeling awkward and then going into a bookstore two blocks away. I must have floated there because on the return to my car I didn't remember at all that we had covered two blocks. Spacing out

7

in the bright lights and browsing through the books, not really seeing what was before my eyes, I just wanted to get away from her for a moment and think.

And then we left sort of bumping the way we do when we walk shoulder to shoulder and then I thought that I would put my arm in hers as I had done or we had both done that night two weeks before when we walked the long way up to her house in the cool evening of Berkeley, me seeing for the first time another part of the city, seeing the houses and the trees interlaced through the hills and the sky and stars. I can't remember how I felt — I think some of the sensations and excitement of being in Europe.

That night in Berkeley it was a warm closeness and excitement as we mounted the hills and I loved feeling her arm in mine or when we took turns my arm in hers as we carried the huge box containing a birthday cake. I guess one could describe our meandering as a kind of merriment — sort of thrilled or pleased with our silliness, of buying a birthday cake and deciding that it was for someone's 40th birthday who was neither near forty nor nearing the date of his birth. We had stopped after purchasing the cake for a delightful dessert — creme anglais in a French restaurant that I have been wanting to go to for two years in Berkeley which added to the delight of our merriment as it seemed such a perfect extravagance after a Chinese dinner and purchasing the cake at the Co-op. A perfect simple dessert with cafe expresso or capucino served in the perfect silver dessert holders the perfect amount and the atmosphere of a good French restaurant . . . merriment yes, that is what I would call it.

8

As we left the restaurant I stole a cherry that was in one of three fruit baskets that was next to our table and heard her giggling behind me as we hurried down the stairs. I think that she thought it was an apple, but laughed even more as she finished the remaining bit of my first cherry of the season.

I never know how to explain an experience with another person. Is it presumptuous of me to describe how they were feeling or that they experienced the same feeling as me? But then the delight of the experience was in part what was happening between us, so I would have to know to be able to describe the event. Hadn't Jessica said that I had captured the thing that had happened between us?

I just squinched up my face as I thought of giving this page to my friend to read — being embarrased or going out of my mind until she finished reading it.

But this night I didn't put my arm in hers because she put her arm around me first. She put her arm around me and then I grabbed her with my arm and we each placed our arms around each other, putting one arm above the other — her putting her arm above mine and me putting my arm above hers around her back (as Larry and I had done walking in Georgetown years ago. Only he would get mad because I put my arm up above his — he thought the man's arm should be higher) until we were adjusted walking arms around each other. Giggling I kissed her on the back of her neck on her hair as we walked together.

I was as surprised that she put her arm around me as I was with the ease and quickness of my response. I kissed her and told her I loved her easily and so quickly that I surprised myself. As we walked in our capsule I felt proud and very powerful. She said "Did you see that woman and the way she looked at us?" I hadn't noticed or looked at how anyone looked. I was so caught up with being with her that I didn't really focus on anyone else.

As I retype this now I recall recently speaking with one of my old roommates from Aberfoyle about this book. Meg asked me did I mean all women should make love? I explained that I wasn't urging that all women should make love to each other, but that I did not want the fear of sexuality to keep them apart. My old roommate was uncomfortable. Her husband chimed in: "Of course, Meg, you have felt what Ruth is talking about. That's the reason that you and your best friend Kristine aren't physically affectionate with each other, because you are threatened by your sexuality."

NIMH

In D.C. I worked for the National Institute of Mental Health for seven years. I was a very dedicated social change person there. Some people considered me with my long bushy hair running down the halls advocating the rights of youth to be the house radical. I was very aggressive and angry. A sense of moral indignation underlined my work. I was conducting a one woman battle against the establishment and its rigid qualifications as to who it would support doing work in the mental health field and what type of work for whom.

10

Looking back at my work in D.C. I realized that I moved between two groups, belonging really to neither: the radical hippie youth and the government bureaucrats. In one of my staff roles as a funder or program developer, I saw myself as giving energy and support to good people who I felt were involved with important community-based projects.

I was supporting groups that were encouraging people to be their own authorities in health matters and that were attempting to fill some of the gaps and serve some of the people whose needs were not met by traditional mental health and medical health services. I was supporting free clinics, hotlines, women's centers, runaway houses, and demanding that they not only be supported by NIMH but that the people running these programs be given recognition and power on the NIMH funding review committees which were 95 percent composed of Ph.D./M.D.s and mostly white males. Those without traditional credentials who had learned by experience were sneered at and their abilities paternalistically questioned. There was the youth initiated halfway house that almost was not funded because it was questionable whether it was deemed right for adolescents to have responsibilities for their own lives. I think the statement in the critique went something like this: "There is also the central issue of whether the Federal Government should support a project which professes to say that the adolescents themselves can do a better job than professionals or their parents in terms of guiding them toward their future."

That terrible social change thrust that I banged my head on for seven years at NIMH and for two or three before that in the poverty program wore me out. Of course I always carried with me my moral indignation, and a tenacity for honesty. I have learned since that there is something indignant about moral indignation.

I have always felt that nothing is going to change in our society unless there can be a new approach to the doing of social change. If one plays the same old game of politics, the end results will be not unlike the ways that one is opposing. What kept me going and the thing that marked my style was a belief in honesty and that that was the only way things were going to be changed. I also had a tenacity to relentlessly hammer home what I believed so that many times in those years I got what I wanted. Some clinics were funded and an experimental peer review committee staffed by youth from women's centers, free clinics and communes was initiated, but in the end I lost part of my soul. I did not protect myself or take care of myself. I came to California a beaten woman. There was not much elasticity left in my being. I felt very brittle and hollow. I couldn't take much more stress, I needed to take a year off and get myself back on my feet.

Here I am giving you my direct NIMH spiel instead of presenting what I intended — a loving book about women loving and women's feelings. It is not easy to learn new ways.

ISOLATION IN D.C.

I HAD flown to Boston for a Task Force on College Mental Health. I remember being devastatingly lonely the day I flew there for the meeting. It was one of those Sundays that seemed to weigh very heavy on me and underlined my loneliness in D.C. Suddenly I was eating dinner with Phil Burns and my sense of loneliness seemed to vanish. Phil was one of the graduate students I had worked with for years. We talked for hours. I felt that I had made a real connection with a human being. Phil asked me why I was not married. I suddenly blurted out "Because I think I may like women." This was for me one of the first steps in openly dealing with who I was. It felt good — and I felt strong. I felt entirely isolated in Washington, and to tell someone what I was dealing with felt really good. I told Phil how I had been thinking of propositioning a friend of mine who I suspected loved women. I was sick of wondering for so many years who I was.

15

I talked to Phil about how lonely I had been feeling since Mandy, my closest woman friend, and Larry, my lover of one year, had gone away in the Fall. Larry had gone off to law school and Mandy had gone to work in Africa. The last year that Larry and Mandy were in D.C. I spent all my time with both of them. Mandy and I had been friends for three years and had taken most of our major vacations together. Though both relationships had their problems, they were very enjoyable. Mandy and Larry met my needs for intimacy.

Phil and I also talked about alternative life styles — the pros and cons of being non-monogamous. He told me about his wife and how she had similar feelings, feeling ugly when she was very aggressive, and also having love feelings for women. He told me how Pat had slept with a woman in her house in the same double bed for many years, but they never touched. That is the same way that Mandy and I had been many times in Europe on our first ski trips. What was marvelous is that this is the first type of conversation on the subject that I ever had with anyone who knew about or had shared similar experiences. Granted it was with a man, but my knowing Pat made the experience feel very close and poignant.

Of course, there were conversations with my male therapist, Dr. Tilbet. But this information always seemed so second-hand. He'd say, "Yes, I have had some patients — women in therapy — who have loved women." He was very proud when one of these women sent him a post card: "Once she even sent me a post card."

As I retype this now, I see how I shared my love feelings for women more easily with men. I wonder how often women communicate about feelings for each other through men. I had told Larry of my strong love feelings for Mandy before I told her.

Often as I have written this book I have experienced what Carl Jung called synchronicity.* Either a person would call on the phone at the exact moment I was writing about her (I was so pleased when I saw this same synchronicity in the writings of Vita in *Portrait of a Marriage*); or the very day I would write up or rework a piece about an event in my life I would discover it was the very day a year or two after the event originally had occurred.

As I was working on this piece about Pat and Phil — they arrived from Boston for a visit in Berkeley. On this occasion, for the first time, Pat and I spoke directly to each other about our love feelings for women and about feeling ugly when we were aggressive women, and lastly how scared we were of each other! We were so busy being professional women, "competing" we hadn't shared our soft sides.

I, of course, was not the only woman dealing with these feelings in Washington but often I felt I was. My close friends did not seem to share my feelings. My isolation was extreme. It was not until my last few months at NIMH that I discovered other women who shared some of these feelings. It is quite true that often we have been afraid to share our feelings with each other. We had been taught to feel alone.

---

* Synchronicity is the phenomenon so called when two interrelated events appear to occur simultaneously without obvious causal connections; acknowledging the influence of unseen compatible forces in our lives which help us make contact with deeper parts of reality.

On a recent visit to the East Coast I spoke to Mandy and some other old Washington friends about my loneliness in D.C. I went back East to see if perhaps had I stated my wants more clearly or if I had seen what was really there I could have had more strokes from other women and would not have had to leave. When I visited Mandy and Pam in Boston, Mandy said to me, "You should have left. You didn't fit in here." And Pam spoke up, "But she had to leave the people she loved." And then Mandy explained how she had to leave her old lover, David, because it just didn't work. She exclaimed "I've always said, You just hold on to old friends. I'm amazed how you keep in touch with everybody." But when she said to me, "I'm sorry Ruth, I just do not find women as exciting and as important as men," I was angry.

Crisp Lettuce

BIG BULLSHIT LADY YOU ARE A LIAR. WHAT DO YOU MEAN THAT YOU ARE "Sorry that you have just not found women as exciting and important as men?" Do you recall what good times we had in Canada, how close we were and how we teased the men, how proud we seemed at dinner laughing and teasing them about who we were? I remember the crisp lettuce . . . and our talking about how much fun we were having that we didn't want to be with those others, and how much, I think we said this, that we were our own best company and entertainment. I know I had those feelings and to some extent we both verbalized them. And then when the bus hit Washington you told me to move, to untangle my feet from yours. "Our feet" were your words and then all seemed cold between us as we hit the NIMH parking lot at midnight in the fog and searched for your car, and then for the exit to the main street. "I'm sorry Ruth, I just do not find women as exciting as men." I was surprised and angry, hadn't Mandy and I traveled all over Europe together, gone on countless ski trips, had incredible good times? Then why did I fly over to Europe and Africa twice within two months if she felt that men were more important than women? This I felt through my heldback tears that wanted to turn into rage. All I could think of was the pain of her not coming to California to join me well up within me, and her voice saying I should have left D.C.

RAGE
UNEXPRESSED
TEARS

Though I knew that on some level it was unusual to like women as much as men, find them as exciting, why else the confession in Versailles of loving women? I am still shocked about the reverse — still feel incomprehensible when women that I know and love verbalize to me that they find men just much more exciting, more important.

Mandy in Africa

After a wonderful trip with Mandy in Africa, feeling very close and warm with her, enjoying our present closeness and feeling so good that I was envious of the times when we didn't know each other and would have enjoyed being with her or knowing her, such as when she was editor of her high school year book. Sitting at the out-door cafe in Lisbon when she told me her story of high school, I had that wonderful feeling that one gets sometimes when one is so pleasureably fond of someone that one is just content being with her — that it didn't matter what I did — being with her made me so happy. I would have been content sitting there listening to her for hours. I felt those same emotions with Anne at Chalker Beach wishing I had known her in college and in high school.

I had told Mandy those last few days in Lisbon that I was or that I thought that I was going to be bisexual. Mandy and I had travelled all over Africa together for two weeks. We slept in double beds numerous times, and I had been incredibly turned on to her. We stopped in Lisbon as a vacation from Africa for her, and as my last stop in Europe before I went back to the States.

It was a balmy spring-like evening in Lisbon. We had gone to dinner and had come back to our room after strolling through the narrow winding streets of Portugal. We were lying on our respective twin beds, and I felt the chasm between us as I lay with my hands at my side trying to get up the nerve to tell her who I was and what I had been struggling with all year in therapy. Suddenly I sat up in bed and said, "I think I am going to be bisexual." Then there was a long silence.

Mandy asked me if I ever wanted to be physically close with her and I said "Yes." I asked her if she found this threatening, and she said no, because she knew who she was and how she felt and that just wasn't her.

It felt good to be able to share with Mandy that "I was going to be bisexual," but we didn't talk much further. Although during our conversation earlier at the cafe Mandy had talked about the social conditioning we have been taught and said "We have been taught not to touch."

What I didn't tell her is that I wanted to make love to her — and that Dr. Tilbet had been urging me all year to try. I had come to Africa very focused on expressing my feelings to Mandy and on telling her that I loved her and wanted to make love to her. I was always trying to get up the nerve to hold her in bed, but never actually felt able to carry that through.

One night we had gone out dancing with two men who had given us a ride to Marrakech from the Atlas mountains. We got very high and turned on from the dancing and flirting particularly with one of the men. I remember being turned on as I watched Mandy make out with this man on the dance floor. When we got back to the room, Mandy and I lay together in bed. I was turned on, I would imagine she must have been too as a long number had been going on with the men trying to talk her into spending the night with one of them. We went to sleep talking and lying close to each other, talking about the struggle that had been going on with the men. Mandy said she wouldn't have gone to sleep with the man after he had put me down, and I remember wanting to put my arms around her and hold and kiss her. Instead I think that I masturbated quietly and fell asleep. We both had on our long underwear. And I thought it would have been wonderful to hold her, and probably would not have been as threatening had we been undressed.

It has been my habit to tell someone something personal that I wanted to tell them just before we are about to part, so scary for me is the telling. I had traveled with Mandy for three weeks. I had planned to tell her about myself all through the trip but only when we had two days left did I even say anything. In Lisbon on the last night we were together, a night or two after I had told her that I was going to be bisexual, we had gone out to dinner late, and on the way home Mandy suddenly got very nauseous and had to go straight to bed. So I never got to test me mettle. But if she hadn't gotten sick I probably would have gotten up some other excuse and not carried through. We had become so close after having spent almost a month together that I thought it would have been easier then to hold or make love to her.

After the intense closeness that I had experienced with Mandy in Africa, underlined by my sharing with her who I was and what I had been struggling with in therapy, I returned to the States. Landing in Washington was like landing in an abyss of hell. It was all too familiar. I knew every street, every sound, every smell. I did not want to be there anymore. I was very much alone. I was again alone.

My thirtieth birthday had come. I would read Simone de Beauvoir for hours and clutched her to my side. I wanted to be as close to a woman as possible, and the way I could do this was to read books about women. I told my friend, Gloria, that the reason I was reading these books was to be close to women, and she said that yes, she knew.

I remember when I left Africa, I kissed Mandy goodbye. I mention this because I think that it was the first time that I had ever kissed her. On the plane leaving Lisbon I felt the emotion, for the first time in my life, of what it must be like to have a daughter. I had never particularly felt motherly toward Mandy, but I loved her very much. I thought how can Mandy's mother bear this? Her daughter is 5,000 miles from home on some unknown foreign continent — Africa — a non-reality. Europe is like being some place familiar, like California, but Africa seemed to lie at the end of the world. If something happened to Mandy or to me one could not easily pick up the phone and call. I was aware that it was partly a mind/feeling thing that the unknown strange environment took her further from me.

Landing in the fog in Tunis, had underlined this feeling when I began my trip, as I searched for Mandy in the airport and then took the long journey in the taxi, looking for her in the fog, unable to speak anything to the taxi cab driver except the word Carthage. Mandy wasn't at the airport to meet me as I had been held over in the Orley airport waiting for a connection to Tunis. I remember the Orley airport was crowded with people, because flights were fogged in. At last I had been able to find someone to help me find the flight for Tunis by constantly going up to the schedule board and talking to a stewardess who finally told me to go to gate 5 right away. Suddenly I found myself dashing with two other people to an Air France plane that was going to take off in five minutes. We were racing along in an airport service car, searching between planes for the mysterious Air France plane that was about to take off for Africa, while all the other planes remained on the ground. We finally found it and climbed in, and then, of course, waited for what seemed to be another hour before we took off. I don't remember the exact time. I fell instantly asleep, and vaguely remember one of the stewards coming by my seat on the empty airplane and covering me with a blanket. We flew through the night over a never-ending land which was sprinkled with lights below. The feeling I experienced was I didn't know where I was or where I was going, only that at the end hopefully I would meet up with my friend.

Imagine raising a daughter like Mandy, loving her and then having her go to Africa, wanting her to do what she wanted and to be happy yet missing her. Loving her and watching her go so far away from you that letters crossed paths in the night and time sequences became inconsequential. I knew this was how I felt; I wondered how her mother felt.

For two weeks after I returned from Africa I pretended that time just stood still. I wrote Mandy . . .

January 23, 1972
"Dear Mandy,

I imagined when I left Portugal that when I got home I would have a letter off to you quite soon, but instead I did my best to keep busy over the last two weeks so I could pretend that I wasn't quite back. Plus, the feeling of seeing you was so good that I wanted to keep an illusion of permanence by pre-

24

tending that time and events were standing still. I am now voraciously reading *The Prime of Life* by Simone de Beauvoir. The book is just delightful. I have again told or promised myself that I will try to write one day. At the age of thirty I really should not talk about one day but get to work right away.

I am really feeling good. Today is the first day since I got back that I have had to myself. I read most of the day. I will be sending you a copy of the book as soon as I get organized. I think that you will enjoy it quite thoroughly. I, of course, am completely identifying with Simone, especially in her pains of searching for her identity. She has a fantastic sense of humor! She states that at one time she had so many complaints against herself that it was hard for her to determine which was most important.

Her descriptions of her strivings to maintain her independence are quite delightful, and you will have no trouble identifying with her as she pours over maps to chart her adventures so that she covers every bit of the area surrounding Marseille, wanting to make sure to avoid all group activities. Marseille is the town she went to the first time she went away from Sartre. Also I was quite excited to read that one of the most elating experiences she had in Marseille was her trip to Cassis. This is the resort that I told you about that I went to by myself, where mostly the French go for their holiday. It was for me also one of the most exhilarating trips that I took in France. If you get to Marseille you must go.

I told Gloria about the book and the fact that Alice had given it to me because she felt that I should read about being an independent woman. Apparently Sartre and Simone, in addition to their working out a relationship based on essential love with contingent love affairs, practice bisexuality. (I haven't gotten to that part of the book yet.) Gloria thought that Alice was quite perceptive in giving me that book and told me that the book made perfect sense to her. She also told me that she did not differentiate between a relationship with a woman and a relationship with a man. She said that she felt it was absurd to draw the line at which any affectionate relationship would stop. She told me all this over dinner at the Japan Inn, where we went for my 30th birthday celebration. I was interested to hear this, though a bit overwhelmed, if not uncomfortable.

Gloria also told me of a relationship she had with a man who I have always admired. She said that he was the one man she would consider marrying if she ever wanted to marry. This was all very interesting to me as I would like to understand how or what led her to decide she didn't want to marry, though the latter affair leaves me suspicious that she doesn't entirely mean what she says or more fairly that what she says is more complicated than how her statements appear. She says that she just decides what is right for her and recognizes that society has made some absurd rules or has a weird perception of what is right and wrong. It is sure hard to know yourself that well and be that confident. Gloria is 35 or 38, so possibly age helps to some degree, but she kiddingly told me as I asked her "if she knew all this at 30" that she realized it *ages ago.*

The Beauvoir statement that "it was hard for her to determine which of the many complaints she had against herself was most important" underlines how I felt during this period. I was so confused and so unhappy. I identified with Simone completely. I searched. Did I need a different structure, such as hers, an essential love and then other loves, so that I would be non-monogamous? Would this structure help me be happy? How was I going to be independent and not lonely? Alice saw me as an independent person at this time. Thinking back I am quite sure that I neither saw myself as an independent person nor as a strong woman. I remember that this idea came up in therapy and I couldn't believe it when Dr. Tilbet insisted that I was a strong woman.

Gloria

I had sought out Gloria earlier in the year, seeing her as a strong person without a man, wondering how she survived. She was the first woman I had ever met who said with such conviction that she didn't want to marry that I wanted to know how she survived without a lover, a Man. How could she be so independent and so self-contained and do her work well? I remember her telling me that she had someone that she loved very much. At the time she said that I didn't think she meant a woman. It was not until we spent more time together that I slowly began to realize that the person Gloria loved was a woman. And even longer to realize that the woman she lived with was her lover! So resistant was I to know.

I propositioned Gloria in the month between my first visit to Mandy in Africa and my second visit in Europe. My 30th birthday had come — the pressure was mounting. I had to know who I was and what I wanted. Did I indeed want to make love to a woman? Gloria was the only woman I knew who loved women.

I remember driving downtown and then going into Gloria's office and closing the door. I had on my suede jumper and yellow turtleneck. My hair was long and bushy — I felt very attractive. We chatted for a while and then I asked her if she were non-monogamous? She looked up and smiled. She said she was very flattered. I wasn't in love with her but I admired her and told her exactly why I wanted to sleep with her. Later she told me a story about two people getting involved who agreed that the minute their relationship got painful, they would end it quickly. Then she looked me in the eye and said, "I'm talking about you and me."

Image: breasts coming out of walls.

Memory flashes after I first kissed Gloria. I went to a party and I saw breasts coming out of the walls — on a Picasso of a woman. It was as if everything were three-dimensional, a 3-D movie. Breasts seemed to be coming out of everywhere — and seemed to be standing out prominently, even on the chests of my women friends.

My first time making love with Gloria was very traumatic. We had kissed once or twice at my house and that itself was scarey enough to me.

Gloria did not want any quickies. She wanted us to be able to spend a whole day together if indeed we were going to make love. To be able to talk and to make love, to go for long walks, that was what she thought love-making was all about.

One day in the middle of the week we set out for the Eastern shore. I had been quite reluctant to spend a whole day together and to give up a full days work. We left late in the evening to avoid rush hour traffic, and took four hours to do a two hour trip. We stopped for a leisurely sea food dinner. That was pleasant enough — but then the rest of our journey was unbelievable. For some reason Gloria had to use her lover's car, which had been having mechanical difficulties. So we had to drive more slowly than usual — below the speed limit. Twice we were stopped in small towns, by police with flashing red lights because the rear tail light of the car was out. Gloria felt that her lover had unconsciously hexed our trip and I felt that the eyes of society were on us. I was so nervous and tired from our journey I couldn't wait to get to bed and go to sleep. When we arrived in "our wonderful cabin by the sea" I could barely keep my head up. I was exhausted. I hopped into bed and cuddled up to go to sleep. Gloria still wanted to make love and I was petrified. She got real passionate instantly and I instantly got diarrhea — the worst case of the runs I've ever had. I spent an hour in the john that night and half the next morning on the toilet. We never did make love. Gloria had to get up early and search the small shore towns for an open drug store. It was winter and the middle of the week and very few were open.

An hour or two later she returned with Kaopectate. I took some and fell back to sleep. When we were ready to leave after our designated day for love making — without making love — the trip home was very silent. I remember rubbing her neck and asking her if she were tired of driving and she said no and we kept very quiet.

This happened with Gloria shortly before I went off to Europe to see Mandy again. I did not dare tell Mandy about it. I only mentioned to her in my letters my conversations in Boston with Phil about having more than one lover — being non-monogamous — and reitereated about feeling ugly when I was aggressive and a driven woman.

February 16, 1972
"Dear Mandy,

Well, as you can guess, what is bugging me is that I am so damn fucking lonely! I feel better already. It is just that I am absolutely driving myself mad with my work, since that is literally all I do. I am simply a driven woman. I just want to achieve, achieve, and that just doesn't seem to make me happy. I am so driven that I get exhausted from all that I do. I am so driven to achieve and I think that when I reach the top, whatever that is, that I ain't going to be any happier.

I wish that I was working more because I enjoyed it and not because I am driven. I just keep on thinking about work and getting someplace else because I don't like it here because I ain't got no one to take care of and no one to take care of me. It was interesting that my friend Phil said he saw me both as an independent person and as someone that likes to be mothered or taken care of. He said that he had always wanted to do for me or take care of me but that he had stayed away because he didn't know how to deal with these feelings. He felt a man could be mothering too. Phil is married to a lovely girl, Pat, and his main complaint so he told me is that he is also in love with another woman and wouldn't mind living with both of them. In a way I got angry that he told me this. I was feeling so lonely, I was jealous.

I was surprised that he recognized in me a wanting to be taken care of. I didn't know that anyone knew that about me.

I am sorry that work has gotten rough for you . . . what a pain. I hope it is fun to fantasize about working with me and Alan Smith in California. I think it would be really fun if we got a grant. Traveled around the world a little after you did your alpine skiing and then did a project together in California. I hope that I am not just dreaming. I am afraid that I will become buried in my work because of my success drive. That's probably ridiculous but I have BEEN SO BUSY I haven't had time to do my bills.

Well I should stop rattling on. This will crack you up. I hope that I haven't sounded too bad, but things are really going so well in my work that it is just so frustrating I am not happy — a typical Falkism. Phil told me that his wife Pat is also a driven woman and sometimes has trouble feeling feminine when she is very successful and aggressive. I am not even unique.

See you soon."

My California Scheme

Alan Smith was a man I met through work, a young psychiatrist. He sought me out because he was excited about the work I was doing at NIMH trying to support youth-initiated programs — free clinics, runaway houses, women's centers, and other youth alternative services. He himself was working with a free clinic in D.C. and was most interested in innovations in mental health created by youth programs. He asked me if I would be interested in working with him, and perhaps developing some sort of mental health program in California along the lines of these youth projects. This intrigued me. He kept saying "You're wasting your time and life here at NIMH. Why don't you try something new? They aren't going to develop new programs here."

I knew about innovations in alternative youth services well. Alan knew about large human services, and had been working to break down the stronghold of psychiatrists in the mental health field. We came together as friends and colleagues excited about our mutual interests and shared frustrations.

Our common belief, that professionalism and the academic mode of learning emphasized by the mental health institutions had nothing to do with actual effectiveness in life or for that matter with the delivery of human services, brought us together. We believed that real life experiences and common sense — the quality of the person delivering the service — were much more important.

Our plans changed often but from the start we hoped to develop a non-hierarchial organization — a collective with our friends. We were excited about the collective work being done in alternative service projects and by their attempts to integrate work, life and play.

I was sick of my life being so isolated. I looked forward to working with people who I didn't have to fight, who would push me further in my ideas yet be supportive of me. People who were my friends.

I was of course doubly excited about our plan, as it presented to me a way that Mandy and I could work and be together again. Mandy had become more and more discontent with her job in Africa. I was hopeful I could get her to come back and work in the states and I soon went to see her in Europe to vacation and talk about this.

In some ways during this time period I felt my life was standing still. Yet, I had met Alan and also had become closer to Gloria.

Mandy in Europe

Two months after my trip to Africa Mandy had quit her job in Tunis, and moved to France. I returned to Europe to see her and to talk about our possible plans to work and be together in California. I had written her several letters about Alan Smith. In her letters Mandy indicated a strong interest in working with us. I flew to Luxemborg and then took the train to Florence to meet her and Pam, my old Aberfoyle roommate, who was now living with an Italian lover she had met there on an earlier trip. After vacationing with Pam for a few days, Mandy and I left Florence to travel together in France.

But my anger and resentment reached a strong crescendo in our tense car as we drove from Mandy's new location, Grenoble, to Paris for our short vacation. Paris was the place I was going to get my train to Luxembourg, where I would catch a homeward-bound discount Icelandic flight to the States.

My Body Flying Out the Window

The silence and tensions were stifling between us the night before our long journey to Paris. I remember the emotions I felt. My resentment, my anger and my feelings all locked hidden inside — my supreme isolation.

We stopped the first night of our journey after traveling many hours through the dark spring night across the French countryside in a hotel next to a train station. As we climbed to the third floor we talked little, turned off the only light in the room and got ready for bed. Only I didn't sleep — I stared out the window. I was so angry and I only recognize it as anger now. I wanted us to talk, to make contact, but I didn't know how and was sick of always being or feeling that I was the one who brought things up when something was wrong. I wanted Mandy to take more responsibility for our relationship. The only problem was that our friendship was not recognized as a relationship; it was something pushed under the table, not really acknowledged.

I had always looked for hints that Mandy saw it as a relationship. I remember the time that she said that my relationship and the pain I was having with Larry made her feel like she was watching someone she loved have an operation. Yes, she indirectly admitted that she loved me.

I just never felt comfortable bringing up that we related this way or that way because I felt uncomfortable making the

34

presumption that we had a legitimate relationship that could be recognized.

My emotion was of my body going out the open window, and part of me holding tight to the bed so that my body did not fly out the window open to the French night with its train noises, and whistle noises from the station below filling the cool evening.

My emotion was my body going out the hotel window. I thought of Mandy alone with my body travelling back to Paris for shipment to the states for burial. I wrote this in 1973, and only now as I type it over do I see that such a fantasy, Mandy alone suffering from the shock of my sudden death, having to make all the arrangements in a foreign country, was indeed a sign of how angry I was at her. It was two years later that I recognized anger in myself and accepted it as legitimate. On a recent visit to D.C. I expressed my anger the best way I could. But it is hard sometimes to express new ways with old friends (something ironically Mandy often told me in her letters from Europe).

My emotion was my body going out the hotel window. I thought of Mandy alone. We had barely talked. Mandy wanted to know what was going on. Did I indeed want to work with her in California? I was resentful for coming all that way to see her and talk to her about coming to California with me. It always seemed that I was coming to her. I had the distinct feeling as I helped Mandy move into her next location in Europe to study French after having quit her job that I wasn't at all living my own life, that as I put it to her I wasn't affirming myself. I traveled with her to find a place to study, and then we traveled to Strasbourg, and then later on to Paris. Tension got outstanding. And in all that anger I remember feeling better as we slept close to each other — we were close in the night. But my anger resumed during the day. Mandy asked what was wrong. What was wrong was that I wasn't being a full person and asserting what I wanted. I loved Mandy. I wanted to make love to her. I wanted her to be with me in California. I wanted her not to put so much of the relationship on me, because I couldn't come to meet her at a certain time. Or put the intercontinental phone calls on me. I wanted her to understand that I had my work and my life and couldn't just leave any time to connect with her. That she had decided to travel more so the responsibility of the calls were also hers. I wasn't able to tell her this until later, after I moved to California. I wanted Mandy to see our relationship as ours. I wanted her to put as much energy into the relationship as I did.

I still felt that Mandy had left me when she left Washington, and it broke my heart. I felt like a fool following her around all the time. I wanted to be with her; why did she not come to be with me? The whole issue around my going to Europe or her coming to visit in D.C., which I never brought up, irked me. I was paying all that money to get to Europe. I was having trouble feeling good about myself coming all that way, not daring to ask her to come to the States to see me, or telling her how I felt that she left me.

I feared her anger if I expressed my wants. My father would always get angry when I expressed my wants. We talked later in Versailles about how it made more sense for me to come to Europe, more fun to travel there (after I had already come, had already built up resentment, felt a fool and made the decision on my own). I hadn't said what I wanted.

Meeting at Versailles

After Mandy and I had travelled for two weeks through the French countryside, upon arriving in Paris — overwhelmed by the intensity and noise of the city — we went off to the Palace of Versailles. While the Palace itself was closed, we wandered through its formal gardens, allowing their peaceful calm to envelop and soothe us. Because our trip had been so difficult, we needed to talk about the bad feelings and tensions between us. When we were in the midst of our long conversation I thought of other peace talks and summit meetings that had gone on there before, and that this talk was indeed a very important one for me and perhaps for her (that I don't know).

I asked Mandy if she had ever fantasized or considered sleeping with a woman. Mandy said yes. I was quite surprised and said wow! I did not fantasize sleeping with a woman until Dr. Tilbet suggested I see what it would be like to fantasize about Anne. I had very strong feelings for her and I didn't understand the pain and tension we had been going through. It was the same period I was also working out my relationship with "a nice Jewish boy." I had never allowed myself to even consider sleeping with a woman, let alone fantasizing such love making — for fear that if I did I would automatically be a lesbian.

37

I asked Mandy if liking women was ever an issue for her. She responded that she pushes those things back and decides not to deal with them. She said that she saw me as willing to confront myself, and that she saw me as courageous, but also she felt I gave myself a very hard time.

It wasn't that I was courageous. This was what I felt. I must explore these feelings — this is what I was. To do so was the only way I could go forward. It was the only way I could be. I did not push myself to love women, the feelings were always there welling up in me. I did however when I finally made love to a woman push myself. My feelings were exactly those expressed by young people in Keniston's book *The Young Radicals:* "This is what I was made to do."*

Mandy brought up the time that I had rappelled off a cliff on a camping trip. One of the fellows on the trip was teaching us rappelling, a technique used in rock climbing to descend a very steep face of rock. I was scared and petrified by heights, but I wanted to do it so I pushed myself to try. All the men were learning the technique and I have always gotten a charge out of doing something as well as men, performing in a way that they wouldn't expect for a "girl." Mandy said that she just wouldn't push herself like that. Then I recalled how painful going down the cliff was for me. When I finally touched ground I remembered being so relieved my legs just shook. They were weak. But at the same time I remember feeling angry. I was so terrified, so nervous going down the cliff, that my excitement turned into pain. Though I had accomplished the feat, it was not at all enjoyable.

I remember thinking that I had crossed that line, that

* Harcourt, Brace, Jovanovich.

nebulous vague, indefineable line between excitement and terror, different for each of us. I had crossed the line where excitement became painful and turned to terror.

I explained to Mandy that my love for women was not an issue that I took as a challenge as I had when I pushed myself to rappel off the cliff. My pressure was internal. I loved the women who were my close friends. I wanted to touch and hug them, have them touch and hug me, and be close with them.

Touching and Hugs

That for me was always a terrible, painful problem. Was it right for me to love my friends so? My women friends have always been as important to me as my male friends, and sometimes more important. I have always loved them with the same intensity as my male lovers. It is very painful to love someone that intensely and not be able to touch them.

I feared hugging my close women friends because I was afraid they would get upset and reject me. I feared they would not only get angry at me if I touched them, they would be angry over an ugly thing — over something very taboo that people don't do but might whisper about me. I had asked Anne not to tell anyone when I told her I loved her. I felt very vulnerable, and that I would be exposed. But I loved her and wanted to touch her. We are still very close friends but we have never talked about those times when I told her about these feelings.

I told Mandy how I once spent two weeks with Anne at the seashore and remembered loving her so, loving to be physically near her and close to her. Loving her so much that my body literally ached to touch. It was like my whole body ached and pushed out energy to touch, but did not make contact. I don't think I would have had such intense feelings if there had been room for hugs and affection in our relationship. When you can touch, touching is not as important a focus. It is a total part of your relationship.

When I finally told Mandy how my women friends have always been as important to me as my male friends and sometimes more important, I remember that I felt relieved by my confession as if I had committed some crime, done or felt something wrong. Imagine feeling that it is wrong that your women friends were as important as your male friends and sometimes more important!

THAT IS ENOUGH TO GET YOU ANGRY. I had at some level bought into how society taught things ought to be, for why else the relief when I told this to Mandy?

Working these two days I feel like I am in Europe again in Strasbourg. The morning air is cool and I can hear the cars when I go to the front of the house through the open window buzzing by to work. I just flashed to my room in Strasbourg my junior year in college, the last day that I was there studying for the last final and then walking through the city chewing cherries before the exam.

Last Night in Paris

Then on the last night in Paris, neither of us sleeping close to the other, having trouble finding the hotel. Mandy said "It seems that neither of us wants to get back." We had been having such an incredible dinner. I was turned on the whole time that we were talking. I am sure that Mandy must have felt something. Why else the long drive through the city going in circles? Maybe it is just hard to say goodbye, but I really suspect that it was much more than that. Maybe Mandy just isn't as aware of her feelings. She said that she pushed them back, or maybe she didn't have them.

When we finally got back to the hotel we fell immediately to sleep. We slept completely apart though during that two week trip we often bumped or leaned against each other or touched as we slept.

The next morning we got up and rushed to the train station. I almost missed my train to Luxembourg, where I would catch my flight back to the States.

Running from Gloria in Tucson

After I got involved with Gloria the issues of loving women changed for me somewhat. Gloria commented on what she called my problems of intimacy: "If you would just stand still for one second so one of us could touch you, get close to you...." She was referring to my always being on the go. After returning from Europe I stayed home for one day and then flew to Tucson for a conference which Gloria was attending. I was so turned on from being with Mandy for two weeks in France that I literally flew into Gloria's arms.

Seeing Gloria was one of the reasons for going to Tucson but I also wanted to attend the conference on New Lifestyles.

At that time in my life, God only knows why, I still had the hope that if I went to an academic conference I would learn something about how to run my own life. The conference was a bomb but my time with Gloria was just wonderful. One of the best experiences in love-making that I have ever had. I was so perfectly relaxed. The first time we tried to make love I had focused so much on the sex rather than on the closeness. I was so tense and scared. Maybe that is to be expected one's first time. I am becoming aware that there is an incredible amount of pleasure that I miss in my life that is available out there in the universe if only I can let myself take part. But then the next morning I got up early and flew back to Washington. I left what was after all incredible love-making. It was so intense, so slow and light that it almost reached the place of pain.

Pleasure

"I had wasted what should have been the nicest day of my life. I dislike then and I dislike now those who spoil pleasure or luck when it comes not so much because they refuse it — they are a different breed — but because they cannot see it or abandon it for blind nonsense."

Pentimento, Lillian Hellman.

I went back to Washington because a friend of mine told me that her boyfriend and his house were holding a huge party and that there would be a lot of new men at the party. I thought that I didn't want to miss such an opportunity. Because maybe if I just met the right person, the right man, I would not have to leave Washington, which was something I desperately wanted not to do. I was very invested in my job. I wanted to carry it through and I was invested very much in my old friends, though they just weren't as exciting to me any more. They didn't hold that magic like they used to. It used to be if I spent an evening with one of them I was completely cheered by their presence. Later when I went out to visit them in the suburbs that excitement was no longer there; often being with their families magnified my loneliness.

Anyway, I left Tucson early and flew to the party in D.C. Of course the man of my life wasn't there. I had operated on the outside not on the inside. I was afraid that if there was a good party and I didn't go to it that I might miss a wonderful opportunity. That was the way I structured my space, just acting or responding to events rather than ordering parts of my life the way that I wanted or needed them to be.

I don't mean to imply that I was the only one feeling intense isolation and franticness in D.C. Most of the women I knew my last years there on 29th and 30th streets who spent time together with a motley crew of men — sometimes because there was nothing better to do — felt a similar pain in their loneliness. But it was not really ever discussed between us in the terms I think about now. We seemed to have no sense of having our own selves and focused so much on outside things to make us happy. It would be very interesting to me to talk to some of these friends now, and see how they would react to this material. Our terms then were and we all know them: "We are so unhappy because we don't have a man." "What are we going to do, our loneliness just consumes us!" One of my friends who was an extremely bright, attractive woman went out with literally every man that would ask her in the high hopes that she could meet the right man. We once had bells to our phones placed in each other's apartments because we might miss the phone if *he* called when we were visiting each other. This phone trip was somewhat like the scheme for prime time at Aberfoyle, but not done with the same sense of humor. We were older women in Georgetown and our feelings reached a tone of desperation.

One time my Georgetown neighbor, Katherine, and I had a fight because a man that I met and was dating had asked her out, and she had decided to go out with him. My ego was hurt that he asked her out instead of me. But I really didn't like him very much. We used men to validate who we were. In that last year in D.C. I had stopped going out on dates. I hadn't dated since I lived with Larry, and was surprised that I got myself into this conflict, but then men were so important and we competed so much for their attention that the quality of the men or our feelings for them hardly mattered.

When I did stop dating in D.C. it was a relief. I had in fact learned early at Aberfoyle that I would much rather be with a woman that I liked than go out on some boring date. At that time I didn't get too much support for my view, since going out with the right man always was of prime importance in our lives.

Early Years

I had lived in Washington for eight years. I came there straight from college. The early years were very good years, though of course filled with the usual joys and pains of growing up. I thought Washington would be my permanent home.

I chose Washington because I wanted a different place than Philadelphia: I wanted to be away from home. I did not want a big city like New York where I felt or feared that I might be gobbled up. Washington to me was like a small country town with its trees and residential areas. At the time Boston somehow just wasn't in the running. My view of the East Coast went from New York to D.C. and anywhere beyond was not in my vision.

I recently went back to D.C. with its heaviness and new constructions reaking of the corruption and power of Watergate. I don't think that I ever will think of it as a small country town again. But that is how I felt when I arrived there my first year after college. I was scared of the big cities, and I had to see Washington as a small town to survive.

So Washington it was.

I was also scared about starting out in the big world after college. I remember being very upset when I graduated, and I graduated early too. I was hoping that someone would just tap me on the shoulder and say "We want you." I was scared about going out in the world. My feelings were that it was so big and so vast that I felt like I was plunging into outer space. I was overwhelmed by the incredible quantity of directions that I could go. Reminds me of a California friend's favorite Pogo quote: "We are confronted by an insurmountable quantity of opportunities."

In college at Penn State I had majored in liberal arts — arts and sciences. My folks would constantly go crazy about my not choosing a specific major. "Why don't you at least major in teaching or computer science? Your aunt and uncle think that is a good career. How can you not major; you have to choose something!"

But I didn't choose a specific major. I didn't want to. I wanted a broad education. I studied art history, science, theater, sociology, music, religion. I didn't want to box myself into a specific category. I wasn't sure what I wanted to be, but I knew for sure what I did not want. Certainly not a teacher or a person in computer science. I felt being a teacher was a dead-end career especially for a woman, and not very exciting. The idea of computer science was an indication of how well my aunt and uncle didn't know me.

When I arrived home from college I began an incredible search for a job in the Philadelphia area. At that time there seemed to be jobs that I could have taken but I wanted work that I would enjoy and be interested in. That also drove my parents crazy. "Why don't you just get a job?" My parents grew up in the Depression when people were pleased just to get any job that would bring them earnings. To me a job was not work just to get money. I wanted to do something meaningful with my life.

After much pressure from my parents I finally took a job with Almond Pies and Cakes in the personnel office for $90 a week. This was pretty good pay in those days and I was proud that I persevered until I got something close to what I wanted. I could have some major responsibilities there and my ability to type well was not a major requirement. Though indeed I had launched my career in social change at Almond Pies and Cakes.

The day I was hired Mr. Mace, the head of personnel, and I talked for hours about recidivism rates and making factory conditions better for employees. He showed me a diagram he had developed about the multiple aspects of people's personalities. Mr. Mace seemed like a very sensitive person and I felt I could be open with him.

The first two weeks on the job I talked about women getting pay equal to men's and about employees having more determination over their work. I also expressed my displeasure to a fellow employee that the race of each employee was being recorded on job application forms (light pencil check marks in the right hand corner meant black) though the federal law had been passed against such practices.

Two weeks after my job began I was fired. I remember crying all the way home on the commuter train to Chestnut Hill, "How could anyone do this to me!"

The Friday I was fired all the employees in my office area quietly left early. I was all alone when Mr. Mace called me into his office to inform me that he was letting me go. He said my typing was not fast enough and that I did not have any finesse. One of my little chores had been typing the lunch menus for the employees' lunch. I never could center the desserts and vegetables at the bottom of the menus correctly.

I cried to my mother. I was really hurt. My neighbor Millie Stein said she thought I was fired because Almond Pies and Cakes had a reputation for being anti-semitic — she was surprised they had hired me in the first place.

A month later the opening for a job in Washington, D.C. with the American Friends Service Committee which I had been hoping for became available. I had applied for the job at the Friends' Philadelphia Headquarters. I gladly took it, and began my life in the capital city.

Aberfoyle

I remember when I answered the ad: "Four college girls wish to share house with same." A friend of mine drove me the long way up Connecticut Avenue to Chevy Chase Circle and then down Western Avenue to the house on Aberfoyle Street. Years later whenever I was sad and lonely or just depressed or alienated from the absurdities of the bureaucracy, I took that same journey down Western Avenue. Tall trees formed a wonderful delicate green canopy.

The house felt like a long way out from the city compared to where I was living temporarily on Capitol Hill, a one room rental behind the Supreme Court. Chevy Chase was unfamiliar, an unexplored area for me. My first year in Washington I had lived in Suitland, Maryland.

I remember meeting Anne. She was sitting on the couch cleaning out her purse. She didn't seem that attractive to me. Her hair hanging loosely down to its natural curl around her face seemed very unstyled.

Later when I decided to move into the house I found that Anne was an extremely attractive person. Her looks and manner were very exciting to me. She had long hair that she wore in the style of the early 60's, some version of the sassoun, the front end tips coming right to her face. Mandy used to describe Anne as someone who liked things just so, precise and bright. That quality was definitely reflected in her art, in her decorating, her dress style, her manner and even in how she organized her closet. She unquestionably had the best organized closet east of the Mississippi.

Anne had a very happy manner that I loved. She hated to get depressed and I loved to play with her. I admired the way that she seemed so easily to greet with a big hug the men that entered our house. During our three years together she helped me select clothes and I remember consciously copying her dance style and some of her manner. Pretty soon we were competing for the smartest outfit in the house and for the men that darkened our doors.

Anne was four months older than I and taller. I loved the way her nose was sharp and how it came to a precise point. And how she rarely let things get her down. Gradually over the years I became very attached to her.

At
Aberfoyle
a secret
was
something
we told
each other
one at a
time

There were four of us living there at one time. Meg, Kate and Anne had grown up in California and had driven back from there to live in the East. I think I remember correctly that one of the reasons they moved East was to meet a man — they felt the men in San Francisco did not have the substance they found in the men in Washington. When Kate got married our second year at Aberfoyle, Pam, who was a friend of Anne's from the National Institute of Health, moved in and filled the refrigerator full with beer. Kate and Meg were school teachers and Anne was a nurse who did research at NIMH.

At Aberfoyle we gave many big dinners for ourselves and our dates around our huge dining room table. It was there for the first time that I learned about California artichokes and avocados. Long before I ever visited or lived on the West Coast in California, Senor Picos, the B.V., Big Sur, the horse on the way to Sam's in Tiburon now passed away, the Pierce Street Annex and other San Francisco high points were alive and part of my life from those dining room discussions.

Though we were very close and suffered together through our numerous affairs with men, tensions around the house focused primarily on getting married and doing so before we were 30. I was younger so I didn't have to worry about turning 30 like Kate and Meg who had only one or two more years to go.

But I was just as determined. The summer before I moved into Aberfoyle the two women I had lived with the previous year had gotten married. I attended both their weddings, and at one of them I caught the bridal bouquet.

My roommate threw the bouquet into a crowd of young women and I leaped in the air above everyone — my basketball jump shot came in handy — and I caught the bouquet. I hoped it would bring me luck and a man.

It was not until I returned from my summer vacation in Europe in the fall that I learned that when I returned to the ground after my "great leap forward" I had swung my elbows back and gave another eager young woman a bloody nose.

Saturday night without a date.

Tension in the house. And many Saturday nights I would be in my room and Anne in her room and we kept separate. We were lonely. She was watching of all things "The Marriage Game" on TV and I used to think then that we could have slept together and held each other. We loved each other far more than many of the men we ever dated.

Anne

Anne, I just read through the beginning of my journal. I was then going to finish the section that I had begun writing on you in response to your recent letter and I came across my feelings for you. I knew that they were recorded on the first few pages to my entry to my journal, because my journal and the reason I left for California had a lot to do with you. I wrote "Shit I want to scream. I am about to type my entry to the first page of my journal about my feelings for you. But I want to scream and cry and pound the typewriter. Do you know how much we loved each other? Do you know how much and now eight to ten years later we are finally telling each other openly. How does that make you feel? It makes me god damn angry. What a waste. What sadness that we had to guard our feelings from ourselves and each other. How uncomfortable we both felt, how unsure, how frantic. Well my dear friend I loved you ever so much. I have told you that you meant much to me often and you have showed me by your caring. You taught me another way to make love that I had not known or seen in my repertoire — that of doing for another person. You and Larry had that trait in common and the intensity of my feelings for him equalled the intensity of my feelings for you. When I held him so tightly and squeezed him I realized that I liked him as much as I liked you. I thought of that then.

Sometimes late at night when we were lonely and didn't have men that we loved to be with, to go out with, we stayed in our separate rooms protecting ourselves from the cold feelings of loneliness and "what's wrong with me feelings," I wanted to come in your room and hold you. I used to fantisize about your hips. Those hips that you used to talk about. Those hips that you said if you lost all the weight in China they would still stick out. I used to fantasize running my hand down them and over them. How many times did I have that fantasy? When you write you kaleidoscope events and feelings. Maybe I had that fantasy more when we lived in separate houses in Georgetown but then what's the difference? I had them, and felt them strongly. You used to describe your body as having breasts that stuck out just perfectly, not too big and not too small. They just stuck out. Anyway, it makes me feel good now to say I love you."

52

Prime Time

That was what we called it when the men would call us to ask us out for the weekend or for Saturday. We had to be off the telephone then. Often the yell through the house was "Prime time, get off the phone!" Prime time started at 8 p.m. Wednesday evening. "Please get off the phone!" I was a talker. Finally to resolve our tensions we installed a push button phone. That is we gave up our old number in favor of two lines so that if someone called, if *He* called and one line was busy, the call would automatically switch to the second line.

One time Pam had two men on hold, one called to ask her out and then another called. She put her first man on hold and answered the second line. She told the second man that she was on a call on the other phone and put him on hold. Flash flash the lights go on the buttons. Two men on hold — wow e e e e — a Full House. "Damn it!" I yelled down to Pam. "That is not fair! You can't tie up two lines! Which one are you going to go out with?"

It got so bad that whenever I would come home I would ask right away if anyone called. Pam always seemed reluctant to tell me. I asked her years later why and she told me that it was because I didn't say hello to her first.

Then there was the time very early in the morning when my boss John, who lived down the block, called for a ride to work. Pam panicked and put him on hold. I had spent the night out with my lover Ken and wasn't home. She didn't know what to tell him. In the 60's people weren't open about sleeping over. Pam left him on hold for five minutes until Anne rescued me with some excuse that I went to work early. I never ever went to work early. I was always on the side of late.

53

At Aberfoyle there were many Friday nights bar hopping and going to singles bars — Young Republicans, Crazy Horse — looking for men. I must admit that two husbands out of three were met in this manner. We used to go to Gentleman's

II in the early days. I believe it might have been the first singles bar in D.C.

Sometimes we used to have so much fun dancing. This was when Aretha Franklin's rock period was really big. *Sweet Sweet Baby* (Since you've been gone) was a big hit. I just craved her music! Gentleman's II had just opened, and I remember all four of us out on the dance floor at G-II dancing in a circle. We were having so much fun and the music was so good it didn't matter that no men were dancing with us — we were our own fun! That was in the 60's when women's dances were unheard of and that just wasn't done.

Before G-II we used to go to regular bars in Georgetown — with me trailing reluctantly behind and not until the second year fully joining in. You see I didn't approve. Single women just didn't go bar hopping. But apparently they did in San Francisco, so I finally agreed to join in with my California roommates. But I found I only had fun when I went out for a good time and to be with them, not in search of the elusive Mr. Right. That quest usually was a disappointment which brought back feelings of standing all alone on the dance floor wearing white gloves and patent shoes in the 6th and 7th grades.

For some reason it seemed to be somewhat okay to be single under 30, but over 30 was a crisis. We all felt the pressure.

When Meg reached 30 and the bar scene was not fruitful, she tried computer dating. She had just a wonderful sense of humor and was full of short quips. I believe one of her computer dates brought her a dozen long stem roses their first date, and then by the time they reached Chevy Chase Circle,

Meg quipped, he proposed! Chevy Chase Circle was five minutes away from our house.

Sometimes I used to say I wish Meg wouldn't worry so about getting married before she reaches 30. "Why doesn't she forget it and have fun and then worry about it after she turns 30?"

That kind of thinking from me was quite amazing at the time as I certainly was a worrier myself and very much like Meg in this respect. I of course did not think it was okay to be unmarried after 30; later worrying was in order.

Like my roommates I had many a painful affair during my Aberfoyle years — but one of my affairs and most pleasant and exciting memories was with one of my favorite people, Ken. Ken not only helped me through my painful affair with my nice Jewish boy but I absolutely craved him. I have often thought of Ken and wished we hadn't parted so awkwardly when he moved away to New York, but it is only now looking back that I realized not only how much I admired him but how often I used him as a model for myself. I liked that he was independent, that he seemed content with his own life, and that he was a sensitive person.

Image: a strong independent gentle person.

Sometimes I would look at Ken so at home in his apartment and admire the way he lived. He seemed to have a command over his life living based in himself — perhaps my fantasy. He lived alone. I wished that I could be like him —

seemingly independent and with a way that was his own. I remember how pleased and proud he was of his new home. I admired that. He seemed to be satisfied with himself and to have direction. He seemed not to need people, which I am sure looking at all the people that he was involved with is far from the truth. But that is how he seemed to me. I really loved him.

Jenny, my closest college woman friend, and Ken have always reminded me of each other so it should not be surprising that as I write of one memories of the other flow from me. Ken, a soft male and Jenny, a hard female. Their quality the same but reversed. I felt more comfortable with the likes of Ken. Jenny was very sensitive but afraid to show it behind her hardness; her harder outside was more apparent at first.

I saw Ken as masculine with a feminine side, which I saw as more pretty and would prefer to be than Jenny, feminine with a stiff masculine side — the way I often felt in D.C. Ken wore his soft side well. Jenny and I wore our aggressive sides awkwardly.

"When we see another person we identify with or admire, she or he is expressing a hidden or unexpressed side of ourselves."

Anais Nin at a speech in San Francisco, 1974.

Carol Lancy, a friend from my new job in the poverty program, had introduced me to Ken sometime between my first and second year at Aberfoyle. Ken had gone to law school with her husband and at the time had just arrived in D.C. to take the bar exam. I instantly liked him. On our first date he found he had no money and borrowed money for the beer we drank. I remember that we spent the evening lying in the grass at the Washington Monument, watching an outdoor Shakespearean play. I think it was "As You Like It." He was an incredibly sexy man. We made out on the couch at Aberfoyle when the evening was over. Carol warned me that he had a girl friend in Boston and that I should be careful not to get too attached to him, that a lot of women liked him and that he was a bit crazy. By crazy I guess Carol meant his strong individuality, which was precisely what I liked about him so much.

I remember visiting him at the Georgetown School Library with Carol when he was studying with her husband for the bar and later watching him decorate his new Georgetown apartment. He was enthusiastic about his new life in D.C. and was exciting to be with. We did not become lovers for over a year, though we became good friends.

Shortly after I met Ken I became involved with a nice Jewish boy named Jared. He too was a lawyer. It seemed to me that in Washington most of the men were lawyers. Sometimes I thought in terms of dating lawyers rather than men.

Jared was my big love — I thought he was Mr. Right on a white horse — a tall Jewish boy from New York and a Harvard lawyer to boot. I met him when he first moved to town to join the government. I fell madly in love with him and thus began one of the most painful relationships I ever experienced in my life. In the beginning everything was wonderful. We played tennis, went out to dinner, to the theatre and to art shows, and went skiing in the Poconos with my old friends Lisa and Gary from Philadelphia. A perfect dream. Then Jared told me that he had another girl friend in New York. He complained that I wasn't flashy enough. He couldn't decide what to do. And then I kept on telling him that wasn't important, that we were so in love. Instead of telling him to go to hell. I kept trying to please him, to figure out how I could be more attractive. When the relationship with him became unbearable, I entered therapy to try to end it. We kept on breaking up but neither of us could completely let go.

I had thought our early love-making was fine and was surprised to find Jared was upset about it. I was naive. I didn't understand why it was so important that I have an orgasm. But I wanted to please him, so we tried and tried. Our sex life became awful. I was a mark on his masculinity. My love-making experience with the man I went with my first year in D.C. was easy and exciting. We didn't have intercourse and orgasm was easy and never an issue.

Therapy

It was during this period that I met Dr. Tilbet, my male therapist for three years in D.C. He was tall and seemed to me lanky though I am sure he would not describe himself that way. He used to run up and down the stairs in his office building to lose weight.

I got his name from my general doctor. I remember at our second session I met Dr. Tilbet late one evening because I was so upset with Jared. Jared had come by Aberfoyle to tell me about how well he was doing at work and about his new apartment in Dupont Circle. He said he was still seeing the other woman and did not want to date me. I did not understand why he kept on calling me. But I was still in love with him so I did not turn him away. Dr. Tilbet said he wanted me to tell him he was doing well. And he said: "When a man drives all the way up to Chevy Chase Circle for a compliment, tell him he is doing well." And I said "What's in it for me?" and Dr. Tilbet said "Not a God damn thing!"

During this period I remember thinking as I drove home over the Connecticut Bridge: "This is so painful, what must it be like to get divorced?"

After I broke up with Jared I became closer to Ken, who was very comforting. We soon became lovers and this relationship became one of the healthiest I had had with a man. It was not as intense as my relationship with Jared and at first I tended to take it for granted. I wasn't used to things going along so well. I don't want to give the impression that my affair with Ken was a major event in his life. He had lots of lovers. What was important to me is that we were close.

I realized even then that his having other women allowed me to get close to him. It somehow was safer for me. It made us more equal — sharing our feelings about the other lovers in our lives. With Ken I never felt one down.

My painful relationship with Jared motivated me to enter therapy but at the same time I had developed strong emotional feelings for Anne I wanted to explore. There were tensions between us that I did not understand. I had worried at times that some of my feelings for Anne and other women might be homosexual ones. It was with Dr. Tilbet that for the first time I began to look directly at my feelings for women. When I allowed myself this new honesty my feelings for Anne intensified. I wanted to be closer to her.

I remember that I would like to be near Anne when we had parties because that is when she would get high — everyone was always a little looser — and she would sometimes grab my arm to introduce me to someone . . . or I remember sometimes that I would lean back against her as she walked behind me to another part of the party . . . the room was so crowded by everyone standing and talking and drinking that it was an easy feat, as one could not walk through the room without bumping into people . . . maybe that is one of the unconscious reasons for cocktail parties in the East — people get to be able to stand close to each other, bump and touch even though they were not "supposed to touch or hug."

It was Dr. Tilbet who first encouraged me to explore my sexual feelings for Anne. He suggested that I fantasize about her when I masturbated. I said "Oh my God I couldn't do that!" I had never allowed myself to fantasize anything sexual about women. But when I finally tried it, I found intense, exciting feelings. I wasn't quite sure what to do with them. I couldn't bring myself to hug my women friends before therapy and now, with these new exposed feelings, I was even more confused, but more excited too. Dr. Tilbet felt if I worked out my feelings for women it would be easier for me to be closer to men.

He encouraged me to hug my women friends and to express my affection for them. I exclaimed that would be really difficult. Often when I would sit and talk with Anne late at night, I would put my foot against hers gently as we talked. She would move away. Giving her a hug seemed like an herculean feat.

Dr. Tilbet would say "Come now, you see women all the time giving each other hugs as greetings, particularly when they haven't seen each other in a long time."

In those days in D.C. I didn't think of wanting any hugs, I hadn't felt the needs for hugs, that wasn't in my repertoire. I wanted just a touch or a kiss. I don't think I could myself handle a hug that was total body and close, and such a thing could hardly be hoped for; it just didn't happen or I never saw it happen between my women friends.

Anne was standing before my door in the living room of my apartment in Georgetown. I remember grabbing her arm and trying to kiss her goodnight. We had gone to the movies that evening. She said "Oh Ruth, please honey, don't!" and then left. I remember she was gentle in her rebuke.

The next day I was so devastated it seemed like a wide open Sunday — that I would fall into and never come back from. So I went to see *Funny Girl* to hold onto the world.

Anne and I have never talked about that incident.

Anne, you and I have never talked about our past exchange of feelings for each other. At one time in our friendship we were able to reach a place where we could talk — I can't remember exactly when this occurred or whether it was only once but the pattern in our relationship seemed to be that we would be tense and apart, then there would be a coming together, and then another painful tense distancing. It was only during those calmer periods when for some reason we both weren't terribly threatened that we could talk about our feelings for each other.

Once when I began therapy we were able to be open about our feelings and I told you that I loved women and that I loved you. I remember that day we were sitting in Mandy's old apartment in Grosvenor and I told you that I loved you and that Dr. Tilbet saw no reason to draw the line between loving women or loving men. It was then that you said "You can't make love to everyone you love."

And I said, "Don't you want to help me get married? Dr. Tilbet said if I worked out my feelings for women I could more easily get married."

You said "No."

Anne and I sometimes competed for the same man. Once I had discovered that she planned to see a man I was dating, though he had broken the date. In those years dating the same man that your woman friend liked and was still interested in was considered wrong, though competition between us was keen. The day I made my discovery we had a big argument and talked about our jealousies. Later when we had dessert — ice cream cake role at Howard Johnson's — I felt very loving towards her and looked at her through my fingers over my face. She said "Who are you hiding from?"

Once Anne Gave Me A Hug

For some reason I just thought in this section of the time that Anne once grabbed my shoulders and sort of shook me and gave me a hug. It happened in a split second. We were in her room by the door which let in the only light into the room. The room was dark except for the pale light coming through the door.

Or the time at National Airport dropping Pam and her mother off — Anne and I walked back to the car in the rain and under the umbrella. Anne grabbed my arm. I loved it. Or the time when Meg's sister died — Anne answered the phone and received the news. She grabbed me and I heard her heart pounding.

There were other times — sometimes they all blur into one — when she told me that she knew that I loved her. She said "I could just tell the way you watched me in the movies. I told Janice I think Ruth really likes me."

Or the time in Georgetown when I would come over to talk to you and tell you not to tell anyone — that I just loved you — loved to hear the tone, murmur and sound of your voice. You were sitting on your bed and I was on your pink shag rug — trying to tell you how I felt — probably saying something like "I want to tell you. . ." And then the long silences that were so painful to us both. You would say "Just say it." I am just beginning to understand why it is so painful to the person waiting to hear me. Maybe I don't understand it but I realize how often I go through telling a person I want to tell them something and then just go through agony and a lot of time before what I want to say is out. Instead of just simply saying it without the thought or precursory statement that I am about to say something that is hard for me to say.

I don't know why sometimes saying my feelings feels like the voice of doom or why I sometimes feel so awkward when I finally get them out. This occurred the other day after I completed this section. I told a friend in Berkeley my feelings for her and asked her how she felt about me. I had found myself expressing my feelings to her through writing this book rather than in person — repeating some of the same patterns I had with Mandy — holding back my feelings.

Dr. Tilbet once asked me to bring him some pictures of Anne so that he could see what she looked like. I had spent months talking about her and he wanted to know who she was. Anne gave me some pictures to take. Years later a mutual friend, Janice, told me that Dr. Tilbet's request really ticked Anne off. She felt her privacy invaded, but she hadn't wanted to express her anger for Dr. Tilbet to me.

When we used to plan our Aberfoyle cocktail parties Meg and Kate and Anne used to ask if Dr. Tilbet would come. And Dr. Tilbet even used to have some fantasies himself about that. He insisted that he be invited to my wedding. "Miss Falk you must invite me to your wedding." If I ever got married he would meet all the people in my life that we had talked about for two years.

Anne and I became close during the period when my mother was dying. I was watching a healthy woman slowly deteriorate before my eyes. It was so painful to see that I didn't want to visit her. My relatives (gradually none of whom ever saw her, just my father went consistently everyday) kept on insensitively insisting that I wasn't seeing my mother enough. I felt guilty, but seeing her was ripping me apart.

Like the day I walked into her bedroom. She was lying there looking up, falling in and out of sleep saying "I'm not dead yet." And I thought on hearing that "I shouldn't have heard that."

I tried to thank her those last few years for the things she taught me, and tried to hug her and be warm. I remember awkwardly sitting with her and talking about her old recipies. Dr. Tilbet had encouraged me to thank her for what she did for me.

I had blocked her goodness to me and had only felt anger towards both my parents when I went off to D.C. to work for the American Friends Service Committee. My starting salary was very small and my parents and all my relatives were down on me for not marrying or falling in love instead with the wonderful person who was a stockbroker from Shaker Heights. My parents didn't approve my career wishes but weren't as verbal as my relatives.

My wanting and needing to get away from home and at the same time not wanting to think of my mother dying was an avoidance. I did not want to think of my mother's death. I, Ruth Falk, was the child of a mother who was dying.

That my mother was dying. Even now when I look at the topics covered in my book there is some unreal quality to it — that I had a dying mother — that that happened in my life. I remember those long drives to see her in Philadelphia from D.C. and how my shoulders were practically up over my head after the journey in my VW down the Baltimore-Washington Pike, so tense was I from the visit.

The sad part about the way my family handled my mother's death is that for the most part she had to die alone — face her ordeal alone. The seriousness of her disease was not revealed to us or to her until she became very sick from the M.S. I don't know if she ever talked to anyone about her fears. Perhaps to my father. Our family was so guilty about her dying, God forbid they had to do something. Her death made them face their own. Mother was still healthy enough to know she was dying. Perhaps we, her children, could have been more supportive.

This period in my relationship to Anne should not be underestimated. I used to love to listen to Anne talk to her mother on the phone and lived through her relationship with her mother vicariously. Her mother would send Anne long letters that were very warm and really very interesting. Anne used to read them out loud to us at Aberfoyle. And I would wish that my mother and I could have been able to communicate so openly and warmly.

The beginning of my third year at Aberfoyle I took a vacation to Mexico with a friend from work. Just before I left for this trip Kate announced she was getting married. I wanted to stay for the wedding but I had already made commitments at my job, and with my traveling companion.

When I returned from Mexico, Meg picked me up at Dulles Airport. It was a sweltering warm day, you could just see the humidity in the air as we drove on the Beltway to Chevy Chase. When I arrived home, I literally found a new roommate in Kate's bed. There was a big mound of covers and the room was dark. Anne had asked a friend, Pam, from her office to move in.

Under the covers, Pam was in a depression over something. I was to learn that this was her way of coping when things got too much. She would just hop into bed and hide.

Meg would sometimes talk about climbing into the great white biscuit to comfort herself. But her comfort was more a fairyland type of comfort than Pam's animal type burrow.

I remember two things about Pam's moving in. First, I lost my position as the "youngest" in the house, which I had thoroughly enjoyed, and secondly that we worried that our dating behavior might shock Pam. We weren't sure about letting her know we sometimes slept with men. But the first week she lived with us, at 2 a.m. we heard her little feet run downstairs and out the door. Within minutes she was reving her MG engine and was out into the night to meet one of the men she was seeing. Our fantasy of the innocent youngest was quickly dispelled.

That third year at Aberfoyle I purchased a huge lithograph of Carol Summers, which I hung over the couch in the den. I was very proud of my piece of art — and had it framed in chrome.

Buying art or even a stereo was a big step to me. It seemed a statement that I wasn't going to wait any longer to get married before I could have nice things. It was also a statement that I was an adult, or was becoming adult.

Alison, my friend from the poverty program, once criticized my hesitance to buy a new stereo. I said my boyfriend Jared had a stereo and if I didn't marry him any other man I'd marry would. In those days men came with penises and super stereos. Alison thought I was ridiculous. Why should I wait to enjoy good music?

When I brought the Carol Summer's picture home my roommates were incredulous. They were not at all into modern or abstract art and couldn't understand my excitement. Meg instantly dubbed the picture Moon over Miami while Anne and Pam discovered that they could comb their hair in the reflection from the glass covering. And they did not hesitate to use the picture as a mirror in front of me to tease me.

During this period I had quit my job at the poverty program and eventually got my job at NIMH. The poverty program job, though exciting and controversial, was filled with conflict and became increasingly tense. When I began the job I was doing "social action research in the monitoring unit." Though much of our reporting was "purely descriptive," some of our work was never released because it was controversial. I learned early in the game that any research study, no matter what its intention, is by its inherent nature political. And most social action research is used to support and maintain the political status quo.

The graduate work in research that I was taking at this time at George Washington University was not helpful to me in conducting social action research. I came to NIMH hoping that I would learn the type of research skills necessary to conduct and evaluate social change projects well.

By the time I left the poverty program I was helping to code cards for a data bank. That was the direction research in the section was taking. Numbers and units and where bodies lived were recorded on IBM cards. This was the data bank system which later became (and still is) a controversial issue in minority communities.

I had been wanting to leave the poverty program for a

while but I just couldn't seem to make myself make a change and take another job. I finally quit, figuring that if I put myself against the wall by leaving, I would be forced to seek a new position. I had found job offers before, but none of them had suited me. This period, when I was out of a job, was very frightening for me. It was the same sensation that I experienced after college. I was going to fall into a great big void.

I was very anxious without a structure, a nine to five structure. When I wasn't looking for a job I would try to play tennis and relax but I was so nervous and anxious that I did not enjoy myself. I just couldn't play tennis in the morning in the middle of the week. It just didn't seem right. My parents were furious at me for quitting the job. My father especially just couldn't understand it. He said "Wait until you get your next job before you quit."

Suede Coat

During the last few months I worked at the poverty program I had purchased a suede coat at one of the dress shops along Connecticut Avenue and had it shortened at a highly recommended cleaning and tailoring shop.

Unfortunately, my tailor shortened the coat one inch more in the back than in the front, so that my dresses hung out in the back below the hemline. There went my Parisian look. I was angry and not about to pay 25 dollars for such a bad job.

I offered to pay the tailor less but he insisted on full payment which I felt was just too much for such a poor job.

Within weeks I received notice that I was to appear in small claims court, since the tailor was suing me for nonpayment of the 25 dollars.

I called all my lawyer boyfriends for their advice. They all insisted that the tailor was going to lose. And they agreed to coach me on how to defend my case in court.

When my day in court arrived I took sick leave from the poverty program, picked up a woman friend for moral support, and purchased a yardstick on my way to the municipal court building. I soon found myself standing before the judge, with the judge's assistant down on his hands and knees reading my yardstick to determine whether in fact my coat was an inch shorter in the back than the front. After a long pause, the judge asked "Well, what is your decision?"

The assistant replied that he could only see that everytime I breathed the measurement was different. The courtroom was in an uproar. The judge had to bang his gavel to get everyone to sit down and order restored. After much measuring and counter-measuring it was finally determined that my coat was indeed one inch shorter in the back than in the front. Ken had come to court to support me, and at the last minute he stood in as my advocate. Then the tailor spoke. His face got so red that I was sure he was going to have a heart attack in what I thought was a very serious but amusing situation. It was so very painful to him that I felt guilty that he was in such agony.

With his red face and big belly he insisted to the judge that it was the principal of the thing and that "the customer got away with murder," that if he measured the judge's own shirt he would find at least one quarter of an inch difference between each sleeve. Thereupon the judge decided against me. He stated that though it was determined that the coat was indeed one inch shorter in the back than the front he felt it didn't make that much difference. I had to pay the tailor 25 dollars.

Later I felt that perhaps had Ken not come to my rescue I would have won. With his slick style I hardly looked like the down-trodden consumer.

After the court trial I met two young reporters who wanted to take a picture of me in front of the court house with my yardstick. But their photographer wasn't there. I was a bit uncertain about having my picture in the paper since I had called in sick and didn't want to get caught with my face on the front page of the city section of the *Washington Post*.

The reporters were unable to get their photographer, but took down my name and indicated that they were going to write a story about this case. One of the reporters was Carl Bernstein, who later became nationally famous as the Pulitzer prize-winning investigator of Watergate.

A few weeks later Meg and I were at a cocktail party at a neighbors across the street from our house. I said "Hey Meg, that's the judge who decided against me." Meg grabbed my arm and pulled me over to Judge Browne. She said "Do you know who this is?" to the judge. The judge said "Oh my I have never met anyone I decided against before." He pulled his wife over and said "You know what, my wife thought you were right. I just never thought an inch meant that much to a woman."

Later in the month I was attending a semi-clandestine

meeting on abortion and I bumped into Carl Bernstein again. He looked at me and said "It is bad enough that your tailor sues you, but to need an abortion!" He told me that he had written up the tailor case and handed in the story but that his editor didn't think it was funny.

At the time of my suede coat case I was not at all aware of the women's issues involved and thought of the case only as an amusing event in my life.

My fourth year in D.C. we moved out of Aberfoyle. The day we moved Pam was away sailing with her latest beau and Anne, Meg and I did most of the work putting the house back in order the way it was originally. The long heavy old drapes were put over the windows again and the Mona Lisa was put back over the green couch.

Toward the summer of 1968 the house had begun to break up. Anne said it was time, that 3 years was enough. I didn't want the house to break up. I loved Aberfoyle. And I was also really scared about what I would do next. (Anne had always said looking for a new apartment and/or looking for a new job were the two worst things in the world to do.) I didn't want to live alone and I also wanted to continue living with Anne. I remember talking to Anne at the Hot Shop. She said "For God's sake, it's not so hard to live alone. I did it once in San Francisco and liked it." I remember sometime during that period coming home and being so mad that I ripped up the picture of the four of us — so intense were my feelings.

Dr. Tilbet said "Well if you are so scared to live alone why don't you try it? If you find you can live alone, when you live with others you won't be so demanding on them because you will know you don't need them."

I decided to try it. I began to look for a place in Georgetown — though indeed I was scared to death. It was during that summer when we were all moving that I met Mandy. She had just come to D.C. and found work in Anne's office. Mandy was a young Ph.D. whom I heard Anne talk about long before I met her. Anne said she is so bright and cute. She is the littlest thing, it is hard to believe that she has a Ph.D. at such a young age — twenty-six.

Mandy was living in the same apartment complex in Grosvenor where Pam and Anne had sublet their apartment for the summer. I met her there when I went to visit Anne.

When I found my apartment in Georgetown I was thrilled. It was in a huge house on 29th and N Streets that looked like it had been built in colonial times in the South. It faced a large yard with two Mulberry trees whose mulberries would later get all over my red rug in the spring rains.

My apartment was a hit. Mandy was so excited by it that she decided that she definitely had to live in Georgetown. She immediately started hunting for a place and Anne told Mandy that if she found a two bedroom apartment, she would move in with her. Mandy found one at the other end of N Street in a building which since has become an historical landmark. I was jealous and angry that Anne moved in with Mandy. But by then my relationship with Anne had become very tense. We were hardly talking.

During my first year in Georgetown I became increasingly close to my married friends from Philly, Gary and Lisa. My feelings for women were becoming very intense and Dr. Tilbet was putting more and more pressure on me to explore sleeping with a woman. He said "If you like and are turned on to both Gary and Lisa, why not try sleeping with both of them?" The idea was exciting, but it seemed far-fetched to me that it could actually happen.

It was during the time of the second sweep of peace demonstrations in D.C. that Lisa came to visit me. She told me things she and Gary were discussing about their sex lives. We also talked about our feelings for each other. Lisa said Gary and she were thinking of sleeping with a third person. And I told her what Dr. Tilbet said to me. We both laughed and she said she knew that I liked women and thought in college that my closest friend and I had been lovers. We weren't.

Our conversation got really threatening. Lisa tried to get close to me and I moved away. She said "Why are you so scared?"

Lisa and I had first met as camp counselors in our teens in Philadelphia. When we were younger our mothers used to say we had a mutual admiration society. I liked her a lot, especially the way she flirted. She was a very warm person and was one of the first women with whom I experienced very intense emotional exchanges. When her lover of five years died, I was in Europe on a Quaker work-camp program. I felt for her strongly. I wanted to love and comfort her as much as I could so that all her pain would go away.

Somehow, someway, Lisa, Gary and I did sleep together in Philadelphia. It was very scary at first, but very exciting. I really loved it. Lisa was the most uninhibited of us all. She was able to touch me easily. I remember how upset Gary suddenly became when Lisa and I got so excited touching each other. Lisa said "Let's hug Gary, he's upset." When Gary and I made love it seemed even more scarey to sleep with someone else's husband. After we all made love we sat in Gary's and Lisa's big king-size bed saying "If only our parents could see us now."

The next morning Lisa split from bed quickly and Gary and I made love again. Gary said after I left that Sunday evening they had the most incredible love-making they had had in a long while. I had to drive home alone to D.C. to be there for work on Monday.

I was very excited by this experience. I liked our closeness and the idea of being a family. I encouraged Lisa and Gary to read the *Harrad Experiment*. They were interested in exploring group families too. Later they tried one such experiment with another couple. Once after that I slept with Gary. Lisa and I remained good friends but she kept her distance. There were tensions between us which I never quite understood. Years later in California Lisa told me, after she had a relationship with a woman lover, that I scared her by wanting to be close, that I was as she put it "too advanced for her." She was really afraid to be close to women.

In a sense, being with Gary had given us permission to touch and avoid those painful scenes I went through later with Gloria. In fact, I never counted making love with Lisa as making love with a woman because Gary was there and Lisa would not make love with me one to one.

During my last year at Aberfoyle and the beginning of my first year in Georgetown my job at NIMH became very difficult. I do not know how to explain why my job was so painful — other than it produced a slow eroding away of my core. At first I worked as an assistant to a man, Jack Peters, who had come to NIMH six months after I began my job there. He and I started the Center's Section on Youth which I later ran for 3 years. We were pushing a position that was very unpopular at NIMH — giving power and responsibility to young people. We were alone for most of our struggle. We began our work in the late 60's, during the advent of the counter culture revolution, the increasing controversy over the Vietnam war and over the learning functions of our universities.

Jack was very supportive of me, though we had our hassles over the written papers and whose ideas were whose. It was during the period I worked for him that a lot of administrative negativity came down on me. It was also a period in which I was growing professionally, taking on more staff responsibility. Jack and I traveled together visiting youth programs and universities across the country. There was pressure at times for us to stop traveling together — to do our traveling separately — because the rumors were we were having an affair. We weren't. Later when Jack left NIMH and I wanted to continue our work, I was told I couldn't travel alone because I didn't have a credential.

Before Jack left my promotion had come up and I was turned down. With his support I fought the division's refusal to promote me on their grounds that I didn't have the right credential. I argued that I actually was doing the work and had the responsibility of a grade level higher than my rating. After I wrote what felt like a thousand memos to the Civil Service Commission, I won. The rumors then of course were that I was sleeping with the man in personnel who processed my appeal.

It would never have occurred to me not to challenge their refusing my promotion. As it would have never occurred to me to stop fighting for projects or grants I felt should be supported. Often I was treated poorly by male colleagues but I persisted. And sometimes I was also treated poorly by one or two of the secretaries particularly my first year at NIMH. They were upset at my taking the same privileges as their bosses — the professional male staff. Older women secretaries were not supportive of me as a young woman and I was not particularly sensitive to them or aware, until the women's movement, that they had been doing "shit work" for others for years. How the structures of this society divide us!

I felt that if I could build a good program and develop my skills at NIMH I would develop an independent power. I wanted my work and the projects I was supporting to be recognized and I wanted to be treated with respect. My work was slowly recognized inside and outside NIMH: outside by youth groups and by support on the hill from Senate offices; inside by a small group of colleagues, both female and male, committed to youth programs. But one thing that remained constant was the pain I felt from the hostile treatment I received from time to time by some of my male colleagues.

It was during this period when I worked with Jack that I met Thomas Linney, who was one of the reasons I was able to survive at NIMH.

Thomas became a very important person in my life. He was a student activist who had just resigned from National Student Association in Washington, D.C. and was about to begin a commune called Dragon's Eye in Berkeley, California. He and another friend, Michael Rossman, were organizing a group of people to live and work together. The focus of their work was to be education.

Our first meeting was a bit tense and awkward. Thomas had just participated in an educational caucus in Urbana, Illinois. I kept asking him to explain exactly what an educational caucus was all about. I don't think I ever knew.

It was from Thomas that I first learned about educational reform: learning by experience, breaking down one's boundaries between work, play and life, and about the new alternative families. Though our first meeting was a bit awkward I found Thomas to be a very supportive friend. What I remember most about him holds true today too — his openness for other people's ideas. Though he felt strongly about the counter culture movement and educational reform, I could easily talk to him and wasn't afraid to express my uncertainties about the movement or about my job in the government. While other radicals I met tended to be intolerant, I found in Thomas a soft, understanding and at times warm teacher.

Thomas and I found in each other a mutual support base. I gave him support and energy for the work he was doing with community-based projects. And he and several others were important liaisons for me into the student and counter culture communities, and my outside support at NIMH as well.

We spent long hours talking about ways to fund youth programs and about current new projects and government policies. Clearly there had to be some way into this closed power structure.

Over the years it was Thomas who I told about my relationship with Lisa and Gary, about my feelings for women, and about my search for an alternative family. I was one of Thomas' links to the bureaucracy and funding sources and at times Thomas was one of my links to sanity.

Thomas told me about non-monogamous relationships at the commune and the joys of integrating work and life and living in a "non-hierarchial community." When I first visited the commune I was very impressed and excited by the people I met. What struck me most was the warmth and sense of family I experienced there.

But by the end of my first year's living in California, Thomas was saying that he thought monogamous relationships made more sense and he certainly was not extolling the joys of living and working with the same people — integrating life and work.

I had already experienced a painful jolt myself trying to integrate my life and work and exploring non-monogamous relationships. I complained to him — "I bought your whole bag and now you tell me it doesn't work!"

What I never bought was whether the commune and/or other alternative programs that tried to work collectively really in fact had non-hierarchial structures as they claimed. Most projects I knew, and these were male-dominated, had one or two very strong male leaders.

The second year we all lived in Georgetown Anne got married.

Anne's Wedding — February 18, 1969

Yes, Anne's wedding. It seems like an event to describe some place on the bottom of a long list. I don't know how best to explain my feelings about her getting married. There was the long drive up to New York with Mandy and Pam. I was just miserable, the car seemed so cold. Pam had borrowed her brother's old convertible which was very drafty. My back and neck were hurting. I had hurt my back playing tennis the week before and the long ride up in the cold car increased by my anxiety that something was seriously wrong with my neck was excruciating. My mother's illness had been getting more and more severe. Anytime something was wrong with my health I suspected I was dying of M.S. too. I felt alienated from Pam and Mandy. I remembered this only after Pam remarked in California later that she was mean to me at Anne's wedding. The night after the wedding I spent with a lover. How awful that was! Pam and Mandy picked me up late Sunday at his apartment. It was snowing for the long cold ride home.

The next day — a bleak and cold Monday morning in D.C. — I went to therapy. Dr. Tilbet said "No wonder you are upset. You lost the person you love most in the whole world!" All this was inside me. Mandy, Pam and perhaps

Anne did not know. No one knew how I felt, except Lisa who knew how much I loved Anne.

And yes that last lunch before Anne and Eric went up to New York to get ready for the wedding. We all had lunch together in Georgetown at the French Restaurant — Meg, Anne, Kate, Mandy, Pam and I. I remember ordering orange juice and getting tomato juice. I remember the linen table cloths and then the long walk back to Anne's and Mandy's apartment and remember watching from the stoop as Eric hitched up the trailer and put Anne's things in it. I remember watching Anne and Eric turn around on N Street and then leave.

But the wedding itself. There almost was not going to be a wedding with Anne and Eric's friends. Anne and I didn't talk about it directly. I was getting all my information from Pam, Mandy and Meg at the time. I believe Meg was with Anne when she first met Eric. They were out dancing at a bar. I was really upset when I learned I wasn't going to get an invitation to the wedding.

But the invitations did come. I don't remember the details, but the couple, family, parents and friends all have different ideas of what a wedding should be and what often happens is usually a compromise of everyone's wishes. At first a small wedding was planned for Anne and Eric with family members only, not friends. Someone must have talked them into inviting their friends.

Janice was maid of honor.
Pam took the photographs and set Anne's hair — electric
    hot rollers.
Mandy and I watched, Mandy's camera was used to take
    the pictures.
Yes, I got to button Anne's dress. 100 tiny buttons on her
    long wedding gown.

Anne used to send a scrapbook home each year for her
mom of pictures from her life in D.C. — Aberfoyle, trips,
parties, dates, her whole life. One year there was no picture
of me in the book.

"In the beginning we would hug goodbye, things like that
and then that sort of stopped. I forget that that's really a sign
that things are too intense a lot of times." — from an interview about women loving women.

The wedding service itself was lovely. Anne looked beautiful of course. I remember being in the car later with Janice
and Ben — Janice talking incessantly about wanting to marry
Ben. Ben was drunk. The actual service and party were fun
and wonderful — it was the period before and after that was
so painful to me.

Anne, I loved you and felt that the person that I loved
most in the world had left me. It would have been so much
easier for both of us if we could have talked about it. I wished
you could have verbalized your feelings for me but we were

scared and desperate — you for a husband and me too for a man. Why am I always liking women who seem to like men first?

There were times that I saw myself as more charming and lovely than the men my women friends chose as their lovers. I thought that they certainly would have been happier if they had chosen to live with me and remain part of my ongoing life. Anne and I could have been buddies and stayed together too, though now I certainly wouldn't want to be committed to only one woman or one man. But a few good buddies that were my essential loves, and the freedom to have others. At this moment in my life, I wouldn't want to be in a couple.

I once commented to Meg that I didn't know how Anne felt about certain things anymore and that I was afraid to ask. Meg said that she thought that of the roommates I was closest to Anne. I said I doubted that. What is true I said to myself but didn't feel quite right in saying to Meg was that I loved Anne the most but I didn't know at all whether that would mean that I was the closest to her or that I knew her the best.

So Anne would live out my fantasy about living happily ever after in a suburban marriage. I had said to her earlier that I envied that she could be happy with this life she had chosen. I regretted having to go through so much to be happy, including moving away from the people that I loved. When I said that to Anne she looked away.

Married Couples

Mandy would say that when women get married it would change their friendships because the husband wouldn't want his wife so close to another woman.

Dr. Tilbet would try to teach me that just because your women friends get married it doesn't mean you lose them. I would think maybe if I could learn to look at it differently it wouldn't feel like a loss.

Dr. Tilbet pointed out that sometimes with Anne, after her marriage, she and I seemed closer.

The feeling of liking women who chose men first — Anne, Mandy, Jessica. I remember saying to Dr. Tilbet "All right, I'll sleep with a woman! Where are all the lesbians in Washington? How come no one ever propositions me? How come none of the women I love ever try to make love to me?" And he said "You seem to like women who like men."

How many women have felt strong feelings when their best friend got married? Sometimes the marriage marked the end to their closeness or their emotional relationship or their seeing each other at all. And sometimes the marriage made no difference.

Meeting Larry

During my years at Aberfoyle I took it upon myself to buy a football. I became exasperated depending on my dates each fall to supply me with a game of catch. None of the lawyers I dated came with footballs. So I purchased a football at

Korvettes and kept it in the back of my car. It's there now. Each fall I just love throwing it around. I met Larry in the Fall of 1970, or rather our relationship began that fall. We would pass the football around for hours.

We met on the tennis court that first summer in Georgetown. I was sitting waiting for a court when Larry came and took the first court that was opening up. A fight ensued between he and the man who was sitting down from me on the bench about whose turn it was to take the court. I clearly saw that the court was not Larry's. I spoke up. The man got his court and Larry got furious. Jimmie, the court mayor, had to hold Larry back as he yelled at me. "Girl," he said, "the next time you come around here you bring your boyfriend!" That was the beginning of our relationship.

I had observed Larry the summer before. He was a great tennis player. He had a lot of energy and seemed to be a lot of fun. At the time I noticed him, he was having an affair with a Congressman's wife who I admired, and that added some excitement. I was frankly curious about him. We played tennis a few times at end of the summer we had our encounter and slowly began our relationship. We both liked sports and we both were very competitive. I loved playing Larry at net and he loved trying to impress me with his passing shots. Then football became an irresistable sport for us and we would throw my football in the street for hours. We had fun but at times Larry was over zealous and threw the football so hard it hurt when I caught it. A few times I exclaimed when this happened "Hey don't forget I'm a girl!" Forgive me liberationists.

Sometime in January Larry and I began our affair. I took him to a party at Runaway House on Dupont Circle and he walked me home. We made out for a while and then began the most exciting love-making I had experienced in years. We were up all night. I hadn't planned to make love with him — I was ambivalent about that — but he insisted and I was glad. I only tell this because that was one of the reasons I liked him at the time. He wasn't afraid of me, or afraid of telling me to do something, or that he wanted something.

Most men I intimidated. Larry made me feel (I hate to say this) feminine. When we began our affair he was still involved with the Congressman's wife. As our relationship became more intense, he eventually broke off with her, but not for a very long time.

Our relationship was exciting. I fell madly in love with Larry. At one time I even thought of marrying him, and he moved into my apartment for about a year. As time went on we fought a lot and I was constantly jealous of the women, many my friends, that he would flirt with. Though I liked the fact that he wasn't afraid to tell me what he thought, it became tiring to have everything I said or I wanted taken as a challenge. At times it got so bad that if I wanted to do something Larry would choose the opposite just so he wasn't doing what I wanted. I became exasperated and I complained bitterly. Dr. Tilbet said "If you want an equal relationship so badly why don't you try a relationship with a woman?"

Sometimes the things you like about a person are the same things that drive you crazy about them. Originally I liked Larry because he played and liked to be silly. I like someone who is fun, but when I want to talk seriously I want the person to be there. Larry was a mover. He couldn't sit still for one minute and when I wanted to talk seriously he would always kid around.

Mandy

Mandy and I became close when my relationship with Larry intensified. Our relationship really began right after Anne married. I remember our first talk together. I was surprised that Mandy was so open. Most of my contact with her previously had been through Anne. I discovered I didn't really know her. She told me her feelings about D.C., about how she didn't like the people there and was planning to leave.

We found we shared some similar work experiences, and for the next two years we took major vacations together skiing in the Alps and often weekend trips as well. Sometimes we would flirt with other men, sometimes compete for them, but for the most part we spent our vacations enjoying each other's company.

When things became painful with Larry I used to call on Mandy. I liked seeing her often and in fact sometimes I used a problem with Larry as an excuse to see her. I felt very strongly about her and shared my feelings for her with Larry. The last summer that Mandy and Larry were in D.C. the three of us spent a lot of time together. They were my best friends.

Dr. Tilbet kept on encouraging me to express my strong feelings for Mandy but sometimes would add "If you keep scaring your close friends, they'll all keep getting married. You are going to scare them into marriage." This always made me angry at him. Looking back, it almost seems cruel.

At one time I felt that since I couldn't make love to Mandy, I wished Larry would. I had told him this fantasy and he couldn't understand my feelings — or how this would make me feel closer to her.

In the last year that Mandy was in D.C. every night I went out with her or with Larry. My life was very full being with these people I loved. Those relationships, though each had their problems, were very enjoyable. Mandy and Larry met my needs for intimacy. Though my relationship with Larry was frought with incredible problems, it had its warm moments and I do believe the fact that I was in a relationship to him allowed me to get close to Mandy. This is my view, it is not necessarily hers. But I know that I was more comfortable in getting close to her and feeling that it was okay because I had Larry.

When Mandy finally was about to leave for Africa I was somewhat shocked and upset by the fact that she, as I put it "left me," when she had been planning to leave all along. Hadn't she told me our first conversation when we became close that she didn't like D.C. and was planning to move?

That summer as Mandy was getting ready for Africa I was available to be with her whenever she wanted. I was ready to play tennis and go out to dinner or to the movies whenever she was done packing or doing the research that had to be finished before she left. I hated thinking of her leaving. We had so much fun whenever we were together or when Larry joined us.

On her last day I remember going over to Mandy's house. I found her on the floor tying boxes together to make the 5 o'clock mail so that everything would be done by the time she left. She was sending most of her belongings to Africa by mail. She was frantic as we tied those packages and screamed at me when she asked for the string. Then we ran to the post office and got there just in time. I dropped her off at her place and went home to have supper with Larry. Then he and I went over to Mandy's to say goodbye. I remember that she thought it so silly that her folks insisted she call them to say goodbye that very last night before she went to Africa instead of the evening before. She couldn't see what difference one day would make, but I knew exactly how her mother felt.

Our goodbye was awkward and painful. Larry kept on joking the whole time. He gave Mandy a big hug — thank God he was there. Then I remember saying goodbye to her standing on the stairs. She was above me on the landing. I touched her hand. She hardly moved. And I felt that maybe I shouldn't have done even that. Can you imagine, here was one of the women that I loved so much and we could hardly touch even in our leaving?

I remember going home and feeling awful. I was sitting on the floor using the telephone, calling to make arrangements to go to New York the next day with Larry.

Larry said it was a shame the world has to be this way, that people have to lose their good friends. I could barely let myself cry. The next day Larry kept me busy. We drove up to New York, to the tennis tournament at Forest Hills. Later I would be devastated by Mandy's absence when I returned to D.C. and Larry left for law school the next week. Then that pain, that awful loneliness and loss were there.

I remember when Larry left that raw pain coming home from work to an empty apartment after having spent an intense day at review committee. I was hoping to find a note from Larry. There was one. He told me to take care. It was the first time he signed a note to me "love."

That year I resolved to write this book. It was as if everything in my life had reached a crescendo. My 30th birthday had come, Larry had gone off to law school, and Mandy had gone off to Africa to do research. Their absences intensified my feelings of aloneness. I worked and never stopped working until I dropped from sheer exhaustion, or until I was overcome by depression or loneliness and then I would go out with new friends made to replace the loss of Mandy and Larry. It was true that if Larry had not gone off to law school we would have broken up, but the loss was still there and I felt it.

I remember in those early days after they had both parted going to see *Sunday Bloody Sunday,* and asking myself how anyone could leave people that they loved. I especially felt the loss of Mandy because we had been so close. Not only did I love her; she was my buddy. My close women friends many times helped me fight the loneliness and the isolation that I had felt so much in Washington.

After Mandy left I became friends with Greta, a woman who lived down the street from me. Greta had just separated from her husband and was looking for close women friends. She was the first woman in D.C. that I tried to be openly affectionate with. We would kiss hello and goodbye and shared some warm moments. Once we talked about holding each other in bed when we went on a trip together — but then we were quite distant. I felt that had I been able to connect with her I wouldn't have had to leave D.C. But we didn't connect. If Greta (or Anne or Mandy) could have at least entered my world and acknowledged my feelings, it would have been easier. They didn't have to make love to me.

I tried to keep as busy as I could now. I was up in the air, traveling the country as much as possible. After three months Larry dropped out of law school and returned to D.C. We fought more than ever, and I tried to break up with him a dozen times. Traveling for my job, traveling to see Mandy, and planning my next year was one way to avoid seeing him.

When Mandy and Larry left my life was at a dead end. I had to get out of Washington, but I was ambivalent. I was very much invested in my job. I wanted NIMII to adopt the youth-initiated program that I had developed, and I didn't want to leave until it was adopted. I had some fantasy that if they adopted it of staying and running it, but mostly I knew that I needed to leave. I had already talked to some young people about taking my position if the program was adopted. And they did agree to run the program if I went away for a year so it wouldn't be dropped.

I was simply attached to Washington. I never thought that I would leave the place. It was my home. I loved it and had spent some good years there. My job was often exciting: I was able to travel a lot for work and for vacations. I went to Europe almost every year for a ski trip. My roommates from Aberfoyle and I had gone in different directions but I was still very attached to them and didn't want to leave them, though there was nothing for me in their day to day lives now. Often it was sad to be with them because I was so lonely. I knew I needed to get away at least for a while. Time was standing still. I had to try something.

So that year I applied to Harvard for graduate school. There was a program that if I could get into it I would be able to maintain some contact with my job at NIMH, and still change my life to some degree. I had found that it was a really hard thing for me to apply there. I was scared to put myself on the line.

In my personal statement to Harvard I indicated that one of my reasons for pursuing graduate study was that I thought I would be more effective in my role at NIMH and take a few less lumps if I had academic credentials. I argued "that people in power might be able to hear my position and deal with me more comfortably (and I may be more comfortable with them) if I had credentials — it may indeed be true that one needs to have a Ph.D. in order to effectively say that academic credentials are not a prerequisite for knowledge and competency."

I also indicated that I wanted to be with people who would push me further in my thinking. I was sick of pushing people at NIMH and doing battles. I wanted people that were going to teach me new things and I was sick of being isolated.

I was very lucky that a young woman, Alice Hill, whom I worked with was so supportive of me by helping me edit my personal statement, as she had so often done with some of my papers at NIMH.

At the same time that I was applying to Harvard, I wanted to maintain my contact with the outside world. Learning by experience was very important to me. I didn't want to be cut off from work — I had a tremendous fear of that. I saw going to school as a complete withdrawal from the real world. I wanted to keep current with developments and the activities occurring in the community health field. At NIMH I continuously stated and had in fact one time testified at a Senate sub-committee that often education was a withdrawl from life and I urged the funding of alternative youth programs and research programs that demonstrated the importance of direct experience.

So I decided to try a series of alternatives — graduate school, law school, the job in California with Alan Smith who had asked me if I would like to start a mental health delivery system with him there. Alan and I had talked about hiring our friends and I was of course hopeful that Mandy would join us. I had sent away for some law school applications but then never did fill them out. The applications were just too long and involved and I knocked myself out on my personal statement to Harvard. There were also other alternatives. I forget what others. I know that I had wanted to write a book about my feelings — my struggles with women for a long time but I couldn't envision how to do it full time. My fantasy was that I needed a husband to enable me to write because it was just too frightening for me to think of out and out quitting and writing full time. I was so lonely and scared of being lonely and so much of writing is alone and being by yourself. I also considered being a hippie and dropping out and retiring, but I was too scared to do that. I felt I would be floating free in the universe — the same feelings I had experienced when I graduated from college and didn't know what to do with my life. Gloria said that with all my energy if I were to retire for a year they would have to put blinders on me. I felt I needed contact with the outside world through work even though it seemed to be beating me down.

I almost felt like I was playing some form of Russian roulette with my life. I remember one lonely Saturday afternoon returning from shopping in Georgetown and Dupont Circle with books in my arms. My neighbor asked me what I was up to, and I showed him a book for the graduate record exam and one for the law school boards and he said "Oh, the natives are restless." I saw myself putting my life in the hands of fate and trying for doctor, lawyer, writer, Indian chief or whatever would turn up — that is what I would be for the next few years.

After I returned from my second trip to see Mandy in France, I was so lonely I continued to travel as much as possible. I resumed my journeys to California. I had been going there often that spring for work, having funded several programs in the Bay Area. One contract with Dragon's Eye to do a self study on commune life was about to begin. On one of these trips I met Alan. We took some time to look for a location for our proposed human service center. We had decided it would be easier to get grant monies if we first had an institutional base to apply from. Our concepts changed often. At that time they included art stores and galleries, restaurants and mental health services, all supported and run by the community. We interviewed at Kendale, a public health institute and then Alan interviewed at Topeka Community Health a private organization which provided mental health and health services in Northern California. But when Alan landed a job at Topeka, everything changed.

While we were interviewing for the job at Kendale, Alan and I fantasized about working with our friends and integrating our work and play. We talked a lot about this.

I took Alan to Dragon's Eye to meet Thomas and the other commune members. We both wanted to change our life in some way. Alan kept on teasing me that I would never be happy in a commune, I was much too middle class.

I remember that evening at the commune when we were all on the floor in Howie's room doing back rubs while Michael and Howie did animal fights on the floor, and Alan was lying with his hand on my knee. That felt strange. I always kept a certain distance from the people I worked with at NIMH and though we had discussed integrating work and life, I had not thought of getting it on with Alan. I was in the place in my life where I wanted a man for me. I was not into having affairs with married men. It was this same period in my life that I found it disconcerting seeing a blues singer and guitarist I was very fond of because he had so many women lovers. I wanted someone for me.

I had fantasized developing some form of group family with Alan. He felt his wife wouldn't be open to such an arrangement, but promised "We'll see when we get to California." I felt if I slept with him now and he did not tell his wife that it would be like having an affair. I wanted a relationship more like the one I had with Gary and Lisa. One that would include us all and give me some sense of family.

I had read *The Harrad Experiment* and *Proposition 31* and anything else I could get my hands on that talked about alternative families during the period I was exploring my relationship with Gary and Lisa in Philadelphia. Earlier that day I had talked with Mark, a commune member about group sex and group families. He said he and Millie tried with good friends and were hurt when it failed. I remember him saying as he worked in his garden "You hungry for that, huh?"

I also didn't want to have an affair with Alan since that was not my habit with men I worked with, despite all the fantasies that abounded at NIMH about my sex life. I was always afraid that if you had an affair with a colleague, a man, it would be especially difficult for you to maintain your equality. I wanted Alan to deal with me in terms of my intellectual prowess and not my body. I just didn't like being the "little woman," it never has fit me. Also I realized that I was especially hurting then and didn't think I could handle a relationship with a married man.

When Alan left the commune that evening, I felt his moodiness and his weightedness on my knee and on me.

Then when we met the next day I remember telling him I didn't want to have an affair with him. At the time he and I were driving onto the entrance on the freeway going to another job interview — going on the ramp I felt very powerful and sure of myself. Alan was no different than other men I worked with. I just didn't want affairs with them — even friends I had been very close to. I didn't sleep easily with people. When I reached California things did change.

So Alan and I didn't have an affair; we didn't even keep an equal relationship. As soon as he landed his job at Topeka, our non-hierarchial relationship went out the window, and all the haggling that one does with someone about money occurred between us. Alan was to head the mental health services for Topeka in Sonoma and Marin Counties.

It was then that I learned I had been accepted at Harvard. So I had two opportunities come through. Alan began to tease me about being status conscious, asking "Why did I want a credential?" I remember being very defensive and irritated each time he did that. It took me several trips to California to sort this out. The bastard had an MD! What kind of shit was I letting him give me?

My opportunities were varied and innumerable. I could go to Boston, attend Harvard and maintain a liaison with my NIMH job and keep my residence in D.C. Or I could take the job with Alan in California. I decided I wanted both the job in California and to attend Harvard. I called my advisor and asked if I could do my field work in California. He said yes!

So halleluiah! I was so excited! And there was even the chance of being with Mandy in California if Alan would give her a job.

It was also possible that NIMH would support me for this year of graduate training. A month later they agreed!

Now I had two more options. I could take a permanent salaried staff position with Alan or take a position as his deputy assistant but be paid by NIMH and maintain my NIMH position.

I decided to go as Alan's deputy assistant, though I wasn't sure whether I wanted to be a member of his paid staff or be paid by NIMH. I also was somewhat torn between wanting a reflective academic year sitting back absorbing and studying a non-hierarchial organization as it developed and being active and running a program with Alan. One thing was decided, however. I was to play the role of sounding board for Alan and remind him of our original plans as we struggled with the day to day operations of the program.

Over the summer months the tensions mounted. We haggled over my future role and my demands for a salary comparable to my NIMH salary. In the end I decided that I wasn't ready to leave NIMH, and turned down the salaried staff position with Alan. Furthermore, I felt I would be in a more powerful position on my own and not on Alan's paid staff.

Nurturing

Larry and I that last year in D.C. were always breaking up. Once that year after tennis around 8 o'clock at night I remember Larry stopped by to visit and we fell asleep together on my bed. I think we were playing and hugging each other when we fell asleep, me on top of him. I just loved that kind of closeness. And I remember the next day in therapy telling Dr. Tilbet that it was so wonderful to sleep holding each other (saying something like when things are like that I really love him and want to be with him or I don't want us not to see each other.) Dr. Tilbet said "Well, you have to weigh whether it is worth all the pain that you have been experiencing."

That kind of nurturing and closeness I love to experience with men or women. I had at that time experienced it only with Larry — no I take it back — when I slept with Gloria she had told me that what she had done in our lovemaking was given me a lot of holding and nurturing. From Gloria for the first time I believe I heard the word nurturing used in this way and at the time I didn't know exactly what it meant.

Mandy

At first I was going to travel with Mandy one more time in Europe before I went to California but I decided I had too much work to do at NIMH. Mandy had decided to travel through Europe and was going to come to the States when job positions at Topeka with Alan were settled. However in her meanderings she met up with an old friend with whom she proceeded to fall in love. But she continued writing about joining Alan and I. When I reached California I was still hopeful that she and I would be working together.

Those times in Washington were my last months of agony waiting to leave. I had made the decision, now I had to decide when the moment of truth was to be.

Was it going to be in August or September? I wanted to finish some things that I had started at NIMH before I left and I made one more attempt to get NIMH to adopt the youth program. I do know I went through much turmoil in my leave-taking. I am not a person that easily lets go.

I wrote in the first page of my journal:
September 30, 1972

Leaving Washington on September 20, 1972. Warm feelings with Anne looking for or more like savoring her tears and red face. She likes me too and will miss me. Didn't I know that anyway? Do I need proof? She has always been there, (through my months of preparing to part from Washington) as she said of me often years before — "You are always there."

Self consciously I write. Somehow I want my first entry to my journal to be — not my earlier writings of Harvard registration day or my transition feelings of parting — but my feelings about Anne and leaving D.C. Anyway, I want the above moment recorded. I leave Anne because I come to Berkeley so that I can hopefully express my love of men and women more openly and more physically. I love Anne, went through pain and agony — literally because I didn't know what to do with those feelings — and in fact did not know that maybe they were okay.

Well, it's nice having someone who is there all the time. And that last evening and morning before I left when Anne made me dinner and took me to the airport, I thought maybe all those days of agony are coming round with her.

102

Anyway it makes me feel good to say "I Love You Anne," and tears come to my eyes as I write. It is a good feeling. I hope one day I can show you this journal.

I will be exploring my sexuality in my new life. I see myself sometimes like Ken. I want to be independent, attractive, sexy, and be able to make love to the people that I love. Men or women.

CALIFORNIA

W E HAD gone horseback riding that day up the winding hills of Marin. The two of us on our horses. Jessica on Nepenthe, with his head always lurking forward, and me on Shadow, his firm body as calm as his brown-toned skin. We had ridden up the ridge above the trees. It was all very romantic. I turned to watch Jessica as Shadow and I climbed to the top of the hill. Jessica was rounding the edge of the ridge, and behind her I saw the tree-covered hills way down below looming like the backdrop to an incredible 3-D movie. Seeing her I was able to see myself on horseback in this beautiful countryside. It was unreal and was like a movie.

Before we had rounded the crest of the trail where the land drops off below, we had ridden side by side on our horses — and kissed each other as our horses inevitably pulled and pushed us apart. We giggled at our joy and precarious touching. How romantic I thought. I just loved it!

What I always wanted was happening to me. To be able to kiss and hug the woman that I loved. Dr. Tilbet was right — it was possible!

Meeting Jessica Albrick

I remember the day that I drove across the Richmond Bridge to San Rafael, to the Community Center, wearing my long black dotted swiss skirt and shirt. It was hot and I was nervous as my car blew in the breeze across the bridge. The sign said CAUTION, high wind area. Trailers slow down. All I know is that I held onto the wheel for dear life. My car was almost blowing off the bridge. "You got to be kidding! How am I going to make this trip everyday?" I planned to buy a new car, so that I would avoid the pitfalls of having this VW.

Alan Smith was in his office. First we discussed positions in the organization. Then he gave me two names and told me to look up these people at the Topeka Community Service Center. One of them was Jessica.

I remember driving over to Larkspur on the freeway, over the hills of Marin. I entered the Community Health Center and looked for the people whose names were written on my piece of paper.

Jessica was in a meeting of the crisis team. I entered the room and sat on the floor beside her. We talked a little, and afterwards we talked for quite a while. She was very friendly and took my name and number and offered to help me find a place to live, and to do something with me so we could visit and talk. She also invited me to a party.

I remember that she asked me what I was doing as the deputy assistant but after that, that part of the conversation was dropped. Unlike all the others who kept on asking me what the deputy assistant did and who she was, who kept scrutinizing me and watching me, that never seemed to be a concern of hers.

What I liked about Jessica was that she related to me as a person, not as someone from NIMH doing graduate work at Harvard who was going to be working closely to the director. We talked instantly on a personal level. Everyone else seemed to be grilling me to the wall. "Who are you? What are you going to be doing? How will the new organization work? What were you doing before? What are you doing in school?"

We became fast friends. Jessica Albrick was her name. We were both Capricorns and almost instantly trusted each other. We talked about our lives and what we wanted from our work.

Alan had said "You have to meet Jessica. She is going to run the unit in Sonoma and West Marin which is a piece of land that broke off or is constantly moving away after the earthquake. It always has fog over it." Alan told me he once drove over there with Jessica and Ned and Chris. He felt West Marin was an erie place. He wasn't sure that he would want to live there, but that a lot of rock music stars did. Jessica had met one of them. I think it was Jessie Collin Young.

He said that Jessica had just gotten over a divorce, but that he thought she would handle the job well enough and that she had her life in hand an that the divorce wouldn't affect her doing the job well. That is all I remember, but he did urge me to see her and was sure that I would like her. I did.

Later when Alan separated from his wife there was never any discussion about whether he could handle his job during his divorce.

Jessica asked me to go horseback riding. I didn't know how that came about, but it was wonderful. I think she asked me to go with her the first week of work. It was so wonderful that very evening I bought a horse. His name was Shadow. Jessica and I rode through the Redwoods and through a stream where Shadow stamped his foot and splashed water around like a playful child. When we trotted down around a hill and went under a bridge over the stream I decided that I just had to have a horse! It was just like the cowboy movies when we went "around the bend under the bridge." I was going to live out all my childhood fantasies in the glistening waters and magical hills of Marin, wet with moisture captured by the Redwoods and ferns. For the first time in my life I had made a choice to buy something major that wasn't flashy or expensive but easy to take care of. Instead of a quarter horse that had a sensitive foot that had to be watched carefully, I bought a buckskin gelding. He was delightful, a layback horse, a mellow horse.

Emma, my roommate, was real surprised when she met Shadow. She said "A speedy lady with a layback horse." I had purchased a horse before I had a permanent place to live or before I even had decided whether to live in Marin, Berkeley or San Francisco.

110

When I arrived in California I was still going through my 30th year identity crisis. I really wasn't sure who I was or who I wanted to be. I didn't know what to be — hippie, woman, middle class lady, girl, or professional woman. In part I could not see a role or a model in this society for who I was.

For me the commune in Berkeley where I first stayed was an important transition point. I was aware after my conversation with Thomas the other night that the commune during my early months was holding me together. The folks there were supportive of my adjustment to California. On earlier visits I had told them about my feelings for women and my isolation at work. They had urged me to come to Berkeley, and when I did arrive Karen said "Hurray for our side, another good person has joined us!"

My hopes when I went to work with Alan were that we would learn a new way to do social change in a large institution. I thought that if Alan and I were at the top of a large organization I could learn how huge organizations were run. Why it was often not clear who made the decisions and why decisions were made in institutions like NIMH. I was hopeful that I might help in making decision processes clearer and in clarifying power.

At NIMH people were reluctant to take responsibility for decision-making. Often you didn't know who had the power to make a specific decision and consequently one had difficulty determining what one could do to influence a decision about their program priorities. In the case of the youth program I couldn't find out who ultimately was objecting to it and so I couldn't ask him the reason for not wanting it so I could make it more attractive to him, or to meet his own power needs. No one wanted to be responsible for a decision. Consequently issues were kept diffuse. The tactic used by administrators was to delay decisions — just wait or just rewrite a memo again and then wait again. Rewriting memos when it comes to making decisions that involve power distribution have never to my knowledge contributed to decision-making. They may of course be used to justify the decision but not to make it in the first place.

No one wanted to make a decision on something that could be unpopular, i.e. giving power to youth. If they said yes and a program became unpopular in Congress, they could get the ax and if they said no on it and it was backed by someone in power like a Senator, they could get it too. So the tactic was to delay and not to make a decision until one was absolutely sure. Most people didn't want to take a stand or risk their necks.

Phil said (I)and the people that I associated with tended to be ahead of our time and for that we take a lot of heat. No one likes changes or new ideas, so they focus their anger on the agent of change. At NIMH I was ahead of my time. I served as a catalyst and hurried things along. It may be that I had to leave to have the youth program happen. I became the bureaucrat's enemy and they weren't going to let me have my victory. But perhaps they would institute the program when I left. I need to learn to do things in a more receptive way so that initiated changes are made to be everyone's programs and the power structure is dealt with in such a way that programs are allowed to happen without two opposing sides forming and issues seen in terms of victory and defeat.

Phil said "Often you can be respected or loved but not both. People might let you have your victory. They may respect you for it. But they are not going to love you for their defeat." NIMH was perhaps going to do the youth program but not for awhile. As in all issues, a variety of forces cause change. The murder of 18 runaways in Texas sped up the long needed Runaway House funding, by a bill initiated in Congress. Only after a public crisis do we act. When I left I told the division director: "You can delay the youth program but you can't stop it. It will happen in two or three years anyway, and you have the opportunity to do something innovative now."

At first it seemed so easy. I wanted a woman I loved who loved me that I could hold, and there was Jessica Albrick.

Mandy did not come to California and that was very painful, but her replacement was right here and available. (Mandy had gone to live in New Hampshire with the man she had been traveling with in Europe and later married.)

Jessica and I became very close friends fast. So fast that within a month's time I had told her how I felt about women, that the women I loved I wanted to be able to hug and/or make love with. I didn't want ever to be in that painful place again of loving a woman and being unable to touch her. I didn't want to love another woman and have to hide who I was or how I felt. I wanted to be able to express my love, to hug her, to hold her, or just to say I loved her. I did not want to fear that if I expressed my feelings I would lose her.

I don't know whether Jessica learned about the idea of integrating work and life from Alan or whether I told her right away. I think it was a little bit of both. But I remember that we seemed to agree on our concepts about work and play and friendships and discovered we had similar experiences in our lives.

Jessica and I spent a lot of time going back and forth to Point Reyes and to Bodega City. The first time we went there Ned and Chris drove us in their van over Sir Francis Drake Highway until we almost reached Forest Knolls, where we took a right and caught the Nicasio Valley road to Point Reyes. I remember I thought it was strange territory, and I still feel that strangeness when I drive through it today. The morning we first drove it was September and there was plenty of water in the lakes against a barren bleak land with a tremendous wide open expanse to it. Alan's description of this piece of land that broke off from the coast deep in fog and had floated up from Mexico of course added to the erieness. It was beautiful here but also very desolate.

We stopped in Point Reyes Station for a little while, sat in the hot sun which I remember was just wonderfully soothing. We sat opposite the Cafe next to the Dance Palace. I let the sun soothe me as I rolled up my pant legs and my shirt sleeves. This was heaven I thought as I watched the horses and cows roam over the hills behind the Kings' grocery store. I could be inside the Parklawn building at NIMH right now!

After a quick meeting there we drove to a town ten miles down the coast called Bolinas. On the way we stopped for some natural food at a grocery store in Olema. I remember Chris and Ned bought some carrot juice, which I found quite strange tasting.

Then we drove to Bolinas and I saw another town on the coast. After a brief meeting with some people there, Jessica and I walked to the beach and sat there watching the waves. I was fixing my belt that had broken. We had stopped on the way to the beach at a store and bought strips of leather to repair my belt. I had decided when I moved to California that I would repair my things myself, do things with my hands that would be simple and pleasurable. Jessica gave me her Swiss army knife to make repairs. It was red with a white cross on it, an important artifact of California. It was something to be cherished and taken care of very well. I believe that Ned and Chris had them too, but had special rules as to their care.

I felt as if I was learning about all the artifacts of California, and riding in the back of Ned's van with its tie-dye curtains, I was getting a first-hand account.

We were to spend a day and a half each week at the beginning getting to know the community, since we were planning to further decentralize the community health program which was presently located in three buildings — one in Larkspur and one in San Rafael and one in lower Sonoma County. Those early days were fun for me; it was all very exciting and I must admit tiring. I would come from Berkeley in the morning — I was staying at the commune at the time — and then meet Jessica or Ned at Greenbrae and drive to West Marin. The contrast between my office in the Parklawn Building where 3000 employees were working off long narrow corridors that were over four city blocks in length (after spending an hour outside driving around looking for a parking place that was never there — the elusive parking place — because they never did build enough spaces to go with the size of the building) was overwhelming. This built-in parking problem was blamed on government employees by towing their cars away for parking "illegally." The building was built in the suburbs only after much protest and without the needed public transportation from the city. It is an example of the system "creating a problem — and then penalizing the victim for his behavior in trying to survive."

Sometimes, when I would park on the south side of the building, I would have to use the longest hallway to reach my office. As I walked down this hall it took me so long to get to the other end that I could actually see people at the far end walking in and out of nearby offices conducting and concluding their business during the time it took me to walk the length of the corridor. The contrast of winding down Sir Francis Drake Highway through the redwoods and the hills of

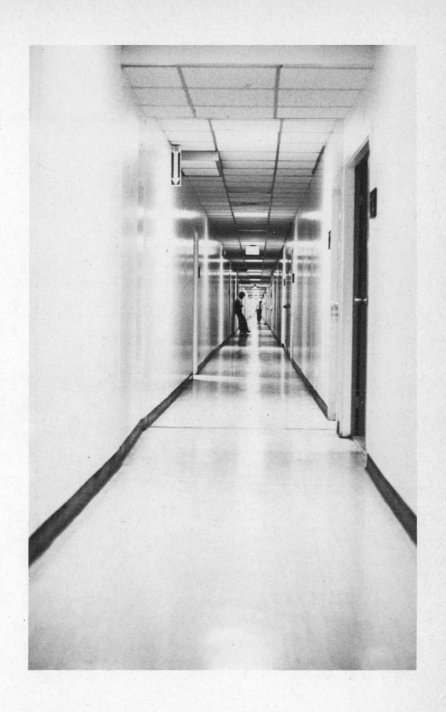

Marin where horses and cattle freely roamed and dotted the hillside was a welcome relief.

I reflected back often. "This is my new life." I had fantisized about it but I never quite dreamed that it would be this fine, this lovely. Life should be more like this — where people can be in touch with the earth, can spend part of their work time in the out of doors. I was very lucky.

The Earth was Alive

We were to determine the best location for an office for the West Marin-Sonoma unit, and what type of services would be best for the community. So we spent time meeting people in the community, talking to shopkeepers and some time visiting a bar in Bolinas.

What I remember most is the long drive along Sir Francis Drake Highway through Forest Knolls, starting from Fairfax, the countryside reminding me so much of Europe. Through the redwoods of Samuel Taylor Park and down into Olema, I remember mostly the trees and the stream that ran the entire length of the highway. I remember the long rides in Jessica's light blue VW, the silences and the talk, the rushing water in a storm. Once we stopped the car in the middle of a heavy rain fall, and got out and stood on a bridge as the water rushed beneath us. We were crazy. Then I got scared the bridge would collapse under the force of the water, but it was so exciting. The earth was alive.

Jessica reawakened me to the earth and its pleasures, its smells, its noises, its song, its colors and then there was no stopping me. I took off on my own trip, my own connectedness to the earth. I loved her for this. She had helped me, put me in touch with it. But only by awakening a part of myself that was once there in childhood, that was once in all of us. "Yellow flowers, smells of the Acacia, the first flowers of spring," she told me.

On Saturdays or Sundays I would usually go horseback riding with Jessica in West Marin. Thomas joked once that he could see us tying our horses to the hitching post, then throwing open the saloon doors, marching in and saying: "Okay, where is Mr. Right?"

One of our very first days together Jessica took me down Route One where she had driven so many times when she was going through her divorce. We went toward Muir Beach and then on up toward Stinson in her VW. She took me out to the coast on a cliff. I remember walking down the narrow path that took us under a haven made by some cypress trees blown by the sea wind into the shape of a flat umbrella, and then out from under them to the cliff over the sea. She was dauntless in her walk, moving briskly and smoothly to an opening on the path where she could stand on the very edge of the cliff. I trailed behind gingerly. The great expanse of water reaching the horizon was breathtaking, a flat blue as far as the eye could see.

She stood on the ledge with her arms open straight up and her hair blowing back. I asked her if she weren't frightened of falling and she said that she had walked here often, and had in fact one time with a lover camped here, and made love under the cypress trees.

As I stood there looking at the blue expanse, I wondered how at that precise moment a war could be going on in Vietnam. I could see how one could come out here to California, drop out, and stop all the silly haggling that we all do. I was afraid in fact that I would be so happy in Forest Knolls riding my horse and sitting near the redwoods that I would not want to work, and I thought "that would be terrible!" Jessica didn't think so at all. I thought of the people who were stuck in hideous offices doing jobs they did not want and did not think to be very important. How could all that crap and status stuff that I left behind still be going on?

Being with Jessica on Sundays that first year in California I felt that my childhood place was right around the corner, that Silver Springs, Maryland was right over the Richmond Bridge.

The Relationship of Jessica, Alan and Ruth

I don't know where it began. I was so frustrated by my relationship with Alan. We were fighting all the time. The tension was mounting. The night before I had told him of my concern about not having an office and he screamed "Your concern, your concern, you are always concerned!"

121

Jessica and I went off to Sam's for lunch that Friday afternoon to talk about work. Sam's is a restaurant in Tiburon. I had visited there years before with my roommate Kate from Aberfoyle on my first trip to California.

Jessica and I talked over Sam's big hamburgers and two gin fizzes. I thought then again "What a life I am having! At lunch break I can go and have lunch at Sam's!" Sam's was a Sunday treat for many people, a special treat which I could take during my work week for lunch.

We talked about my relationship with Alan, the tensions and difficulties he and I were having and the breakdown of communication that had occurred ever since Alan landed the job and moved to California three months before I was to join him. Jessica suggested that I play with Alan, that we just go out and be together and stop talking and arguing, so I asked him that day to go for a ride and to spend some time with me by the Bay. We stopped by the Berkeley Marina on the way home from Marin and threw the football that was in the back of my car. Jessica mentioned during our talk that she had hoped to get close to him too, but we talked about how it would be possible for us both to be close to him. We talked about non-monogamous relationships and how it was possible to love more than one person. We learned only later that sharing the same person is quite a different ballgame from being non-monogamous and liking several different people at once.

The football game and afterward the wrestling-type back rub eased the tensions between Alan and I for awhile, but they didn't solve anything.

122

Desks

I had often told Alan during those early months at Topeka that if I were his *male* deputy assistant he would not be treating me the way he was. "You wouldn't bring a deputy assistant to the boss — a consultant from NIMH — some 3000 miles out from the East Coast to work with you and not give him an office!" Unless perhaps the consultant was female and your male staff, who you were uneasy about since they were resistant to your program changes, was on your back because you gave a woman an office to herself in the administration wing where two men usually shared a small office.

For me it was humiliating working in the waiting room next to Alan's office. Offices in organizations often represent power and respect. I felt little respect from Alan and powerless and humiliated in front of his staff. Worse, when I would bring up the issue of the office — as a woman's issue — I would feel embarrassed and small about it. But that was my first month in California when I was new and disoriented from adjusting to my big move to the West Coast and didn't have the feminist support base that I have now.

I had experienced similar feelings when I confronted an NIMH male staff member with submitting my written work with his name on it to an upper staff administrator. I felt soiled and dirty as if it were I who committed some "crime." With Alan I didn't feel soiled, I just felt whinny and inferior. I didn't feel powerful and indignant over his behavior toward me, I felt humiliated.

The office trip was really about Alan's not being able to tell me that he didn't want me on his staff anymore. I asked him directly if he wanted to work with me, and he said "Yes." There was indeed a shortage of office space, but there is a shortage of office space in all bureaucracies and those who pressured and had the power got what they wanted. At one time I was told I could have an office if I bumped another woman. I refused. I wasn't going to be a part of such male behavior.

The role that I was to play — that of sounding board and advocate of the original plans and ideals we were going to attempt — was no longer useful to Alan, and probably at times even painful. Plus, he had found in Jessica support for his role as a new administrator.

I realized only later, when he was going through his separation with his wife and mentioned to me that he married his first wife just before he went off to medical school, that he seemed to use women as a support for major transitions in his life and got rid of them when those events were over. I felt he needed me to make his transition to California. When that was done I was no longer useful to him. After that he saw me as competition and as a threat, since I watched him run his show from the inside. I must admit I needed him too for my move to California. I don't think I would have come out here without knowing I could work on his staff for a year.

Eventually I got an office. I elected not to quit my job since I wanted to be able to remain in California for the year. But I withdrew from my role as deputy assistant and worked on a new project for Topeka Community Health that I was developing with Jessica in West Marin and lower Sonoma County.

The day before Thanksgiving Jessica and I went to dinner in the city at a Russian restaurant. We joked and drank a whole bottle of wine between us. I got high quickly and felt wonderful and was ready at Jessica's prodding to go and get a tatoo like her's at Lyle Tuttle's off Market St. The previous week Jessica and her sister had gotten flower tatoos on their back hips. It was now or never. If I thought about it, I knew I wouldn't do it. I thought it would be wonderful ritual — a government employee with a tatoo. That would mark a symbolic change in my life. I was slowly becoming a West Coast person and the ritual was a part of Jessica's and my relationship — we were becoming like sisters.

I drew a quick flower like Jessica's and told the man to put it on my back hip just below my bikini suit line. So if I didn't like it, it didn't have to show — and to do it quick before I chickened out. It hurt like hell.

November 24, 1972
Journal entry — written on the plane to my mother's funeral
in Hartford

my mother died today.
I have waited a long time for her death
a phone call in the dead of night in Washington D.C. —
always expected

This morning, bright and sunny — a call in the morning —
mom died at 5 a.m. today.
And it is a fucking shock. I am numb — have been able
to cry a little
numb and shocked
called Anne, Jessica, Thomas at the commune and Jeremy
answered the phone
Ran in night gown with jeans underneath
and shirt above in the cool morning
dewed day to neighbors — knocked on the door, no answer —
no cars in front
fled back to apartment

order a blur — does it matter? talked to Thomas and laughed.
I am going to my mother's funeral with a tatoo on my body.
And Thomas said "At least she won't ever know." Told Jessica
about the tatoo when I called her on the phone to tell her of
my mother's death and she said that she thought of that as she
said "a tatoo, not even healed." I don't want to attach death
to the tatoo but beauty, birth, outrageousness, a laugh at life.

126

My mother needed to die — there in a bed, almost a vegetable, barely able to utter words, and then words that did not communicate in the reality I lived in.

On our last visit she had asked "What are you doing?" What are you doing?" I told her about copying "my old into new" (changing my address book), of California, of Shadow and I looked at her hair gray, long and beautiful. And I watched a tear roll down her left eye as she looked at me. I felt then that she recognized me and really loved me. And now I think of my pain — old feelings buried that will have to surface.

Called Alan. Waited until I had my shit together. Felt like apologizing. Here comes another thing he needs me for and I'm not there. How absurd.

Wanting to be near a woman. Asked Jessica if she would mind taking me to the airport. Jeremy kissed me, she said she loved me. She knows what to do at the right time.
Jessica and I distant in our warmth. We are alike in many ways.

women/mother/closeness

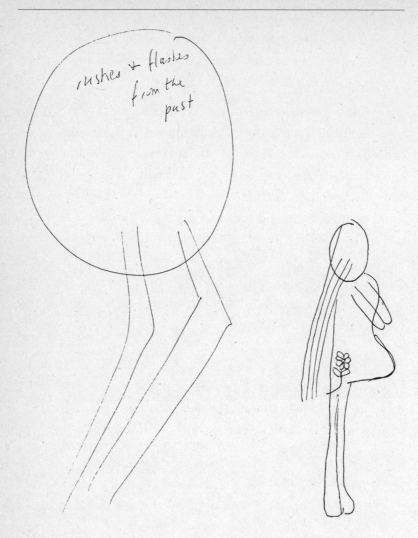

I dreamt I went to my mother's funeral wearing a tatoo.

Somehow my tatoo gave me a sense of reality and humor. When things got overwhelming and horrid with relatives I went into the bathroom, pulled down my pants and looked at my flower from the west.

128

Wednesday, November 28, 1972
Journal entry — written after the funeral

It is sad to see someone you love die even though in so
many respects they have been dead for such a long time.
anger/emptyness. I can't even remember her,
so much being blurred by her disease.
No sweet memories in her death.

When I miss Mandy or Anne or Jessica there are sweet
tears, with mom none exist. I wish I could write a beautiful
poem on her death — to a mother whom I hardly knew — to a
mother I worked out my relationship with in therapy/giving
much to the problems of relating to her disease, not much
practice relating to her as a normal person with mind clear/not
blurred by tangled rotting nerve endings/pain in hands/dou-
ble vision and unexpected emotional ups and downs. Anger
and love in her relationship to me.

I feel physically sick by her death — I could hardly move
yesterday. I hope her death does not take a great toll of my
life in California. Rather I wish to make it a turning point for
me there. I do hope I can turn her death into an energy for
me, focus on happiness, not sadness and loneliness, for I feel
there is hardly much time for any of us. How morbid.
I don't think one can force happiness. I must ease up — I am
wanting it so.

my father. I hope he survives without too much pain
my brother, wife and child give me a sense of meaning in my
mother's life. Jeremy their son is beautiful.
There is maybe no more need to search for a mother — my
mother is dead.

In the category of the unexpected was the death of my mother (but then that was always expected). It was just that I didn't expect that it would reek such havoc on my body. I felt as if the universe had dealt me a heavy blow, beat my body so that walking or moving my legs was an effort. I could not rally one bit of energy to do my work. I thought that I would be able to work on the plane returning from my mother's funeral. I simply couldn't move. I went down to Washington to spend a few days with Anne, recovering before I flew back to the west. It was an unexpected trip and I don't recall much about it. It was hard for Anne and I to talk at all. I remember telling her I was knocked out and she said: "Of course what do you expect?" But I don't think we talked much more than that.

I had expected my mother's death to be relief, something off my shoulders. It wasn't. Dr. Tilbet had been telling me for the last three years in therapy that it would be a relief. So I was surprised to find that I couldn't do my work. The way that I worked in the past was that I could always work. Sometimes it was difficult because I worked so intensely and so painfully and pushed myself until the fuses almost blew and my body became almost rigid — or until I was so frantic that I had to stop to catch my breath, but I had always been able to rally the energy eventually to work to ease my pain. I thought that would happen coming home from D.C.

When parents die, though we might not see them often or be very close to them we still get a sense of no one to fall back on but ourselves.

When your mother dies you are no longer a child.

130

Ironically, both Anne and I lost our mothers within four months of each other. But we never talked about our feelings over this loss but once superficially. I always felt I wanted to say more but decided it would be too painful to Anne and perhaps to me if I upset her. Just as I never verbally told her that sometimes she evokes in me a feeling for my mother. I transferred my feelings for my mother to Anne.

The second unexpected thing was the pain that I experienced with my job. Not only was it not expected, it was the worst time in my life to have it happen. I was down. I was broken. And I had come to California to relax and to repair myself. I did not want to fight anymore. Not only did I not want to fight anymore, I wasn't in a position to fight. I didn't have the energy. I saw my year in California as a bit of a reprieve. I was so wiped out I wanted to retire, but I didn't know how a person 30 years old did that. I wanted to reflect.

I thought that I was coming to a job in which the staff wouldn't be fighting among themselves, that their energy would be going into setting up good programs. There would of course be struggles in setting up innovative programs but not the same old inner turmoil with staff. So many of the innovations in mental health have to do with staff roles and power. There will always be these fights.

How naive I was. I was completely wrong in my expectations. I had thought that I wouldn't have to struggle like I did at NIMH, because this time we would be in power, but in actuality Alan had to deal with another powerful administration over him. Plus the people that worked with us were not our friends who came with us but were part of the package deal. Had we, as planned, applied for a grant from a foundation, we might have been more free to realize our fantasy. So here I was in the middle of a fight I not only didn't expect, but wasn't ready for.

It never ceases to amaze me that the mental health field seems so distorted, the behavior so absurd. It almost seems worse than in other fields. It is strictly political. Who has what power? Who likes whom? One director will be kept simply because he teamed up with one or two men on the board of directors. Decisions are nothing more or less than pure politics! But they call it mental health!

I could also no longer tolerate discriminatory behavior by men towards women. Hadn't women's liberation over the past three years clearly documented discriminatory behavior towards women by men and by this society? The public was saturated with such information, and I somehow expected therefore that this behavior would cease and desist.

I had been aware of how I was treated as a woman for some time and by being made more aware of it and knowing that men were made aware of their practices I somehow expected that all the discrimination, all the insults would magically disappear. And when they didn't, I became more angry. I walked around obsessed with how blacks after 10 years of public saturation and lip service about their discrimination walked the streets containing their anger. And the anger towards men surfaced in me to an incredible extent when I found myself dealing with the same old shit at Topeka.

By January I was at my wits end from work, from my personal relationship with Alan and other members of his male

132

staff. And I was not fully aware of how much my mother's death was eating me up. It is ironic that a man on the staff who was a great source or irritation at this time introduced me to Tracy who opened for me an entirely new world, one which gave me some hope that I would eventually emerge from the abyss into which I had been slowly falling for the past six years or so.

When Tracy and I met, within five minutes we knew the intimate details of each other's lives. She told me about a novel that she had been writing about a woman who was in love with a woman and a man — a female doctor and a male senator. I asked her if the story was autobiographical and she said yes, and then I closed the doors to the outside world and we talked.

We sat in the office of the director — a huge room with wall to wall carpets and a large desk with chairs and tables around the room. I remember seeing Tracy's eyes darting back and forth until I told her that the office was not mine, that the director had lent it to me for the afternoon.

Tracy was the first woman that I had met who loved men and women. I instantly poured forth the painful story of my triangle with Alan and Jessica. Our rapport was exciting. I could not believe what was transpiring between us.

Tracy was committed to loving or accepted the world view of loving both men and women in her life. It was not in her head that she would have to choose between them. Such a concept was foreign to her. She of course had to balance how people would fit into her life, the men and women who were her lovers, but the issue of whether it was okay to love both never came up. The strains of being pulled by two different lovers was there. The struggles and problems in her relationships were problems around intimacy. And perhaps issues of who was more attractive in terms of power, contacts and accomplishments came into play when being torn between a man and a woman, but that is not the same issue. For Tracy it was simply a matter that she loved both.

The other two women that I had met in my life who loved women felt differently. Gloria felt that it was impossible to love both and that I would have to choose. And, Rose, a friend from Marin, was herself in the process of working through whether she would be with a man or a woman and did not seem to have the easy sense that I experienced with Tracy — that as a matter of fact one could love both men and women.

It was the old story, like Gloria said, loving men and women cannot actually be done. One would have to choose, it is too difficult. There was a definite sacrifice, she felt, to having both women and men lovers.

During this period in California I focused on wanting a woman lover. I was fascinated by Tracy. She was unquestionably beautiful and attractive. It was a period in my life when every woman I met who had indicated that she loved women and had slept with women I considered a potential lover, and the question in my mind was whether we were going to make love.

After I met a lot of women and my sexuality became more an integral part of my being, and after I became closer to myself, my intensity for a woman lover or for that matter any lover wore off. My women friends and I became friends first and the focus was on our closeness. The sharing of affection and making love grew out of that. The big question, whether we were going to make love, no longer loomed in the background for me.

My urgency to make close friends went away too. I had a sense that these new friends were in my life for a long time. Now there was time for our closeness to grow. The fact that I had thought I would be returning to Washington, D.C. played a major part in maintaining my sense of urgency. It was also during this early period that my focus was on making love in the context of a triangle with a man and a woman.

Later on in my life in California I told my roommate Colette that I was surprised when a woman friend and I got so close to each other on a business trip. Colette responded "What did you expect?" I had hoped we would make love and I hadn't focused on whether we would get close. It may have been our not making love, contrasted with the closeness that I experienced, with her which brought this realization home most clearly to me.

During the next week the bottom fell out of my life at Topeka. At this time the pressure on me from the men at the office became worse. "If you say any more at meetings, we will run you right out of here." "Sidney, I was hardly saying anything, I am just watching!" As their anger increased towards Alan and I over program changes, the pressure increased on me personally. It was easier for the men to put pressure on me than on Alan. And my relationship with Alan was deteriorating. Yes, we went out to lunch and were together often. That is what the staff saw. But our relationship was breaking down. So that at the same time they were mad at him for our program changes and were trying to influence him through me, my relationship with him was becoming more and more distant.

Alan and Jessica had begun to move away from me to become a couple. They wanted more and more time together, and began an affair. I was devastated and hurting while people were yelling about him to me, and expecting me to defend him. I tried to separate myself from him in their eyes. I had tried to do that from the beginning, to be seen as my own person committed to my own ideas so that people could talk to me freely, but of course that didn't work. People saw us as close comrades. So it hurt doubly when they yelled at me about him because they didn't know what was happening between us. I was also accused of being "hardnosed and insensitive" and not caring about how people were treated on the staff and in the community, when I cared very much. Alan had warned me that people were going to see me only in terms of my position on the staff and not in terms of who I was.

Alan and Jessica met with me after work that week to have a drink and to talk about our relationship. I remember Alan saying that he really liked me. Why couldn't I be satisfied with what we had? He was having an affair with Jessica, and I wanted to be having an affair with him.

We went to the Blue Rock Inn — Jessica, Alan and I — at Jessica's suggestion, because I was really hurting. We sat drinking. I told Alan what some of the men had said to me, calling me hardnosed, and he said "Let's face it Ruth. You talk quick, you are sure of your ideas and when you get an idea

you won't let it go. You are seen as a ball cutter, let's face it."
Wonderful! When you are feeling that you are about to
fall to pieces!

Leaving me in the rain after that talk. Yes, after that talk it
is so hard to believe they left me in the car after our return to
the community health center. They got out of the car and
walked off arm-in-arm in the rain, without even saying goodbye. It was pouring. Alan was going to the office for an
evening community meeting and Jessica joined him. I just
stood there in the rain. I couldn't believe it. It was so unreal. I
walked back to the office and asked "Is Jessica here?" She
came out of Alan's office. I said "I just wanted to say goodbye.
I just don't walk off and leave good friends." I didn't think
good friends should treat each other that way. I was furious
and hurt. My anger was mostly directed at Jessica. I got in my
car and drove off in the rain and shouted at the top of my
lungs as my car steamed up: "FUCK! FUCK!" Gooddamn, it
hurt so much.

Integrating Work and Life

Now as the rhetoric went I had hoped to integrate my life
and my work and get more pleasure. This integration did in
fact bring me great pleasure that first year in California, but it
also brought me more pain than I was ready to deal with. I
remember thinking then that back east it was at least a little
easier. When work didn't go well one had their friends and social life to fall back on for meaning in this world. Here in
California I had begun to erase all these boundaries.

As I integrated or tried to integrate my life and my work,

my colleagues became my intimate friends. That was just a little too much in a new, very political organization complicated by the fact that I was trying a triangle relationship which was even more difficult. Two of the most important people to me at the time were involved in my work so that the pain of work was not very easily assuaged by those friendships. The work and the intimacy were both suffering being one and the same. When I ran for comfort it was difficult to run to the place that was causing me so much pain. And when Alan and Jessica paired up I could not, as was my pattern in the past, go to my best woman friend and ask for solace for my losses, as she was also the lover of the man that I liked so much. And I had wanted it to be that way. Yet it was a double hurt on both sides — around work and losing the man I liked to my closest woman friend who comforted me as much as she could. But I wanted to spend time with Jessica and she couldn't or wouldn't comfort me as before because the time she had to play and be intimate she preferred to spend with Alan.

It was during this period that I began to go to a therapist in San Francisco who exclaimed: "But Miss Falk, you have no sense of boundaries." And I responded: "But no you don't see I am trying to erase all of them."

Jessica and I had agreed that we didn't want our feelings for Alan to tear us apart. We agreed our relationship was important to us, but that we were also competing for Alan. We had spent long painful hours over meals talking about our feelings for each other and for him. We were aware even then how absurd we were, two bright, attractive women competing for this married man. We were attracted to him

138

because he was very intelligent; and because of his power and his position. We were drawn to his "cool, calm, collected image." He never seemed to be rattled or troubled. At the same time we realized we would never be able to have the depth of relationship with him that we had with each other because of who he was, and because he wasn't really in touch with his feelings. He was so flighty. How strong our programming as women!

Just a week earlier before the rain incident, on my birthday, Jessica and I had spent the day together and the night before had slept holding each other. Our closeness was ecstasy for me. That day Alan took me to lunch for my birthday and there was an office party for me. Jessica gave me a book *Only a little planet* in which she wrote "What can I say? I love you as I love the earth. Happy Birthday!" Jessica was giving me everything I always wanted from a woman friend.

It was at this point around my birthday that the three of us had been discussing how we could establish a triangle relationship, a menage á trois. There was a special energy between the three of us. We enjoyed being together.

At the time I was trying to live out my fantasy about having a man and a woman lover — a woman that I loved very much sharing the same man. I got off on the energy in *Butch Cassidy and the Sundance Kid* and wondered indeed whether they had slept together. I was also fascinated by Trufeau's movie, *Jules and Jim.* I had held on to recreating that fantasy often with close women friends — no doubt as a way to get close to them in a way that I felt I couldn't without a man. Mostly however, the triangle fantasy was mine and mine only.

Alan told me at lunch that he would be interested in getting involved with me as a lover if I had another lover. He was afraid that he couldn't meet my needs and suggested that I get a primary lover. He said it was easy for him to get involved with Jessica because she already had another lover, Michael.

. What I got the sense of during our talk was a sudden flash — if I could find someone to be my primary lover — everyone would be willing to be my contingent love. It felt like a card game. If I could get the right card, I could get everyone else. A full house.

If I could find an essential love I could easily have lots of lovers. It was the essential love that was supposed to unlock for me the key to happiness.

It was this conversation with Alan that prompted me to write in my journal:

who will be my primary love
who will hold me, love me, stroke me
crave me, the long long nights
of my life?

It was fine that Alan would sleep with me once in a while but I wanted someone who wanted to be more an on-going lover.

I recall that in D.C. I felt that this structure — having essential and contingent lovers — would give me the ultimate in independence and would enable me to have intimate relationships. I seemed to naively think that if I could just get the structure set up the rest — intimacy — would come easily with both male and female lovers.

140

I had thought
Such perfection: to have
the best of two worlds —
being married and having a woman lover;
having a man and a woman lover.

One day I told a friend in Berkeley how I used to fantasize that if I had a woman lover and if we shared a man, it would be an easy thing for me to do. I wouldn't expect so much from the man in terms of intimacy because I could get most of those needs met by my woman friend. That is what I had fantasized with Mandy and a male friend of ours who was extremely sexy but not reliable. If I had her in this relationship I wouldn't care so much about what he did because I could get my other needs met by her. My friend commented that is what many women do and don't realize it. They have their husband or man but have a close woman friend who fulfills many of their needs for intimacy that he doesn't. "He is called her lover or husband and she is merely her "girl friend." " The importance goes to the husband and lover but many real needs are met by the woman friend.

Earlier in the week Tracy had called to invite me to a dinner for women the following Saturday. She had held several such dinners that past year. It was my understanding that she brought women together who were involved in the women's movement and who would enjoy meeting each other. This was my first introduction to the "salon," a term that I learned from her. She was having dinner for six women, and I was to be one of the invited guests. The experience was very important to me, and in a sense was the beginning of concretizing my fantasy of writing this book.

After so much difficulty during the week I looked forward to seeing Tracy again.

The Dinner Party Itself

I remember being excited about going as I got dressed and then drove through the winding streets of Berkeley, looking for Regent Street. I drove up and down the area several times, crossing Derby Street where I was later to live, before I finally found Tracy's house. I climbed the long stairway to an apartment on the second floor to be greeted by Tracy, who introduced me to several women sitting in her living room. I remember sitting against the couch looking into the dining room, watching Tracy prepare dinner and greet other guests, serve drinks and try to get us talking among ourselves. "Ruth works in community health. She just arrived from Washington." I remember watching Tracy, tall and dark. She was just lovely and I wondered whether I would sleep with her. I didn't know her lover Gale would be at the party.

The other women guests included a psychologist named Olga who worked in mental health in San Francisco. I never saw her again. She left early and seemed to be a bit uncomfortable when we talked about Tracy and Gale being lovers and about women loving women. I do, however, remember a very important thing that she said to me after dinner when I was lying on the floor telling the women how much I was hurting and the difficulties I had at work with Alan and

Jessica. She told me "I think you are expecting too much. It takes a long time to adjust to the West Coast after moving from the East Coast. It is a major change. It took me over a year to get settled. Things are really different here, even the groceries and foods . . . for instance Hellman's Mayonnaise is Best Foods here." And I said "Oh God, no wonder I couldn't find Hellman's on the shelves!" (I had just about given up, and was about to switch to another brand.) She was right, I did expect too much too fast and did not give myself the space and the time to adjust to this new culture.

The fifth woman at the dinner party was Gale's younger sister. The last woman and the last to arrive was Silvia. I was fascinated and attracted to her the minute she walked into the apartment. She was tall and thin, her hair was in a shag and there was something very attractive and appealing in her manner. I thought at first that I knew her. She looked very much like a woman that I had been attracted to who worked at the community health center and who was a student at San Francisco State. For a moment as Silvia entered the door I was sure that this was she. The hall by the door was dark, lit only by candle light. Then she came into the room and sat and talked for a while with us before dinner was served. It was not she, but someone equally as exciting to me.

Dinner was lovely. I admired Tracy's poise and ability to run such a fine meal and be so confident as she helped to keep the conversation going. I remember thinking that if I were in her place I would have been petrified. I am not comfortable serving meals or preparing dinners, especially for people that I admire.

The conversation at dinner was amazing, and I was intrigued. We talked about monogamous and non-monogamous relationships, about women in work situations, about having male lovers who were married, about having lovers from out of town who dropped in once in a while and then left, and that in those kinds of relationships it was sometimes easier to get one's work done. About women loving women.

I remember Silvia saying that it is important to have a variety of relationships to keep from getting into former patterns. By then my mind was blurred with wine. I do remember that one of the women told another that she once had an affair with her husband. Even this part of the conversation seemed quite natural to me.

I remember being so impressed that Silvia was out on a Saturday night without her husband. I thought that was incredible. I knew no women in D.C. would consider going out on a Saturday evening, leaving their husbands behind.

Silvia was married, had a male lover, talked about being non-monogamous and about having had a woman lover when she was younger. I was intrigued and fascinated. I remember writing in my journal a description of her that makes me laugh now. I didn't describe the type of person that she was but more the structure that she had around her life — a marriage, a male lover, non-monogamous. I remember noting that she was aggressive and also very attractive in the way I liked myself to be.

Here was something I longed for and now it was happening in a group setting, as if on stage. I wanted so much to find women to talk to who felt the same way I did, who would be open about their feelings, who would talk about loving women, about their relationships, about monogamy and non-monogamy. And a married woman who would talk about these things I found doubly fascinating. My married friends in D.C. tended not to talk about their relationships at all once they got married. When they were single and dating we knew so much about each others lives, but after marriage most couples withdrew into their own worlds.

After dinner we returned to the living room. I remember lying on the floor as I talked with the other women. I remember Silvia saying that she was very much interested in organizing women and that if I were interested in organizing women at Topeka we could get together.

I remember telling everybody about my situation at work and about the way I had been treated, and that I was sick and tired of men being intimidated by me and having them hate me. And I remember Silvia remarked "I can see how you would be intimidating, you are very direct." She sat in a chair directly in front of me.

I remember asking Tracy and Gale about their relationship, asking if they experienced the mirror-image feelings that Jessica and I had, or if they experienced an incredible intensity that was sometimes almost painful. And I told them how Jessica once described our relationship as: "What are we going to do about this laser-beam relationship?" I remember Silvia saying: "Don't you see Gale is saying that it is intense?" She then talked further about the woman she had as a lover when she was younger — a very positive experience for her.

After the psychologist left we talked late into the night. I was simply fascinated to be talking to two women who were lovers — two lovely, exciting women. I felt very excited and positive myself. Is this what I had been afraid of all my life?

At the end of Tracy's dinner party Silvia and I exchanged names and numbers. She told me about two groups that were starting in San Francisco that I was welcome to join. I was the last to leave Tracy's. I felt warmed and thrilled by this experience. Never in my life could I have forseen that such an event as this would occur.

Work and Nourishing

When the bottom had fallen out of my life in Topeka, when Jessica and Alan walked off and left me in the rain, I wrote in my journal:

The End of the Road
The Beginning of Emerging Me

Would you be afraid of her?
She seems nice to me!

I knew I had to get away and a few days after Tracy's dinner I flew to Mexico. Jessica had been encouraging me to give myself time off to relax. I was going to get away by going back to Boston to see my advisor about my graduate work. But I decided Jessica was right. I really needed to relax and stop working.

This is the first time that I ever just gave myself time to mend. I left work without telling Alan, I just left. And said the

146

hell with everyone. I had to heal myself and get myself on my feet. This time I just took time off from the world. I needed it very badly.

Usually when I hurt I would plunge myself further into my work and finish some great project that was due. That is what I was doing when I made my initial application to Harvard — beat myself with my work. But more and more I was unable to push myself when I hurt. I had begun to listen to myself and to do only what I felt like. If I didn't feel like working, I didn't. And when I did, it was not with the painful driven pressure. I began to stop pushing myself so hard.

On Sunday evening I called Anne's sister who lives in San Francisco, and I said "Where do you go when you want to get away and you live on the West Coast?" She said Puerto Vallarta — and I said spell it. Two days later I was on a flight to Mexico.

I went to Puerto Vallarta with six good books and a pile of work at the bottom of my suitcase, which happily I never read.

The morning I was leaving, Brenda, a friend from work called to say she was glad I was going and to take care of myself, but not to expect it wouldn't be the same mess at Topeka when I got back.

The first few days in Puerto Vallarta I didn't quite know what to do — how to be with myself and mend myself. Taking time out to take care of myself was new to me. I felt like I was with a new lover. I was quite shy and not sure what to do with me. I began to write poetry in my journal and read alot. I thought of going out to meet people and to visit art museums. But mostly I stayed just with myself.

January 31, 1973
Puerto Vallarta

The sea breeze

caresses me

its warmth envelops my body

the air is sweet and noble

and I feel good here

Solitude

I like being with me

It seems strange

there is no pain

I do not feel lonely

How do I feel?

I feel red, hot and sunburn

my face wears a big red

glow

around a slow warm smile

Hello Ruth

Body warm and silky

new round stomach

with tatoo to its right

who shall

I be with?

no one does the

magic any more

I shall be with me.

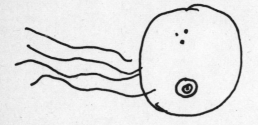 

little snails

in little holes

in big boulders

on the shore

This evening I had a good time with me

as good as if I were with someone

like Jessica

and now solitude

with me

sweetness

and some pain

when my mind

returns to California

And Jessica

"We will get more from

each other

than we could get from

him,"

and where did that go?

Fly, Towards California

Moving from South to North

the sea gets darker

towards gray black

the clouds and mist are gray

and one enters the season

of the North

called Winter

When I returned from Puerto Vallarta I called Silvia. I felt like I was really hurting and I needed to talk to someone. I remember that I did call Tracy. I was hoping that she and I would become good friends. But Tracy was busy and didn't indicate any interest to get together. Silvia invited me to meet her at a women's center in San Francisco. I did, and after the group meeting I went over and talked to her about getting together. She invited me to have dinner with her and another friend Alice who had dropped by the Center.

I remember being nervous when I went to this first meeting at the center. Silvia had talked about all the women who were leading groups. I was quite frankly scared of them. I didn't even know who they were, but I was scared of strong, competent, attractive women and I wanted them to see me as strong too. I thought how were they going to see me that way if I was feeling torn up and ugly and hurting inside?

Silvia's friend Alice was an actress and writer who was married to a lawyer who worked at a local legal service agency. We had a long enjoyable dinner talking about our lives. Alice had lived in D.C. five years ago and we discovered we had many mutual friends. We had even attended the same lecture course once at George Washington University in psychology, but had not known each other as the class was huge.

At the end of the evening Silvia invited Alice and I for dinner the Friday after she returned from a two week skiing vacation. Alice and I met for lunch twice the following week to talk, visit and share similar experiences we had had with mutual friends.

The day that I was supposed to go to Silvia's for dinner I was very upset. I had just found out that I had to give up the therapist I was seeing because my health insurance did not cover therapists who were social workers. Everything I was counting on was falling through.

I was so upset, I was experiencing so much pain in my neck that I could hardly move. I was in pain over my feelings for Alan and Jessica. They were moving further from me. I remember being very angry at Jessica but loving her very much.

Brenda, who was my friend and a therapist at Topeka helped me that day to get a new therapist who would be covered by my insurance, and tried to comfort me. She wanted to give me a hug but I was afraid that if she touched me I would only hurt more. Brenda and I talked about all the anger I had with my father and how I kept on repeating the same patterns of triangles in my love relationships. She said that there was so much anger between me and my father there had to be a lot of good feeling there too. I used to go through my mother to talk to my father, as I had been doing with Jessica in asking her to talk to Alan.

After Puerto Vallarta, I was able to distance myself from the situation at Topeka. I was able to clearly see that a good deal of the anger I received from the men there was directed toward Alan and his program changes. I no longer took their anger personally and told them to go and speak to him themselves. And I also realized that in a sense Alan had placed me and one of the men I was experiencing the most tension with in a very competitive situation by not defining our roles clearly and by giving us overlapping areas of responsibility.

158

What was so upsetting to me most, however, was that people still could not see who I was. When I told one of the men I was upset and hurting from adjusting to my move to California and missing my old friends he could not hear or see me. He just said I seemed so hard driving, so strong, that he made me feel like a hollow tin soldier.

I am like a hollow
   tin soldier
   silver and glittering
worn from the wars
my insides are no
more

The Second Women's Dinner

I had a ball. The energy was high, intense, and somewhat sexual. We drank, smoked dope and sat down for a delicious dinner of fun and conversation.

I had arrived at Silvia's for dinner expecting to meet Alice and a friend of hers from out of town and found instead that I would be attending my second full-fledged women's dinner. Silvia's home was exciting to me. The focus in the living room was a big beige couch which was sumptuous and warm. A huge oil painting hung dramatically above it and accented the room in thick slashing orange, yellow, purple and red hues. The ceiling was high. A red oriental rug covered the floors. I felt very much at home.

The living room was indirectly lit by a single light focused on a white book case crammed full with books which reached as high as the ceiling.

I had covered one whole wall in the living room in my Georgetown apartment with a bookcase to the ceiling, with stained brown long thin boards filled with books and interspersed occasionally with art pictures and a lamp which lit up the books and gave a special warm glow to the room and to my red rug. So it was no wonder I felt like I was "coming home" here.

When I entered the living room Alice introduced me to her friend Vita who was sitting on the couch wearing a beautiful tailored beige silk blouse and dark contrasting skirt. She wore pearls around her neck and her brown short hair softly skimmed her silk collar. Vita's talk was expansive and fast and her gestures wide. I immediately warmed to her and she seemed to adopt me and focus much of her quick talk on me. "Ruth Falk from Washington, D.C. Tell me about yourself!" Vita had just arrived from New York. She had recently moved to the east coast from San Francisco where she had been a writer for a radio station. We exchanged our impressions of the east and west coasts and the individuals that inhabited these lands.

The other women soon arrived for dinner. I found them all as exciting and energetic as Vita. Jill was a lawyer who worked for a private commission running the social policy unit investigating discriminatory practices toward women. She was tall, her eyes set deep in her face seemed quiet and serious. During dinner she told me about her work and asked me about funding possibilities from NIMH. She was concerned about federal legislation which was discriminatory toward women and had drafted several new laws. Jill had worked for the federal government in L.A. for four years. We shared our experiences working for male bosses. Later when I got to know Jill I always found her humorous in the center of any group, so I was surprised she seemed so quiet that evening.

Ginger was an artist. She sat next to Jill and across from me at the dinner party. She had designed jewelry in Boston and worked in an art and design studio in San Francisco. I remember that she wore bright colors, large red platform shoes, and that she was very exciting and refreshing to talk to.

The fifth woman, Teresa, was an ecologist who had taught at Stanford and had recently begun a small Ecology and Women's Center there with some friends. She was very bright, had a keen sense of humor and never stopped talking. She and Silvia kept up an incredible repartee throughout the entire dinner conversation. I was excited by her wit.

Silvia herself was a ceramist who was learning body therapies and exploring female psychology in a women's collective.

I was excited to meet these women. At last a group that I felt I belonged with — professional, committed to work, competent, aggressive women who dressed well and cared about how they looked. Exciting! I had been hanging out with hippies and country folks in California and realized I was hungry for art and style.

After dinner we drove across town to a party given to welcome Kate Millet into the Bay Area. It was my first big party of all women and it felt warm and nice. There were some men at the party but they were peripheral — the focus was women. It was a good feeling. The group singing music *"Will you still love me tomorrow?"* in a circle near one end of the room added to the intense warmth and energy which permeated the room. I was standing by Silvia in the kitchen as a woman gave her a passionate kiss on the lips and commented "I bet that's the first time you've ever been kissed by a lesbian!" Silvia turned to me and asked me if I was okay. I said of course, yes. She said "You know I don't know you very well."

Another woman was standing by the doorway obviously flirting and picking up other women. If this had been a mixed cocktail party in D.C. I would have hardly noticed and shrugged it off as the same old sexual games. But this was a party of women and I was fascinated. The young woman at the doorway later asked Silvia for her name and number. They agreed to meet some time for lunch.

The six of us who had had dinner together sat in one corner of the room on a long couch and played and kidded with each other as we watched the goings on. I was a bit shy as I crossed the room to join them.

Eventually we left to go back to Silvia's house where we had left our cars. Alice, Vita and I said good night to Silvia and the others. We then walked to Alice's house which was two blocks away to have some more dope, wine and coffee and to talk. The others went off into the night in a web of entanglements, of which I was only slightly aware, but which would readily unfold before me as I got to know this group of women.

As we sat in Alice's living room drinking and resting from our night's carousing, Alice suggested that we talk about all the sexual energy in the air. Vita was lying on the couch with her feet touching my lap and her head on Alice's legs. The feelings between us were very warm and close. We had mellowed somewhat from the intense energy of the evening but at the same time we remained high.

Alice explained some of the relationships between the women at the dinner party. Jill and Teresa were lovers and Vita had had an affair with Ginger in New York a month ago. Vita said it was great when it happened but that she worried about it for weeks after it occurred. Alice said that Ginger told her that she really enjoyed herself and had called her and told her about the experience when she had returned from New York.

Vita kept repeating how she had loved Alice for years but that Alice did not want her. I said that I bet that was not true. Alice seemed very warm and interested in Vita. Vita said that she wanted to kiss Alice, and I encouraged her to do so. She leaned over Vita, held her head between her hands and gave her a slow warm kiss. I enjoyed watching them kiss. It was very sensual to me. I was also aware of enjoying having Vita's feet rest against me. This simple kind of touching was something I very rarely experienced in Washington, D.C. I was feeling very special with Vita's feet against me, and I was aware of enjoying this special warmth with Alice.

I said that I wanted to kiss Alice then and she leaned over and we kissed. I felt very close and warm with her. Kissing her was like kissing Jessica, very warm and intense.

We joked and drank some more and Alice said: "Well what do you want to do?" It was late and we were all very tired, and a bit stoned. There was no way that I was going to make it back to Berkeley that night. I could barely make my way in this new city in the daytime.

I suggested that we all lie down on the pillows in the living room. I liked this warmth and wanted to be as close to my friends as possible. I had experienced so much pain earlier in the day, I found being with them very soothing. I was able to forget my pain for awhile. Apparently I didn't say clearly what I meant, and we wound up going to bed in Alice's double bed. Her husband was away for the weekend. I could have made my idea more clear but decided that this would be just as nice.

Before we got ready to go to bed we discussed how we

felt. Vita kept on saying to me: "Are you okay? You are the kid, you are the youngest one." Alice was 37 and Vita was 41. I wanted all of us to go to bed together but I worried about risking my friendship with Alice. She was very supportive of me. I felt that my friendship with her was very important, through her I saw new hope for my life in California meeting new people, both men and women. I told her I didn't want to hurt our friendship. Alice said that that would be no problem. I said "Are you sure?" and she said that she was, and we all went to bed with a let's go and see what happens attitude.

Vita and I got undressed and into bed. Alice put on her raggedy nightgown and joined us. Vita exclaimed: "See, I have to be crazy. Why do I like anybody who wears that!" Vita coaxed Alice to take off her nightgown. There the three of us were in bed. I was on one side of the bed as close to the edge as I could get. Alice was on the other edge and Vita in the middle. I told Alice I wanted to kiss her goodnight and I did. Vita kissed Alice and we turned off the light to go to sleep. I was somewhat struck by this situation of three people in bed. How weird — three women in bed — triangles seemed to be my karma.

It was a very awkward silence filled with anticipation that covered the room. I didn't know what was going to happen, but it was very exciting. Vita was fidgeting and kept on making remarks. Alice said that she wanted to go to sleep. Vita said: "Please don't go to sleep" as she stroked both of us. Alice got mad and told Vita that she always made her feel like she had failed her and that she could never do anything right.

Alice said that she never knew what to do for Vita and that she knew that Vita was often in pain but that she never seemed to do the right thing.

I was surprised at Alice's sudden anger. She had been flirtatious and warm with Vita all evening. I guess that I had expected them to at least hug and kiss in bed as Jessica and I had done.

I promptly suggested that I leave the room. I always get very uncomfortable when people yell at each other. My folks had done so much yelling. I felt that this relationship and its problems was strictly between them. I was, however, very hopeful that Alice and I would sleep together sometime, as we had been very warm with each other.

Alice said laughingly: "No, please don't leave!" And Vita recognized that she wanted me there to protect her. The silence became painful. I identified with how Vita felt. I had been there so many times. Jessica in the past month told me I made her feel helpless and that she did not know what to do. I could also feel Vita's intense feeling for Alice and her pain at not having her physical affection returned.

I told the women how I felt, how painful it was for me to see and hear their struggle, but how lucky I was to have met them. I felt so happy. I felt close to them. And I did not feel lonely. I had been so intensely lonely these past few months in California. They asked: "How can you feel so good? We don't know what we are doing. We are just as confused as you! Here the three of us are lying in bed and we don't know what to do!" I exclaimed: "But I never met women like you, you give me hope. I want to be married like you but I also like women."

166

Eventually the room became painfully silent again. Then Alice left to sleep on the couch. Vita moved over and put her arm around my waist and stroked me. I was lying on my side. I leaned my back into her belly, my legs paralleled her folded legs. I was turned on. My body felt delicious and sensuous against her stroking arm, which rubbed my belly. I didn't know what to do. Vita said: "There can't be anything wrong with this. It feels too good." I agreed and fell passively asleep.

At the time I told myself that I didn't want to make love with Vita because I didn't want to hurt my chances with Alice and I didn't really have a relationship with Vita. Though I found her extremely attractive, I felt that we would "just be having sex" and would risk the possibility of afterwards feeling empty.

When morning came Alice got back in bed with us, bringing the morning paper, The Chronicle. Vita suggested that we talk about what happened. Alice said she felt that she could lie in bed with me but that she did not feel at all comfortable with Vita. She felt that Vita suddenly pounced on us last night when she thought that we were going to sleep. I told Alice that it was hard to read her. It seemed clear last night on the couch that she was open to Vita. She responded that she never knows how she feels until a situation happens. I said I felt that she should have told Vita yes or no, that she obviously was ambivalent. Alice went off to make breakfast.

I sat with Vita and listened to her. She was afraid that she had lost Alice forever. Alice had told me earlier that she felt a great deal of responsibility for Vita because she was the only person Vita had told about her deep feelings for women. I

167

suggested to Vita that she talk to her husband and tell him how she felt.

I recorded in my journal:

"I urged her strongly to start dealing with her feelings towards women openly and to tell her husband. She said that she would just go home and forget it. I said that they would recur over and over. You see I Know, I have, I am the pain and agony of it. I saw Vita as an image of me in her pain and how she dealt with it. She just was all over the place, it was hard to pin her down. She seemed frantic like me. She seemed strong and competent like me. She was complex like me. So many things bothered her it was hard to help her."

I told Vita about the time in Boston when Phil asked me why wasn't I married. I had suddenly blurted out "Because I think I like women." When I told him about my feelings for women I felt a sense of power. It was very positive. That was for me one of the beginning steps I took in dealing openly with who I was around my sexuality. Five months later I saw Vita again. It turned out she did tell her husband and she felt good about it.

Later in the morning in the kitchen I visited with Alice while she was doing the dishes. She said that she was interested in having a woman lover. I said to myself "That is good. I hope we may be lovers." She said that she just could not sleep last night — that she was just too uncomfortable.

Alice complained that she needed more space. Vita had fled in the early morning back to her kids and her husband.

She hadn't called her husband and was worried that he would be furious. Alice said "What do you expect? Of course, he'll probably be upset. It is unusual for a wife to stay out all night long!"

I felt very good at Alice's but realized I should leave now. I remember wanting to stay as long as I could, waiting to see if I would be spending the day with her. The morning feelings I experienced with her reminded me of the times I had spent with Lisa and Gary in Philadelphia — complete with round oak table and old chairs. I awkwardly said I was going to leave and went to the front door. Alice came and reached up, grabbed my shoulder, and kissed me goodbye on the cheek.

I hated to return to Berkeley and the life that I was leading. I remember walking to my car in the morning of the gray misty city, along the white fence under the full green trees and driving home feeling tired but very warm inside. I arrived in Berkeley and went right to sleep in my drafty room under cold sheets.

Until this dinner party, I didn't like the image that I saw of what it was like to be over 30. I didn't know what to do after I was 30. It was good to see other women who were older than me, living the way they were. In D.C. I never saw anyone my age or older living the way that I wanted to. At the time I remember feeling Alice and Ginger were wonderful. It is good to change one's image of what it is like to be older. I don't want to live as an adult like my parents did.

Letter to Mandy on the Feminists
March, 1973

"Dear Mandy,

You're probably wondering about my changing my mind about staying in California. It could change again. I wouldn't be surprised. But two things influence me now.

I have met a group of women here who call themselves feminists. They are a different breed of people (than) I have ever met before. I think that I may have looked at them as some kind of unusual specie, something outside of myself. I asked one of them: "What is a feminist?" When I told her how how I felt about women's issues, she said: "Yes, you are a feminist."

Some of them are very exciting. At times I feel like I finally found a place where I belong. The women are strong, attractive, energetic, working professional people. High energy too. The other thing that I like about these women is that they are dealing with their bisexuality openly. Many of them have women lovers. I finally have found people that I can talk to openly about my feelings for women. I still get freaked out about making love to a woman, but I like being able to be physically close to women and have them to talk with about these feelings."

(The period that I met these feminists was an intense period when many women were exploring their love and sexual feelings for one another. I arrived in San Francisco while much of this activity was at its peak. I was not aware of this while I was in the middle of it, only now am I aware looking back. I was new to the area and so focused most on my own newness. But this synchronous eventfulness came at just the right time for me.)

"Some of the feminists have women lovers partly as a political statement of the movement. I don't want to do that. I want whatever I do to come from the struggle within me, not because it is an in thing to do. This has to do with my intense resistance to rhetoric. I don't want women to love each other, be lovers, because politically they *should* love their sisters. And "in things to do" is the side of California I don't like, as I described to you on the phone.

The other reason that I think I may want to stay in California is that I just got into therapy again. This guy is much better than Tilbet. He is helping me deal with feelings that I am blocking.

I do the intellectual trip really well. He says that I am running from my feelings of sadness and that part of me I don't like. He has had me do fantasies and taught me how to watch myself when I run. I do that a lot. I haven't traveled much this year, but I still find ways to run away from myself.

I am also getting rolfed starting April 2. I feel that I've talked my problems to death and maybe a new approach, working with my body, will help me to settle down and stop running.

I feel like I am taking a journey, will be going back through time but will come out the same (living with three women, having Jewish friends like in my childhood.) It is strange.

California is filled with people who have come out here to change their life style. I still haven't found anyone living successfully and happily as I would like to."

After the second women's dinner party I went to the women's center again. This time to meet Ginger who invited me there to attend a meeting of "heavy feminists." I said "Oh, did Silvia tell you I wanted to meet them?" and she said nothing. They were all acting on their own calling me. And it sometimes was very confusing.

After the meeting we went to dinner and talked with the other women. Someone asked what I was doing. I said "Writing a book about women loving women." I said that having strong love feelings for women had been difficult for me and that I wanted to make it easier for other women. And that I was trying to work out this area of life for myself.

Then the different women at the table talked spontaneously about their feelings and experiences with their first women lovers. It was a fun conversation filled with laughter. I explained that I had been so scared I got diarrhea. Another woman said she was so nervous she vomited. One woman said that she thought for sure after sleeping with a woman that she was forever a lesbian and would never like men again. Another woman said that she cried and then the woman held her in her arms and then another woman chimed in: "And that's what you wanted in the first place!"

We laughed not so much because it was funny to get diarrhea or to vomit — that is not funny — but about how nervous and scared we were to love each other and to love ourselves.

Anais Nin — those relationships do exist!

I recall having read about Anais Nin's intense relationship to June in her *Diary* the first week I was at Dragon's Eye. I was so excited to see a woman loving a woman. I wrote in my journal "What I am seeing and feeling in my life does exist! Those relationships do exist and I want one!"

Because our society has ignored relationships between women and has pretended that they don't exist, one feels a sort of schizophrenia. On the one hand one knows that it is true that women have feelings for each other. On the other hand their very existence is denied by society, not only denied, but condemned.

It gives me the feeling of looking at life through a great big thick glass shield. One can see all the activity, but cannot hear it and cannot make an effect upon it. The world denies love relationships between women exist, but you feel them and you try very hard to make a connection and stay grounded in yourself. Often when women look in society's mirror to see reflected how they feel and think, their image is not reflected back, it's distorted.

Three weeks later I saw Gloria for the first time since I left the East Coast. She was visiting relatives in San Francisco. I was very nervous about seeing her and was unclear about our relationship — what it would be, or what I wanted from it. I didn't know if I wanted to sleep with her. I did know that all those times that I was hurting and driving back from Marin over the Richmond Bridge watching and feeling the shadows and rays of the setting sun bouncing off the beams of the bridge, making a pattern on my car as I whizzed under them, that Gloria was the one woman, the one person that would have been able to comfort me, to hold me when I was hurting so much in California. She was the one person that I knew would understand how I was feeling.

And then she came and I was so scared that I ran in high anxiety. I was afraid to let her hold me, or for me to hold her.

Rolfing

I decided I was going to take the high energy that I used to do social change at NIMH and put that energy into me. If I was capable of doing all these things in the outside world, wasn't I capable of working through the things in my psyche that were causing me to have so much pain? One of my friends told me to slow down, that the body wasn't like an organization. That one had to do things gently. She said: "The body is a fragile thing. You can't treat yourself that way." But I was relentless. I started working on myself. I kept pushing myself. I was hard on myself. I remember running to a friend in the commune and complaining that I hadn't made any progress. I said to my friend: "I don't know what I can do to know I am okay. Even if it were on national TV saying that I was okay — that I was wonderful — I just wouldn't believe it."

By my third month in California I wanted to get it all worked out right away. I had half kiddingly told Jessica that within two months I would be "cured," and then I would

174

write my book. At the time Jessica made some remarks about growth being an ongoing life process but that barely reached my inner consciousness. I expected so much from myself and was so unrealistic.

Making a major move to the West Coast in and of itself was a cause for major personal adjustments. At the time I wanted all things settled in my life — lovers and family instantly. I wrote a poem about instant intimacy. And a note in my journal about wishing I could stop at a quick stop market and just get better right away.

instant intimacy
I wanted intimacy so badly that I
mistook its resemblance
blatant revealing . . .
Just because people in California more readily tell about themselves, it doesn't mean that they are closer to you. I was disappointed that I hadn't made friends like my friendships on the East Coast.

Progress was too slow, so in April I decided to get rolfed. If I couldn't do it myself goddamn I was going to have it pushed out of me. Many folks in the commune had been rolfed. They talked about it as a very exciting body therapy and change process. I was not successful solving my problems by thinking about and analyzing them. Hadn't I already spent three years in verbal therapy with Dr. Tilbet? I kept on repeating the same patterns, so I thought that a different mode — nonverbal and non-linear — might do the trick.

I lasted four rolfing sessions and had to stop when I thought that I might be going crazy.

In fact I was sure that I was. I cried so deeply that there was no stopping me. My poor frame was about to fall apart from the constant shaking of my body. Such deep sobbing I have never experienced before, nor do I ever want to again. The pain was excrutiating.

It was as if my whole body opened up and I could see into open space — into the past. It was scarey and uncanny. I heard the sounds and smells of my mother. I would close a drawer and hear her dresser drawers in her bedroom closing with the familiar sound of the brass handles bouncing against or off the dark mahogany wood, in the cool air breeze-filled room of the early morning, the curtains white flapping with the breeze. I would put a hair brush down or a pin down on my dresser and would hear the click of the lid to the top of her white china dish in which my mother used to keep old pins and garters. I yearned for my mother's supper table covered with a green table cloth, flowers, nice silverware and white china with a red Chinese design of flowers and a perfect roast beef for Sunday dinner. And her caring for me. That comfort I can't seem to find anywhere. Are those days all gone by? That comfort is home and a family.

I felt I was facing death itself. I was confronting death. I remember calling Howie, a friend in the commune, in my craziness because I knew that he had been there.

He said: "You know that it is all about death?" and I said: "That is what I have been crying about for hours."

During this rolfing period I kept reading the song that I had seen in *Ms* by Judy Collins, entitled *Secret Gardens of the Heart*.

I was confronting my death and the loss of my youth and the fact that I had grown to be a woman.

Perhaps my mother's death made me face that I was no longer a child.

The verse that I read over and over again from Judy Collins' song was:

"But most of all it's me that has changed, yet still I'm the same. That's me at the weddings, that's me at the graves, dressed like the people who once looked so grown-up and brave. I look in the mirror through the eyes of a child that was me."

"The death of my own mother made me feel like a deck of cards being shuffled by giant unseen hands. Parents, however old they and we may grow to be, serve among other things to shield us from a sense of doom. As long as they are around, we can avoid the fact of our mortality; we can still be innocent children.*

For ten years my mother was dying and I mourned her. I had expected her death to be a relief. Isn't that what my therapist always told me in D.C.? And then she died, goddamn fucking died, tangled and destroyed from a disease that took her mind and her body, made her into a helpless animal when she died.

When my mother died I was confronted with myself.
I was alone.

I still can't write about her without a tear rolling down my face, without a sob. The tear and the sob aren't as great as they were those days during my rolfing. The pain doesn't go that deep anymore. I see this as a healing, that I have healed myself, that that hollow tin soldier is no more and that my core has walls like the thick walls of the uterus right before menstruation. A pain, a foreign object can lodge there but the pain doesn't go in deep and sharp because of the warm soft moist protection that I have built up for myself.

It doesn't mean that I don't feel. I do but it is a warm comforting feeling, not that scarey painful shattered feeling when the walls covering my core were brittle and dry, weak and cracked. Then the pain, the object, would lodge in them,

---

* From *A Different Woman* by Jane Howard, reprinted by permission of the publisher, E. P. Dutton and Co.

fall through the crack and send a pain through me that would shatter my foundation and send me out into space. It would slip through the wall and leave me open to the pain and the infinity of my past.

I learned that "moving is standing very still." That the progress I wanted in my life came from being still with myself and not by trying to do things.

I had slowly over the summer, when I worked on myself and went through a day of crying about my mother, lost a great deal of my frantic quality. I was more able to sit still and be with myself.

I had learned why I was so afraid to be home during the day, and in fact so afraid to get in touch with my feelings, and why I was always running from them.

The Comfort Came in the Mail

It is not any coincidence that today I received a letter from Gloria in which she told me where I can find Jane Howard's description of what it is like when you lose your mother. Before I took my writing break and went downstairs for the mail I had decided I was ready to type the material which follows about the day that I stayed home and cried and cried about my mother. Nor was it any coincidence that in the same mail I received a post card from Tracy urging me to finish the book. This material on my mother was getting me down, and I welcomed their support as well as their cheer!

The postcard from Tracy was sent from Montana — Peter Brautigan's ranch. The day before I had met a writer at Ron's who was flying to the Brautigan Ranch today. I am no longer surprised by such events. I see them as good omens. Nor am I not surprised that I received a card from Tracy when I was thinking of her. I have been wanting more of the comfort and pleasure I had with Tracy the last time we were together. Last night I thought about her nurturing. I wanted to be in her room feeling the cool breezes and watching the planters swing, having her touch my head and run her fingers through my hair while she read. Then I hear from her, and this is the way it is.

The day that I stayed home and cried and cried about my mother it was a sunny day. And it scared me that I couldn't stop crying, but it was also okay. I remember calling Dr. Simon. He said: "Take advantage of this. Stay home and feel what you are feeling." But I exclaimed: "It is such a beautiful day!" and he said: "But this may happen only once, there will be many beautiful days." So I did stay home and cry and it was a wonderful release and ultimately very warm and joyful.

I washed the dishes and felt my mother in the house and felt like her and how it was to be home. I slowly folded towels and did what she did. I would follow my feelings and do what my mother would have done. I slowly cleaned the kitchen and I felt her, and was crying, and I got the kitchen clean and neat like she would. Then I went and cleaned out my bathroom shelf and folded linen and towels like she would have done.

That franticness, that running that I experienced of never sitting still was from running from the sad feelings that I had for my mother that I just could not handle. I had always felt depressed being home in the middle of the day during a work day. It was the same feeling that I noticed I had at Anne's when she was folding clothes in the mid-morning at her house my first return to D.C. I knew that being in her house with her during the day was sad for me but I didn't know why.

This sudden discovery of good feelings for my mother at home during the day was a joy. There were good feelings of her cleaning and making our home comfortable. And I cried and cried. I felt my mother and felt like her as I cleaned. It was a relief. Now I felt I could stay home during the day with myself and or with my work. That was no longer depressing for me, or frightening.

I found that the feelings I discovered for my mother that I ran from weren't sad or awful or terrible. They were good. But I was apparently afraid to feel them because I believed they would be too painful.

If my mother dies I think I will die.

This past week taking a friend to the doctor and waiting for her in the waiting room, I remembered how my mother comforted me and waited with me at doctors' offices. Afterwards often we would go and get ice cream for a treat. It was very fine and comforting being with my mother and also being with Clara was fine, except for the hour and a half wait while I was nervous about her health. Often times when my mother took me to the doctor I was okay. It was just a routine exam or shot. But I do remember my first trip to the gynecologist. It had seemed so serious.

I was trying to get in touch with why I was so concerned about Clara. I knew that I didn't want her to be sick alone, that I wanted to support her. I hate it when I am sick and scared and alone and want someone with me.

But my mother was alone in her illness. I didn't support her when she was still well enough to be scared. And I thought about what it would have been like to go to the doctor with her and realized that I couldn't have done it. I would have been so upset to find out that she was dying. Her death was my own death. "If my mother dies I think I will die." That was a pervasive feeling I always had. And a pervasive feeling that she was dying even years before it was ever admitted that she was sick. It would have been easier for me to support a friend who was sick. I have done that before. It would have been much harder for me if that same friend were my mother. I felt that we were inseparable. If she cried, I would cry. I had always felt her pain greatly. That time she was so upset when she lost $100. When·she was mad at my father or upset with herself, or hurt, my heart would skip a beat or I would gulp. It frightened me so much that she would be hurting — like the time in Chalker Beach, Connecticut when she almost choked to death.

Or the time when she was taking me to the doctor at Olney Avenue in Philadelphia and jammed on the brakes really quick. My heart leaped. I worried about her. I didn't think she could make it. Like the feeling one sometimes has seeing old people crossing the street. I felt there was something wrong, something too abrupt in her quick last-minute motions. She was dying of M.S.

I just looked in the mirror at myself. There is something fine about how I look. I look soft and lovely. I could never

182

write this now if I were feeling as badly as I felt when my mother first died. I am so much more at peace now. I can look in the mirror and I see an attractive strong woman — and a happy face, much to my own surprise.

I do feel happy and relieved that this part of the writing is done with.

I look okay and not sad like the writing.

Ginger

I don't know how one labels when one begins one's affair with someone. Does it start when the actual lovemaking begins or does it start when the two people meet and know that they like each other and play the flirtatious games that people sometimes do before they get together?

When my rolfing and living in Berkeley became overwhelming and I was unable to get the kinds of strokes I wanted from my friends, I drove down to Big Sur to give myself a vacation. My first night I stayed in a nice lodge, Ginger and her friend were down there and I planned to look them up. But mostly I thought that I would be with myself, and spent that first night running around the Big Sur Lodge just like a kid. I was thrilled to be there. The pressure began to lift for me and I began to feel human again. I walked around the cabins for an hour that night. The moist air was wonderful and the smells delicious from the sea and the sweetness of the wild flowers. The trees and the hills looming above in the dark reminded me of the Alps. I came back to my cabin and lay on the floor to do breathing exercises and sit ups. Then I made love to myself. I had a bottle of Kahlua and I treated myself well. It was very thrilling to be there and to be happy again with myself. The rolfing experience had drained me. I fell asleep.

The next day I called Ginger. I planned to meet her for breakfast and after take a long walk by myself in the hills. I had already gotten a map of the surrounding area. I was going to nourish myself the way I had learned to do in Puerto Vallarta.

I went to the cabin where Ginger was staying with Elizabeth, who was also a friend of mine. When I arrived they were both in bed. I told them how I had been feeling. They both grabbed me into their bed and hugged me and were really warm. We talked about hugging and I told them how I wanted to be hugged. Ginger seemed to be teaching us both how to hug. She gave me a big hug. I remember she said: "But you have to learn to hug back" and she put my arm around Elizabeth. The experience was awkward. We touched tentatively, asking each other if it was okay. It felt wonderful to be with them and to be close.

Later we went out for a drink at the Nepenthe, and watched the birds fly between the hills. Then we sat inside. It was cold. After drinks we went back to the cabin and held each other some more. We did not make love, we hugged and were very close. By then, we were pretty much stoned and fell asleep.

Later Elizabeth had to leave; she had promised a friend to be home that evening. Then Ginger and I were together and it was wonderful. We drank Kahlua and vodka. The record player was on and the only light came from the fireplace. The bed was surrounded by glass windows so we could look out on stars, the sea and the moon. The fog rolled in before I fell asleep.

The fire roared. Its light danced on the ceiling. Carol King played in the background. Lying in Ginger's arms making delicious love I remembered the times I heard those songs and wished I had a lover. That made being with Ginger even more delicious.

Tame me
teach me
not to be afraid
to be close

We stayed in Big Sur for three days. I became happier and happier. On one of those days I called Gloria in D.C. I wanted to share my excitement with her.

When Ginger and I returned from Big Sur we went directly to a meeting being held at a local women's center in San Francisco. I remember that sudden feeling of tightening as we came into the city and went to the center. After the meeting a woman that I admired who was a writer and who I liked and wanted to become friends with came and sat and talked with people in the lobby. I didn't know what to say to her. Ginger talked easily to her and I listened. I wished that I hadn't lost the confidence and spontaneity I felt in Big Sur. This person whom I liked seemed quiet and perhaps as awkward as I.

After the meeting Ginger and I went to Ginger's house. A meeting was going on there to which Lydia had invited me earlier in the week. I sat down at the door and listened. The meeting was about the recent Lesbian conference held in L.A. and the schism or issues that were brought up between working class and middle class women. The women were talking about what it was like growing up as a middle class woman and as a working class woman. The stories they told about their lives were humorous, though often their experiences loving women and dealing with their parents were very painful. One woman, a doctor, told an animated story about her father's discovery of a letter from her woman lover and his calling her at a medical conference to say that he received a call from the American Medical Association, that they had found out she was a lesbian. He wanted her to stop seeing the woman. She was with her mother at the conference and didn't understand at all. She said to her father: "You mean that the AMA is upset because the woman doctor who has been giving speeches and talking about women's health care and political rights and who says she is a lesbian really is a lesbian?"

One woman who grew up in Kentucky talked about her life and her folks and how upset her mother had been to find out that she loved women and asked her if she were a "lesbo."

Here were women who called themselves lesbians — charming, humorous, warm people, bright and incisive. They were all dressed differently, some of them in the fashionable styles and others in jeans and flannel shirts. I was again amazed that what I had been so afraid of all my life was so absurd. I felt "What a shame that that word lesbian holds so much fear for so many women and held so many ugly feelings for me for so long."

I remember in D.C. how sad I used to feel it was for two women who loved each other to live together. I felt that very strongly one sunny day when I called Gloria at her home. She told me she had just returned from walking a mile in the snow to get the mail with her woman lover.

When I had played tennis with Lydia earlier in the week I didn't know her. My feelings of what a lesbian was were very abstract and negative. And Ginger had scared me about who the women were in her house — heavy lesbians. I had felt very uncomfortable playing tennis with her.

But when I went to the meeting that day I was seeing much of the "inside" of these women, who they really were. I was able to lay aside my built-in feelings.

It was now near the end of my first year in California. I had decided to make a trip back to D.C. to visit my friends and complete the work on my degree. I was still unsure whether I would be living permanently in D.C. or California. I spent my last day before the trip with my friends.

In the evening I went to the movies with Alice and Ginger and Abigail and Silvia and Jean to see a film by Kate Millet. Everyone met at Silvia's house. Abigail had called me to come there. I remember being really happy as I sat around Silvia's dining room table looking at everybody. I was certainly pleased with my new friends. It was important for me to see them before I went back to D.C. They helped to anchor my being in California because I wasn't sure yet where I wanted to be. We hadn't become close friends, but we had begun relationships and I knew what I had here and what I had in D.C.

Their support was very important. The next day I would be flying back to D.C. to try to get the okay for another year in California from NIMH to continue my graduate work. I also planned to try to find out where money could be granted for women's projects that my friends were working on. Silvia's note to me at NIMH, she sent me a grant proposal that I didn't bring with me, and Ginger's calls and knowing Jean and Alice were very important to me my last very painful visit at NIMH.

It was that last night in San Francisco going to the Kate Millet gala cocktail party and movies that it was really clear to me that it was not so much that I enjoyed going to the feminist activities as it was being with these friends. What I enjoyed was the excitement of going out with everybody. I remember near the end of the cocktail party I found two of my friends in an office away from the large gathering role playing a male chauvinist boss and his chick secretary. I quickly joined them. I loved playing with them.

After the movie we went back to our cars to go home. Abigail and Ginger were fighting. I felt uncomfortable with them so I walked with Silvia and Jean. I remember feeling that evening as I walked with them that they were like sisters. They walked the same, they seemed quite tall, as they strolled together both wearing the same kind of outer garments, long sweaters — purple, that seemed so slender. They seemed beautifully serene that night as they walked together, in contrast to the yelling between Abigail and Ginger. They were just gliding along, talking, walking close to each other, joking quietly. When we reached Silvia's house they both kissed me goodbye before I drove home. I remember liking so much our parting — the kiss goodbye. It really warmed my heart as I drove back to Berkeley to get ready to leave early in the a.m. for D.C. and a confrontation with my past.

THE INTERVIEWS

I WAS very excited to meet so many women who loved women — independent people who were committed to their work — that I thought it would be wonderful to interview them for this book. Here were women, some married, many similar to my friends back home, who loved women. They were not the imaginary freaks and ugly people that I fantasized about all my life and feared that I was.

I was curious to know who these women were, how they ran their lives, what was important to them; what they looked like, how they felt. If I could learn how they coped and ran their own lives, I felt that perhaps I could learn to live my life more easily. When I began the interview process I was particularly interested in those women who called themselves bisexual or who loved both women and men.

I wanted to know about these women's love feelings and sexual feelings for other women. Did they ever feel conflicted about such feelings? When they discovered these feelings, were they pained by them? How did they act them out? When and how did they first make love with a woman? This latter question plagued me for years around the women I loved in D.C. I used to yell in therapy: "Okay, okay, if there are lots of women who love women how come no one ever asked me? How come none of the women I love seem to want to make love to me?"

This was a period in my life I was just emerging from. How had other women dealt with it? I particularly searched for this theme in my readings about women, in books by women and in books involving female characters. I wanted to know if Simone or Anais ever felt conflicted in their love feelings for women. Did they feel their feelings were okay or ugly? Did they have sexual feelings for women?

I searched for literary examples in which two women exchanged warmth and tenderness with each other. I had to content myself with the slight touching between women in *Proposition 31*, a slight hug and touch before they fell asleep, until I discovered Anais' intense love for June, and saw that indeed what I felt did exist.

As I began the interviews I realized that part of what I have been doing all my life with women has been trying to understand how they feel. After an exciting evening with Tracy, talking about women and this book, I wrote in my journal: "It may well be better said that I have always wanted to know how my women friends felt — about sexuality, about men, about themselves, about me. And now I am formalizing this process — structuring it through interviews so I have permission to do what I have always wanted to do — to get to know women better. This time I won't be prying as in D.C. I may have been accused of demanding too much openness and closeness then, or certainly I may have been asking questions about spaces my friends had not yet dealt with or presenting issues that were threatening. In Washington, D.C. and earlier in Philadelphia (of course there were always exceptions) I found I was overstepping my friends' sense of privacy. But now the women's movement has broken down the barriers and brought women closer together and provided me with the support to write this book.

When I actually began interviewing these women I was very nervous and unsure of myself. At first I felt I knew less than the others, who seemed more clear about their sexuality than I. Later I learned that everyone struggles in her own way. What was wonderful was that I did not have to pretend that I knew exactly where I stood with my feelings for women.

It was not that I wasn't scared or didn't fear disapproval from other women who loved women, because of my ambivalence for sexual feelings for women. But the point was I found support almost everywhere I ventured — and often in the places I feared the most. This book has been a healing process, a place for me and perhaps other women to work through our feelings for women.

I interviewed:
Julia who lived with a group of women and was exploring her feelings for other women.
· Tracy, a woman who lived alone, who was non-monogomous and had men and women lovers.

Greta, who lived with a man and had had women lovers.

Ellen, who lived alone and was also non-monogomous. She had men and women lovers but was now "choosier" with the men she had as lovers.

and Becky who was divorced and was living with woman lover.

As I began the interviews I was determined that I wasn't going to become intolerant toward women who didn't make love to women, or were ambivalent about their sexuality. Hadn't I had enough pain? Didn't I know the fears? I had gained a real strength in myself by being able to admit openly my ambivalence for my love and sexual feelings for women. I had met some women in California who stated very strongly that women *should* love other women and be lovers with women. I felt they did not leave room for explorations and doubts. I felt that by announcing unsureness, I helped others who were unsure.

Gloria once commented that what struck her the most about the interviews was that some of the women seemed unsure. She said that as if it were a negative thing. To me it is not negative. I think once again we have a characteristic that is part of the male dominated society — that one can't be unsure, that one must present herself at all times as certain.

The Interview Process

In the interviews, as in my writings, I had faith that if I went deep enough into my feelings and the feelings of other women I would touch upon feelings common to everybody. My first year in California I went to hear Anais Nin speak and heard her talk about the Jungian concept of the collective unconscious. She said that if we all explored our feelings deep enough we would flow into the collective unconscious, reaching a level at which we all experienced similar feelings. By interviewing a few women in depth I hoped to touch important feelings in us all. I talked with many women besides those I interviewed formally and I found at many levels we often shared very similar feelings.

Each woman I interviewed wanted to stress that she was in the process of change and that things she said today could be different for her the next week.

Since I have completed the interviews, Greta got married, Julia, who stressed trying to learn not to think in terms of labels and categories is thinking of taking on the lesbian label. Tracy who talked about being non-monogomous and having men and women in her life is now living in a couple with a woman and would prefer not to have men in her life as lovers. Ellen is still living alone and looks to living with a group of people. And Becky is no longer living with her woman lover.

Form

I feel that one of the things that women must do if we are going to make the necessary and vast changes in this society is to develop new forms. To take our power and then use the same forms as the male, white, heterosexual society would be to find ourselves back where we began.

I had worried when I met women who were taking their work as their main energy place in life. Yes I was excited to find women who were committed to their work with the same intensity as I. But I worried that we would become like men in our striving to achieve and to become independent people — putting work before relationships, becoming unfeeling as men sometimes are.

When I began these interviews I was determined to create a new form. I came out of a traditional research background at NIMH which I felt was very much lacking, offering little to the people it paid researchers millions of dollars to study. The assumption often made in such research is there is something wrong with the subjects being researched or interviewed. One must discover how they got this way, analyzing minute character traits — constructs developed by social scientists (their reality) which are factored out of a multiplicity of behaviors. As if such a categorizing and analyzing of human beings to determine a specific behavior is really possible. Character traits are studied in order to learn how to improve the behavior of the subjects. The assumption is made — a priori — that the behavior of the subject is not normal, or is below standards — a value judgment of the culture made under the guise of objective scientific reality.

198

I wanted my research to be an exploratory dialogue between women — a place where we would express our love feelings and learn together from each other about ourselves — as total people — not as fragments and categories. Not a place where the researcher comes from outside and asks his subjects questions — him playing the superior role — and then presenting an analysis of his data broken up into percentages and fragments. So often researchers are more interested in communicating with each other than with the people they supposedly want to help change.

One assumption that I had made based on my feelings (as is the "objective work" of rational man) is that people will more readily change by sharing feelings with other people than by reading numbers, percentages and abstract statements devised by scientists about human behavior.

Kinsey in 1944 and 1953 presented figures and an analysis to support his contention that a certain percentage of the population he studied was bisexual, but that did not help those of us in our growth process who were struggling and are still struggling today with defining our sexuality. At that time he clearly and articulately stated that there are people who love *both* men and women.

"That there are individuals who react psychologically to both females and males, and who have overt sexual relations with both females and males in the course of their lives, or in any single period of their lives, is a fact of which many persons are unaware; and many who are academically aware of it still fail to comprehend the realities of the situation. It is a characteristic of the human mind that it tries to dichotomize in its classification of phenomena. Things are either so or they are not so. Sexual behavior is either normal or abnormal, socially acceptable or unacceptable, heterosexual or homosexual and many persons do not want to believe that there are gradations in these matters from one to the other extreme."*

Though Kinsey's work has had impact on all of us and made the discussion of sexuality easier, I feel in order for people to deal with their sexuality they need to share and understand other people's feelings and experiences at a deeper level than the type of research Kinsey provided. And though hundreds of magazine articles on bisexuality have been published, what these articles have most in common is their lack of any depth of feelings.

I want to present women more totally in their lives rather than as fragments or abstractions of some scientist's reality. I feel that seeing and experiencing the processes and feelings women go through in exploring their sexuality can have a great deal more impact on people's lives than the type of objective science that is supported today by the culture. Studies which often observe, describe and compartmentalize a phenomena such as sexual behavior but rarely talk about how people feel about their behavior or how their behavior makes them feel are absurd.

---

* *Sexual Behavior in the Human Female,* Kinsey, Pomeroy, Martin, Gebhard, W.B. Saunders Company, 1953.

Before undertaking these interviews I immersed myself in women's books, women's history and literature, looking for another perspective, a model for another reality. I am convinced that our methods of social change and research are inadequate because of the way we perceive the world. I tried to break down old thought structures and ways of thinking for myself. I also read Jung, Carlos Castaneda, Andrew Weil in my search to see things another way. I was particularly interested in Don Juan's lessons in perceiving the world differently and Jung's discussion of Eastern and Western thinking. I feel our whole way of thinking and seeing the world not only prevents social change but makes us unhealthy.

We focus on curing society's victims, "the abnormal folks" and not on the real causes of social problems. We refuse to examine the structures of our society which cause people to have problems in the first place. We research our problems to death, but do not put any energy into changing the structures that cause them. Such change would require a redistribution of power.

In trying to create a new form for the interviews, in terms of how I collected the information and in terms of how I presented it, I first went to Kenneth Keniston's famous study *The Young Radicals*. He presented student radicals in "pieces," by subject matter. I wanted to present the women in still a more total way, not in abstract analyses of who the women were or a quote of one or two sentences from the interviews used to illustrate an abstraction. I had completed three interviews by the time my journey took me to Kate Millet's *The Prostitution Papers*, in which she presented dialogues with women prostitutes she had interviewed. Her book was very reassuring and supportive to me in my research. It was more along the lines I wanted to achieve. Her statement that she had to put the interviews aside for awhile before she was able to work on them as material from life rather than life itself, so profoundly did they affect her, was very helpful to me.

Sometimes an interview was so heavy and close to me I could not look at it for weeks, though I did struggle to try to work on it right away. After reading Kate Millet's work I eased up on myself and didn't expect so much. I just could not plunge right back into so heavy an emotional experience, especially material which was sometimes very threatening. It often took months before my body could absorb all the new feelings and experiences I had learned. I had many preconceptions about women loving women. It took me a long time to let them go, and integrate a new perspective.

In each interview I tried to create a dialogue, a place where each of us could share and explore our feelings. I wanted the interviews to be an exchange. I would also be explaining my feelings about myself. I wanted the women I talked with to gain something from the interview as well. I hoped that each interview would build on the previous ones. I tried to share with each woman the information and feelings I learned from earlier interviews. I wanted the process of the book to be a reflection of what I hoped the book would be, a loving book about women's feelings.

Usually I spent time with each woman before the interview. Several of the women became my close friends. I told each woman the issues I wanted to explore and asked them to

202

think of areas they felt were important. Then when I started the interview, I asked the women to explore their feelings about their sexuality hoping to have each woman's view emerge uniquely as her own. I thought that would be better than imposing a structure of the pre-established questionnaire on each woman.

Most women expressed concern about their parents knowing that they loved women and asked what other women did about it. This seemed at the time to be a larger issue than the fear of losing their jobs because of their sexual choices.

The interviews are over a year old now. I have elected to keep them the way they were. Like the women I interviewed I feel differently now about many things expressed in them, but they are an important part of my journey and, hopefully, will be helpful to many people.

I have left much of the interviews in oral language and only where I felt necessary did I change them to written prose. I feel that women like members of any oppressed group use dialogue as their main form of communication, and I tried to leave this form intact.

Women talk and often non-linearly. We free associate from one topic to another as we talk and then come back and finish topics we began. Often when our conversation is over a whole area has been thoroughly covered in this manner.

JULIA

THE FIRST woman I interviewed was Julia, a roommate of Ginger's. Ginger had often described the roommates she lived with as a collective of radical lesbians and feminists. By the time I actually interviewed Julia the mystique of their radical lesbian house had worn off somewhat, but I was still scared to death.

I feared Julia would disapprove of me for my unsure feelings about women, and for liking men.

During the period I began talking to other women about loving women in California, there were intense feelings that women who were not making love to women, or who claimed to be bisexual were cop-outs — that there was something wrong with women who related to men because they were supporting the white male heterosexual society. This was the radical lesbian voice. Lydia had given me an article to read that explained this political approach in detail. Needless to say, I was intimidated by Ginger's description of who these

207

radical lesbians were. I was relieved when Julia and I actually sat down and talked during the interviews.

My concern here was describing love feelings between women. I felt what was important was that women loved each other. I felt that the love feelings for other women experienced by women who loved *only* women and those who loved *both* women and men were the same basic deep feeling. I know others will disagree with me strongly. I in no way mean to minimize the pain and problems caused by women who have loved a woman until a man appeared on the scene, and then they ran back to the heterosexual world. Nor do I minimize what this means politically. (See Loving Women/A Stronger Sense of Self.)

In March Julia had heard that this woman named Ruth had slept in her bed. She smelled the heavy musk oil on her sheets. It was the night Gloria had come to town and I ran away from her and spent the night in the city. When Julia and I met we immediately clicked with each other. I think a large part of that was our Jewish background and the fact that we seemed to have so many similar experiences and feelings. I had even known her Jewish psychiatrist! He had worked at NIMH in the same time period I had been there. For much of our interview we were bouncing off each other saying "Right, Right" to our similar experiences. I was scared to do this first interview. Julia was very supportive.

During the interview I was aware of the anxiety I felt about beginning this book. Here I was actually sitting and talking with a woman about her love and sexual feelings for other women. It was very exciting.

208

July 10, 1973

Julia.   For a long time I had a lot of fantasies about women. I had very close friends and there was always a sexual excitement about them. But up until about five years ago I couldn't even think in those terms.

Ruth.   Did you recognize the sexual excitement?

J.   Well, I remember once in high school feeling very attracted to this other woman in the band, and I remember thinking: "Oh Shit! — I'm not supposed to have those feelings!" So I sort of wiped 'em out.

R.   Were they sexual?

J.   Yeah, like one day, she was passing by; I was sitting somewhere in the library and she was walking by and I said: "Oh, my God, I want to kiss her! Oh, too much! Oh no! What am I going to do with these terrible feelings!" So I furiously read all kinds of porny literature about heterosexual sex and all that stuff.

R.   To get yourself turned on to that?

J.   Yeah. Then I had a few good experiences as a teenager, with guys, but I really didn't get into a sexual thing with guys for a long time. When you're raised as a nice Jewish girl, you're not supposed to *do that!*

R.   Right, right.

J.   That was pretty heavily ingrained in me. It took a long time to get through that. In grad school I had this real heavy crush on my roommate. It was *such* a heavy emotional attachment I was feeling. She was a few years older than I and had worked, and she seemed to be much older — and very understanding. She really came across to me — "I know what you're talking about," — and I just ate it up. It was just too much. And I really got turned on to her, I really got very, very crazy from her, in a lot of ways, because I thought I was really big shit and couldn't deal with that. It was just terrible to have these feelings. I didn't want to be relegated to the unknown role of a Lesbian — whatever that was — all my life.

R.   What did you mean, the big shit feeling?

J.   I *felt* like I had — that I was really icky, for having these feelings, and really terrible. You know, you're not supposed to have those feelings for women. They were going to cut me off from the general society. I wouldn't be like everybody else or like my parents wanted me to be. And, it was really from *that* that — when I moved to California — I decided to get into therapy. I had all these fantasies about women and I wasn't fucking men, and there was obviously *something* wrong! So I went into therapy. So I started fucking men.

R.   During therapy?

J.   During therapy, but all my feelings towards women were just knocked out by the therapist — he just wouldn't deal with them.

R.   I wonder why. (both laugh)

J.   Because he was a nice Jewish Boy! And nice Jewish girls obviously don't have lesbian thoughts.

R.   Did you tell him that you feared you loved women?

J.   Oh, yeah That was the reason I went into therapy.

R.   And what did he say?

J.   Well, his whole trip was: "Why don't we get you squared away with men, and then obviously you won't have these feelings?"

R.   You won't have these feelings for women any more?

210

J.   Yes, It was *really* an avoidance. I wanted to avoid those feelings and he obviously did too. When I went to Stanford I was really upset at my feelings, and I told the dorm supervisor. I spent an hour and a half relating to her about these horrendous feelings towards women, and the fears I had, and that I was just going to be out of control. And *so again*, I told the therapist. Every once in a while I'd bring up the subject of these feelings. Then I was in a group for a year. I still had these feelings about women, and I still brought them up. I remember I told the group I had a crush on one of my house-mates and the guys in the group were all pooh-poohing my crush on my roommate and the girls were saying, "Oh, yeah, I can understand what that's about!" But no one really wanted to deal with it.

R.   Because it's threatening to them. I got into therapy because I couldn't get out of this relationship that I was in with a nice Jewish boy and it was so very destructive! And at the same time I also was just madly, you know, I had this terrible emotional thing about my roommate in Washington. I absolutely adored her, and I liked him too, and I just couldn't figure out what it was all about. I had very, very strong feelings. But, unlike you, I wouldn't even *let* myself feel anything sexual. I mean, I just *refused*, I just *feared* that I might be a lesbian. When I did go into therapy, I talked about my whole frantic anxiety, one of the main issues being that I feared I liked women, and I was looking for reassurance that that's not really being a lesbian, is it?

J.   (Laughs, delighted)

R.   He was the one who in fact told me to fantisize, when I masturbated, about making love to this woman. Huh!!! Oh, I couldn't do that!! (Both laugh) It was terrible. He really helped me, he encouraged me to sleep with a woman, which I finally did.

J.   That's really great.

R.   But it sounds like you were freer with yourself — that you let yourself at least experience your sexual feelings. I just pushed them back.

J.   Well, by that time in my life they'd gotten so heavy, I couldn't do anything else.

R.   Did you tell your roommate in grad school how you felt about her?

J.   I finally told her. I went to see her a year later after grad school. She was her usual, understanding self! But I felt really terrible, revealing my feelings, partly because she didn't have these same feelings for me.

R.   You were rejected.

J.   Yeah. But there was also a heavy emotional aspect. I think the sexual aspect was really wanting to relate to that person as close as possible. And I think the emotional aspect was there waiting for the sexual one.

R.   Explain that again, will you?

J.   I'm not explaining very clearly, yet I know what I'm feeling. With my roommate as well as with this other woman that I knew for a few years — I felt very attracted to her, emotionally and sexually, but now that I am involved sexually it's a different kind of thing — it's a different way of expressing or of using sex.

R.   I think I understand. When I went into therapy, I thought — women, they're just *very* important to me. I had male friends and lovers, but sometimes I would feel a little torn that I went out with my lover and wanted to see my women friend later that night.

J. Great, great.

R. My women friends were important, and I *really* loved them, but sometimes I wished that I would feel that strongly about a man. Though I was with a man, and he was very important to me, my deep emotions, a lot of times, went to women.

J. Yeah.

R. Then there was the painful part of loving a woman so much and not being able to touch her. It was just excruciating. And now that I'm becoming more comfortable with my sexuality the intensity goes away, because I *can* express my affection openly — I mean like a hug — which I wasn't able to do before. And *that's* a relief.

J. Right.

R. It becomes more of a total thing — there is not that tense focus on sex relief.

J. And that's what I was trying to get to — that I came into relating to women with a heterosexual head — meaning I related first in a sexual way. The *first* woman I became involved with, I really did it almost like a big macho trip. We knew each other, and there was a certain amount of trust and liking each other. One day we just got in bed with each other. And it really wasn't the thing to do. The focus became sex.

R. What do you mean, it really wasn't the thing to do?

J. Because that wasn't where our total relationship really *was*. It's something that I'm feeling more now. I'm much more discriminating. *Now* the options are open. In other words, I truly *feel* now that I can relate as a friend on a lot of different levels, with affection, with tenderness, with gentleness, with anger, with upset to women and it can also be a very passionate, lusty, sexual kind of thing. Or it can be just a gentle hugging or touching or whatever . . . and that there's all kinds of in-betweens that I never felt with a man — where the focus was definitely sexual, fucking. And that with women — like you said — there may have been some hugging, but if we tried to do back-rubs, or show affection at different times, people would "mis-read."

R. Or, or, at least I was worried, you know, I was just too tense even to touch.

J. Right!

R. And I don't know how much was, they didn't touch *me* that much either, how much was my own uneasiness about it, or how much is their uneasiness.

J. Right, both. But now I feel that I'm in control of that, you know. The women I know that are straight, who either are threatened by gay women, the idea of bisexuality, or whatever their feelings are about themselves — I can be very reassuring with them. One friend I have like that, she knows that when I hug her, it's not a come-on, or anything like that. And we've talked about it, and she understands. And she can *enjoy* being touched by another woman and not feel any pressure on her.

R. Yes. It's quite a relief. And it's so enjoyable, to be touched. I guess that's why it was easy for me to get involved with Ginger. It's easy for her to get involved with people. She seems so comfortable in touching, that when she was hugging, I didn't feel that she was coming on.

J. Right. I think those are the kinds of things that start hap-

214

pening. The total kind of relationship. For a long time —
whenever I would touch, especially like in bed, talking before
you go to sleep, or hugging and touching — I'd get turned on
right away, and would want to do something sexual. But that's
not really what my *body* wanted. My *head* was saying "Oh,
you're getting turned on, so do something sexual." And that's
kind of a heterosexual conditioning that I had. When I was
with men, it was like we'd go out. . . . I only lived with one
guy and it was not a very long time. So I didn't really know
what it was like to sleep with someone without fucking all the
time. So when I changed over to women (laughing briefly),
you know, it's taken me some time to really let go with that,
and to be able to cuddle and to hug and, and if I get turned
on, realize I don't *have* to do anything about it.
R.   Right. It's just nice. And I've learned to enjoy being
turned on. I remember once at the commune, we were all
sitting around the table, there were a lot of women and men
there, and I was just turned on to *everybody*, you know, it's
just nice to enjoy being turned on to a friend, and you don't
have to do anything about it. It's just a good feeling to let
yourself enjoy it.
J.   Yeah. Yeah. But there are so many nuances of feelings
that most people never get to find out what they're about. I
don't know how I'm going to feel about men, in another year
or so. I don't *hate* them, I just don't find that I want to
associate closely with them at this point in time. And right
now I'm very wound up in exploring my own kinds of feelings,
the feelings that I've had for *so* many years towards women,
and I think it's helping me find that if you love a person, then
you can express that, that really is beautiful, and you can find

many ways of doing that.

R.   I've learned so much through the first woman I ever slept with who considered herself a lesbian. She wasn't my ideal woman. I think I told you what I wanted.

J.   No.

R.   I wanted someone like me to sleep with, someone with long hair who was definitely into men, someone that I thought was very attractive, physically, and this person had short hair, and this person was fat. And, you know, I was still into the good-looking men thing, and I slept with her and I was *really* petrified — the first time was just absolutely awful. And I just had diarrhea — I couldn't move — but then, later on, I guess there was one other time we were able to be together and somehow, I got myself to relax, and it was just beautiful. The sex was really nice, it was so relaxed. It was outstanding. And through this whole year of being with Ginger and talking with other women and being more in touch with myself, I've become so grateful to this woman. When I went back to Washington to talk to her, I realized that she's brilliant — she's an outstanding person. I was just really grateful that she let me be close to her then. I mean it is sort of a reverse thing now, in that she's just a beautiful person, she helped me with other people, both men and women, I was so superficial about the things that I felt were important. So that, in terms of my relationships with people, being with women, I think, has helped me.

J.   Yeah. It really hit me hard this one time when Linda, my lover, and I were visiting up north, and we were wandering around the beach, and I became very aware of seeing me after bouncing off her. It was like, I could look at her and see me

216

and see her looking at me, and it was incredible, because we weren't doing roles. There's no roles, as such.

R.   Yeah.

J.   There are aspects about our personalities that have certain things we will play out, but there are no *roles*. Neither of us does a macho thing and neither of us does a, well, I'm in charge of this, you know. If anything, we both take turns doing 'in charges.'

R.   Which is nice.

J.   I think that's why women can get closer in some ways, but I also find there are less fantasies, with women. I might have had fantasies *before* I made love with them, but as soon as I'm involved there's less fantasies, and I think that that can be both positive and negative.

R.   You mean, the reality isn't as good as the fantasy?

J.   Right, right. I think that I'm confronted much more with really who I am and what I'm really doing.

R.   Yeah. I really hear what you're saying. There are two things I was just thinking. The part about the role-playing, that's what I was like with my friendships with women. One of my best friends, Mandy, I just adored her, and I never got it on sexually with her, but I used to think about what it would be like if I loved her that much, sexually. It would have been incredible. It just never happened, but our friendship was so nice, because there wasn't that tension, that you have with men and women, of who's supposed to do this and that, who's supposed to be dominant. Unlike with my lover, Larry, who would get really upset if I took a strong position about doing something. He would really get threatened. With Mandy it was just so *comfortable*. It was such a beautiful thing; there

217

were other tensions between us but it wasn't that — she's supposed to do one role and I another. We took turns being in charge. It just sort of happened.

J.   Right, right.

R.   And the other thing that you said — that I found in my relationship with Jessica. I saw the relationship as mirror-images. Maybe that's what you're talking about, getting to know yourself. It became so intense, I'd like to look at her, like when we walked on the beach and I would say to myself: "Wow, that's someone I'm really close to, and she's just lovely" and I would feel beautiful. I think I saw my own beauty in her. But when we were together sometimes, it was so intense, it was almost painful. I've talked to other women that've been lovers and have been really close, and they have said too that the intensity is sometimes incredible. And I think it has to do with us being women, or being the same, I'm not sure.

J.   Yeah.

R.   Because Jessica and I, we didn't get heavily involved sexually; we held each other sleeping nude, we touched a lot, but we petted just once, and so I wonder sometimes if the intensity would have been relieved, had we really gotten involved more sexually. I can't explain it but it is what we were talking about before, about a more whole relationship, that there's not that intense sexual focus. With Ginger my most recent woman lover, it's nice, it's just very whole, it's not that intense thing, like the way it was with Jessica and I. Sexually, it can be extremely exciting, but there's not that intense. . . .

J.   But that's something that you might never know.

R.   But I guess I was thinking, too, even when you were say-

218

ing it is so nice to be close with women, and not to have roles, that all relationships between women are not necessarily healthy. My friend Gloria constantly reminds me: "Don't kid yourself. Women are into trips too, especially those women who recently were into heterosexual relationships." You must know some lesbian relationships that aren't healthy.

J.   But those aren't *role* things, those are personalities.

R.   Well, there are also women who take on butch and fem roles. There is a definite thing about who is supposed to be masculine, or be dominant.

J.   But that was society's thing that women bought. And most of these women are older women who came out when there was no support for being women loving women.

R.   I'm just trying to make sure within myself that when I tell myself why I am writing this book, that I am not trying to sell something. Tracy asked me if I was committed to social change and if I was trying to change something. I realize I want people to feel more comfortable with their feelings but I don't see myself having a social change thrust with this book. I am not pushing for everyone to be bisexual. I'm doing this as a very personal kind of exploration; maybe other people will be helped, but I wanted to watch myself. I'm not saying: "This is what I see in the feminist movement." I don't necessarily want to be saying that relating to women is better, that all women's relationships are great, that being bisexual is best. Women have problems relating to each other too.

J.   I think, for the most part, that's true. But we're saying that between two women there's not the kind of tension that's between a man and a woman, in terms of the roles. Almost all the women I know are in college, have been in college, or are making some sort of life for themselves within the professions or in an alternative lifestyle. So they all have a certain amount of well-developed survival instinct and a sense of taking care of themselves. That's the first thing.

R. Right.

J. The second thing is that I've seen women, straight women, and I use the word "straight" when we talk about women who don't think about relating sexually and emotionally to other women as a valid relationship — they may have long-time friends who are *their emotional backbone*, but they don't think of it in those terms. I know straight women who have certain ways of relating to each other, certain roles that keep them at a distance.

R. I see what you're saying.

J. Also, the thing about roles is that when I first realized, when it first hit me emotionally, that there aren't roles, it scared the *shit* out of me! All of a sudden, I was faced with ME and relating to the other person, and there were no walls, there were no roles, there was nothing to protect me! And I had to become more of *me*, and more a person, and if I wanted my needs met, I *really* had to say what I wanted. And, for a long time, I thought "Women are intuitive, they can sense that." A lot of times, I think that closeness does come from sensing it, but the reality is that you've still got to *say* what you want. It's a lot of work, it really is. So, I think you have to listen to what women say about what's happening to women. I don't buy what men say about women any more.

R. I agree with that. I think we're the only ones who are going to find out about how we are, from ourselves, and from looking at other women. But I guess when I originally started

220

out that was more of a caution to myself, not to think that the way women relate to each other is better. I discovered there was gaming just as in heterosexual relationships; I sometimes got disappointed with other women because I expected more from them. And, you know, we haven't worked stuff out; we don't have models either.

J.   Though there aren't sex role tensions, women still game. I think anybody can have hangups.

R.   What I thought I'd do now is ask you some questions. These aren't in any order particularly, but they are issues that I want to focus on. Some of them we've touched on; let's see if we can get them into focus.

J.   Okay, fine.

R.   Did your male lover know you love women, and how did he feel about that?

J.   Okay, that's interesting, because the guy I was going with last, Stuart, is the one that really feels good about women. You see, I moved into a house where he and his wife and this other woman lived. And he and I played these little sex-teasing games, but I was really turned on to his wife.

R.   Oh. I really know *that* one!

J.   And, so, finally I told her about it, because I really couldn't deal with it, I was really turned on. She was very, very sexual. It was a big rejection trip, but she really didn't know what to do with it; she said: "Well, that's really neat that you love me!" and you know, that kind of thing, so after I got my feelings together, realizing that she really wasn't going to *do* anything about it, Stuart and I got involved. And I really think it was a transference. She was already getting involved with somebody outside the house.

R.   You mean, that you loved him partly because he loved her, and partly. . . .

J.   Yeah, there was that. And that went on for about six months, I think, that Stuart and I were together in the house and then I couldn't stand it; I went to Europe and the house broke up, and part of the problem was that they hadn't dealt with their relationship at all, whether they wanted a divorce or wanted to work things out, and that kind of stuff. But when I talked with him, when I talked with *her*, I talked with him too, about my feelings towards her, and he thought it was really neat. He could really get into women loving each other, and he could really get into being a part of that, too, if, you know, if we *all* loved each other.

R.   You see, that's what I want. That's how I started out, in terms of really being able to face my sexuality. My therapist said: "Look, if you're turned on to Lisa and you're turned on to Gary, and they were husband and wife, why not both?" And I . . . God! that's the perfect way for me to deal with my sexuality! Here were two people I was turned on to, and I thought: "Wow! what energy!" And that's what I've sort of been trying to do, a triangle, but that's just *so* difficult.

R.   Do you find loving women the same as loving men?

J.   A lot of guys you can't really be close with. Their heads and their interests and their everything are totally different. So you have very little in *common* with them except sex. And I think that's one of the biggest reasons that a lot of women, now that women are saying that it's okay to relate to women, they're saying, "Well, thank God! I've felt close to women all my *life*, and the only thing missing has been the sexual thing, that's been taboo."

R.   What are you feelings towards Linda or other women? Do these feelings differ from what you feel towards men lovers? Sexually, is there a difference between women and men lovers?

J.   Ummmm. My *fantasies* differ. Ummm. Let me think. I think sometimes sex is more diverse with a woman, because of all those gradations of showing affection. So that's a difference. With guys it was like I'd relate to them sexually by having intercourse, and that was the way of relating to them closely. But with women there are gradations of affection, so you, we don't have to have, do a whole number where you have orgasm to be close. Many men focus on fucking; they rarely focus on touching you all over.

R.   Right.

J.   You know, with women there's a whole other way of doing it, and so there's times when I get really turned on and really feel very passionate and lustful, and *that* can be carried out. But there's a lot of times when I just feel very close and warm and don't want to do anything sexual.

R.   Did you ever feel that way with men?

J.   Very rarely.

R.   Are you saying that you feel more sensuous and more warm with a woman lover than with a male lover?

J.   Yeah.

R.   I've asked other women how they felt about making love with a woman and making love with a man. I'm not sure about this for myself — whether they have found that being with a woman is being more sensuous and more warm?

J.   Oh it is. In a lot of ways, it is. But when I first made love with a woman I was very impatient because it is a lot slower than making love with a man. With a man I was really used to being really turned on fast and then fucking. In fact a lot of times I didn't have an orgasm because it was way too fast.

R. Me, too.

J. For *me*. There was something really intense and very passionate about this quick kind of thing. Then I'd sort of want to fuck *again* because I really wasn't that satisfied!

R. Right, right.

J. With a woman, it can be a lot slower, and it's much more intense I've found.

R. Right.

J. Another difference that I have found in making love to a woman is that it is very difficult to make love to each other at the same time. I haven't had a lot of experience, but in experiences I've had with women, I've found that we would start off making love together with a lot of touching and a lot of feeling, and then one of us would start making love to the other. And the other person would become very passive, in a sense, and just enjoy whatever was going on.

R. Yes, right.

J. And — until the other woman felt satisfied — and then if there was energy, or we felt like it, we'd switch over. And we didn't always *feel* like it. I have found that, if I made love to another woman, I didn't always have to be made love to.

R. Get your orgasm, you mean?

J. Yes. Like, it wasn't that kind of *need*. I could be very satisfied, because I *really* felt like I was experiencing *her* orgasm and physical excitement. That's a change from making love with a man, because with a man I don't experience his orgasm. Another difference in making love with a man is often you make love together, intercourse is making love together at the same time. Not only are we going together, but I used to get lost by the wayside somewhere. Things would be going along fine with the man, and then all of a sudden he'd start speeding up, and I just wasn't ready for him to speed up! So I would feel like: "Wow, everything was over before I really got started." But with a woman, you really go at each other's pace. At times though, it's just as hard talking about what you like or don't like with a woman. But, I found there was another thing with a woman that really fascinated me. It was that I could really *feel* what she's feeling.

R. That's what I meant by the mirror-image thing. I remember touching a woman and feeling as if she had touched me. I could not tell, in fact, I got *scared,* I couldn't tell the difference. I touched her breast — we were dancing — and it was just sort of how I wanted to be touched, and I got the stimulation in my breast, and I backed away. It was really intense, and it scared me. And in that article in Esquire, that interview with Kate Millet, she was saying that sometimes, when she makes love with a woman, she can't tell the difference between their bodies. Which is so beautiful.

J. Right. That's what I remember her saying. Really, it's a strange thing. But it's so neat, because I can really get into making love like that, I can really feel the woman tighten up, and I can sort of ride with her as she is going higher and higher. It's a tremendous feeling. I have *no* way of knowing how a man feels.

R. Yeah. I never even know when he comes. I never knew during intercourse when that exact moment was. I knew when it was *over,* but I didn't always feel him coming, I just couldn't tell sometimes.

J.   It depended on the guy. Like, I could usually feel it, especially when guys made noises. I dig the noise-making thing, then there is a definite kind of building and relaxation.

R.   This is a key question: why can't we ask men to make love to us the way we want? I always felt like I was being rushed; I like being touched all over, being stimulated on my clitoris. I've had not that much experience with a woman, but from what you say, you take turns having orgasms.

J.   Yes. It's hard to concentrate after a certain point if you are both making love to each other at the same time.

R.   Like with Larry, he felt there was something wrong with me because I didn't come in the usual way — just have an orgasm during intercourse. He sometimes would touch me before we had intercourse. Usually he would have his orgasm first, then he would stimulate me. If only I could have taught him to slow *down!* Sometimes I wasn't every ready to have intercourse, I wasn't even that turned on. Once I met a man in Aspen who I made love with and he asked me what I wanted. It was just real long love-making, it wasn't get on and get off. And it was just as good as with a woman. He asked me after his orgasm if I had an orgasm, and he said that's not fair and took a long time pleasing me. I think that most women have found that men are just too quick. There are not that many men that I've slept with that like to lie in bed for a long time and touch and hug and really get stimulated.

J.   No, I think that that's true. I mean, most of the guys that I knew, they really didn't like to, although there are a lot of them that like to make *love*, so that it wasn't just a quickie. We might make love for a few hours, and that gave *me* enough time. I think men have no idea how to make love to a woman. It takes longer to get women stimulated, but they are much more *intensely* stimulated. In this society, men aren't really taught how to be good lovers. Most men grow up not really knowing how and a lot of them don't understand what a clitoris is and how the feelings are around it, and stuff like that.

R.   My last year in D.C. I got involved with a man that I'd always been attracted to. I was really *angry* at him when I discovered he didn't know how to make love. He always seemed so sexy, but when we made love he'd really be hurting me. He was really rough, not purposefully, but it was incredible how he could not know!

J.   This is a whole facade that men have and a whole illusion that they have about themselves and which they present to women. And I think the more women *tell* men what's going on, even though men aren't going to like it for a while, at least they'll get to a point where they'll *know* what they're *doing!*

R.   One of the men that I'd become close to and made love to recently was doing Masters and Johnson sexual therapy at one of the Berkeley institutes. He likes me to stimulate his nipples. He was really wanting to open his body to his feelings. I think men have cut themselves off, too. They could be enjoying themselves more.

J.   Oh, for sure! I mean, men have really gone to an extreme of how humans can be, but it's not a very good extreme.

R.   But I wonder if somehow as men evolve, get more in touch with themselves, if maybe the differences between men and women lovers will be irrelevant.

J.   Right. But then it depends on how the person feels emotionally toward men and women or toward specific people.

But, yeah, I think there are differences now, and even with a very caring, loving male lover, it takes a lot of knowledge and a lot of patience to make love sensitively.

R.   Also there's a tension there, making love with a man. I always feel with a man that I should hurry up and have my orgasm.

J.   Yeah.

R.   The tension is in me, but it comes from some place. I mean, I'll take responsibility for it, but there is some pressure, I think, that we've gotten from the outside, too.

J.   Yes. Now that people say: "Oh, yes, women *have* orgasms" we're all supposed to have them, and fast. That's a bunch of baloney. That speeding up kind of thing with men really bothered me; I always felt like I was the receiver of this machine, this jackhammer going on. And I really like the slow kind of stuff. But as guys would get more and more stimulated, they'd go faster and faster. And that kind of thing, it's not a rhythm to me, I really felt like I was a pavement and they were a jackhammer. And I really didn't *like* that. I don't know of any guys who really didn't speed up, and there's no way that happens with a woman. Also you can do a lot more *non-verbally* with a woman, like, if you want her to touch you somewhere you find it's easier to just gently move her hand.

R.   You can do that with a man, too.

J.   You *can*, except, see, if you're being made love to by someone, it's an entirely different thing than if you're both doing it at the same time. So *he's* trying to get his own pleasure, as well as, hopefully, he's thinking: "God, I hope this is going good for *her!*" You know. But he's not really that *concerned*, after a certain point.

228

R.   I guess, well, one of these experiences I had with a lesbian once, there's a thing called tri. . . . I don't know what the term is, but where two women can touch each other, I don't know, it killed me, I hated it, each other clitorally, so that you can both come at the same time.

J.   I've heard of that, but I think it's very difficult to do that.

R.   Uh, my God, and also it scared the shit out of me.

J.   (Laughing) Your pubic bones get really sore!

R.   Yeah, right! But apparently there's a way to do it or something where she really gets off so that *that* can happen. It also scared me then 'cause it was the first time I slept with a woman and that seemed *really* close. Plus I guess my therapist made some remark to me. I just hated it because I felt she was telling me it was like, you're *supposed* to make love that way. I mean, it was okay to do, but she really believed that that was the right way. She felt that essentially, love making, it is so funny we all have these *shoulds,* is genital organs to genital organs, and so there was something wrong, you know — and I remember my therapist making some remark like: "You've decided to make love with a woman, you know, you've finally got somebody not poking at you, what do you want some woman poking. . .?

J.   (Laughing) Your therapist was a real winner.

R.   Yeah.

J.   I mean, really good! That's great! No, I've heard of that, but I've never known anybody who had tried it, 'cause it, it just seems like clitorises are so hard to find anyway, I mean, (laughing) *fingers* are hard to find, and *mouths.* But not with somebody else's, that would be very hard. Linda and I've tried mutual masturbation, but we'd get to a certain point where one of us would have to focus on the other. I mean, it was just too hard to keep up our intensity and get into what we were feeling.

J.   And we both said: "Now how the hell do other people get around this problem?"

R.   Why do you see it as a problem?

J.   Well, that's the *other* thing, you know. Finally, I got to the point where I said: "Wait a minute! This isn't a problem! This can be really nice."

R.   That you thought you had to do it both at the same time?

J.   Yeah, and then we sort of got out of that. And both of us were coming out of a fairly heavy heterosexual kind of thing.

R?   Intercourse is both at the same time.

J.   Yeah. So, but I think this other person, at this time, has probably thought the same thing. It's so much nicer taking turns, there's really no problem. In fact, for me, it becomes like a massage thing, not that it feels like a massage, but that I *really* get into what I'm doing to the other person, like I really get into their *place*, and where they're at, and I like, go out of myself, into *them*. And so, having someone make love to me would be very irritating while I'm making love to them.

R.   Yes, I see. I thought you were going to say that some- times, when you were reaching orgasm, you go out of control and then you can't be focusing on the other person. Let's say you're stimulating someone else. . . .

J.   I'm getting all excited (laughing). I can't handle this discussion (laughs) go on . . . (laughing) what is happening? I was flashing back to all these situations, in order to tell you what the feelings are, and suddenly. . . .

R.   (Also laughing) And you're getting turned on?

J.   Oh not *really*, but I'm remembering hunks of turning-on things, and they're passing back and forth.

R.   Okay. We can just jump over to some regular emotional questions and then get back to sexual ones.

J.   Well, anyway, that is a difference that I've had to really work with, six months ago I thought it was very uncomfortable for me, and now I find it's. . . .

R.   Something you can even enjoy?

J.   Yeah, and it's hard, but I've also found it's harder for — now, this may sound rather strange — but it's harder for me to have someone make love to *me* than for me to make love to somebody. I really get really, really turned on — I really enjoy making love to somebody. But, I *like* to be made love to, but I find that it's a little harder to really just be passive, what I call passive, just to enjoy it and really get into that thing, really trusting that the other person is just going to be with me, and do and keep doing whatever I want them to do, until I feel satisfied. And that seems to be taking me longer to feel comfortable with.

R.   That's funny. What do you mean by: "Them being with you and doing whatever you want them to until you feel satisfied?" I guess I flashed to how I felt. Sometimes I worry that I'm taking too long or they'll get tired, is that what you mean?

J.   Yeah, right, those kinds of things.

R.   To accept them giving you pleasure or to receive it.

J.   Yeah, right. It's the receiving thing, and I *never* felt that way with a guy. But I never really had that kind of control. In other words, you know, I was getting my pleasure out of them fucking me, but I wasn't really telling them "I want you to do this and that."

R.   You see I did. After we fucked, I always asked them to touch me, but then I'd always feel: "I better hurry up and come or their hand's going to get tired." And one man I loved dearly, Ken, after we made love he told me when I asked him to touch me that I made him feel inadequate. I felt awful. It's not that it's homosexual or heterosexual, it's more sexuality with men and women, or women and women, or whatever. I mean, it sounds like there's the thing of receiving pleasure, and maybe trusting the other person will move themselves and get comfortable if they're not comfortable, that they'll take responsibility for themselves.

J.   Yeah, yeah, but it's also. . . . Yeah, it's the head thing of: "Do I deserve to have all this pleasure? Is it okay?" But it's also knowing that, when you make love to somebody else, I think there's some realistic stuff, but most of it has to do with being able to receive.

R.   I remember once being with my most recent lover. I'd cried a few times and I remember she was just hushing me and I guess I reached the point where I could relax. She was holding me and touching me, slowly moving her finger in my vagina, and it was just so incredibly *pleasurable*, it wasn't even to orgasm. I was just lying there wondering and saying out loud: "I just can't understand, I just can't understand," to myself "It seems so simple, why has it taken me so long to get here? Is it okay to have this much pleasure?" And I was thinking: "God, if it's this good for me, and she seems to have a lot of relationships, my god is she lucky!" If I could have that much pleasure with so many people! But I'm usually so up tight that I don't let myself sleep with people easily. I just don't get into it.

232

J.   Yeah, it does have to do with allowing yourself to have the pleasure and the time. I find that a lot of times, people are much more conscious of *time* and trying to relax.

R.   Me, too. I always feel I have a lot of other things to do.

J.   Yeah. But I really *wanted* to make love but my head's into thinking I have other things to do. Shit.

R.   What's more important?

J.   Right.

R.   Okay. Um, what do you think about yourself sexually? Do you ever fear that you may be homosexual. I mean, is that a fear?

J.   No, I don't think it's a fear now, because it always was a fear but once I began to relate to women, I realized there's something . . . a freedom to really *feel*. Part of it is because I'm in a subculture, where it's okay. I think society puts trips down on people that it's wrong, it's bad, it's all this kind of thing. You know, the *ideal* thing would be that people would be free to choose whichever partners they want, whether it's men and women or one or the other sex — depending on whom they liked. Um. I don't fear it. I haven't been in a situation where I'd have to deal with it in terms of parents, and I don't care about old friends because if they can't accept that in me, then. . . .

R   Just too bad.

J.   Yeah, and I'm not that close with many people. I have a sense about how people feel towards me, but my friends now are accepting of it. I'm . . . the big problem would be the family.

R.   It's sort of like, you're not sure whether you will wind up again making love with men or not, but it's not like a fear. It's not a problem?

J.　No, I don't feel that as a fear. Maybe two months ago I would have.

R.　Yeah.

J.　In other words, I can't say to someone, if someone said to me: "Are you gay?" I'd say No. But that's, I don't feel I can put a label on myself.

R.　Well, you're in transition and it's an exploratory time.

J.　Yeah, it may be a transition, and it may not be. You know, I won't be able to know for another year or so.

R.　That's what I meant, like in the beginning what we were talking about was sexuality. You know, maybe it's a phase that we're focusing on, that we wouldn't be labeling something as lesbian, heterosexual or bisexual, just different phases that we go through. Finding out who I am and what I want.

J.　Yeah, yeah. At times it does change, but I certainly have gone through the myth enough that I don't feel hetero-sexuality is *the* way. And I don't think men are *the answer* to women. I think that there's a lot of answers to both sexes. In other words, I'm not *searching* for my other self — in a man or woman — you know, I *am* myself, and. . . .

R.　You're not looking for the other partner to fulfill all the things you don't have, the other half, the better half?

J.　Nobody else is going to *have* those other halves (laughing)

R.　Goddammit!

J.　All those myths! If I'm going to have 'em, they're going to be in *me*. So, I don't have those fears, because it's not a bad thing to me.

R.　You're right. I was always so afraid. Eventually I'll get to think that it's stupid to be afraid of being a lesbian.

234

J.   Well, why don't you change your words, and not say 'lesbian' any more, but say 'loving women'?

R.   Yes, that is very helpful.

J.   And what you're afraid of, maybe, is that you'll *only* love women, where you'll just cut off any relationship to men.

R.   I don't fear that now. I feared that before, that I would only love women. No, I *feared* that I loved women, it wasn't that I would only love them. I thought that loving women was a terrible thing.

J.   Sure, right. But I mean, if you can get away from using lesbian or the word bisexual or whatever, and focus on whether the person is loving women or loving men and women at the same time. . . .

R.   I think I will. I think that's important.

J.   That may expand that kind of thinking for you.

R.   I guess, yeah. What I really want is a really close relationship with a person. Were you ever afraid if you started loving women you wouldn't like men any more?

J.   No, I kind of knew there were a lot of things I didn't like about men, but a lot of the fear did have to do with being excluded from the whole *normal* community.

R.   How did you first get involved with a woman? Did you think about it a lot, or did it just happen?

J.   Well, emotionally, I've always been involved with them, and I had fantasies. Do you mean when I first had a sexual experience?

R.   How did that happen; how did the situation develop?

J.   I was sort of close with this one woman, but I wouldn't say it was a real heavy equal kind of thing. I was more like her mother-confessor you know. She'd call up and we'd talk for a few hours on the phone about problems. I never felt that close emotionally.

R.   You felt better than her?

J.   Not better, different, in the sense that I couldn't feel that if I was having a lot of heavy problems that I could talk to her.

R.   The word would be: *stronger*.

J.   She needed to have me more — there wasn't a balance in our needing each other. But we had a fairly good working relationship and we had good times. We worked together on a few projects. We were at a dance one night, not particularly together, but we were at this dance, and we'd been talking, so as we were cleaning up later, she said that she really had to *talk* to me, that she found during the last month or so when we were together she was very attracted to me. She had to say something 'cause it was really interfering with how she related to me. I had noticed that, in the beginning, we'd hug goodbye, things like that, and then that sort of stopped. And like, I *forget* that that's really a sign that things are *too* intense a lot of times. And I think what happened, that there was a lot of personal pressure from people that if you have feelings towards women, why don't you *do* something about it.

R.   What kind of people?

J.   People that used to live in this house. Part of it was my *own*, I was reading a lot into the things that *they* said, after all these years, I felt I had to at least find out what the hell it was all about, relating sexually to a woman. The next night we had a meeting at her house, and we talked for a while. I said: "Well, I think I'm going to stay and see what happens."

R.   Oh, that's scary.

J.   It was at a place where it was now or never, I mean, we

236

got involved for about a week or so, in kind of a heavy situation. And then I realized I was really doing this bad number. It got to be more of a sexual thing, and I really didn't know what the hell I was doing. And so we stopped seeing each other after about a month. But there were a lot of things that I learned from that. And that I feel sorry about now, because it wasn't that she was doing a come-on like, like: "I'll do this number with you because you want to learn all this stuff." There are women like that, just like there are men like that, you know: "I will teach you, or I will bring you out," or whatever you want to call it. And it wasn't like that. She was really looking for a relationship and she felt close to me. And, in a sense, I betrayed that.

R. Because you had sex with her, because you wanted to find out what it was like?

J. Yes. That I was relating on a more surface thing than she was, and I wasn't really relating as a friend.

R. Did you tell her why you wanted to sleep with her? I mean, when you first did it? Did you feel that it was purely sexual? It sounds as if you liked her, too.

J. I liked, yeah, I cared about her and everything, but I really felt, and *she* really felt, that she was being used. And I think in some ways it was a mutual thing, because there were a lot of things that she talked about, that showed me that it was more of a mutual thing.

R. Had she slept with a woman before?

J. She had been in a relationship with a woman. I think she slept with a few women and then got into a relationship with a woman and that had been very negative. And so she was kind of coming out of that; our relationship was more positive.

237

Now, we're friends, in the sense that we feel comfortable if we run into each other in places, and we'll talk and catch up with what the other person is doing. And I think that there's a certain affection that we feel.

R.   I went through a whole thing with my friend that I first slept with who was a lesbian, about. . . .

J.   Why do you keep saying 'lesbian?'

R.   Because that's how I viewed it then. I mean, it was a big deal with me, to sleep with a woman who *only* liked women. That was very threatening to me. I wasn't sure who I was. I feared that I might be a lesbian; I would rather have slept with a woman who loved both men and women. And that my friend only liked women was very threatening; you know, if she would have liked men, it would have been easier for me. I don't know how to explain.

J.   Yeah, I know what you mean.

R.   And I explained to her — you know, here I was, trying to be honest, maybe I was cruel — that I wanted to sleep with her and even the fact that I was scared and didn't like that she was heavy. It was maybe awful. I was trying to be as honest as I could. But I had to find out what it was about. And she really liked me and she was really kind.

J.   Now that's really nice.

R.   She was wonderful. I mean, it was sort of like, I wanted to try, you know. And I really liked her. I *was* turned on to her but it definitely, part of it, for me, was the experience. She was willing, it was really a *gift!*

J.   Okay, well, that kind of a thing is a lot different, that wasn't the situation that I was in. And the woman I first slept with at this point considers herself lesbian. Only she *did*

238

relate to men, for a while, and she was engaged one time. But she really considers herself relating to women and her whole life is around women and working with them and having relationships with them.

R.   I guess you've sort of answered this: Do you see having women lovers as a phase in your life, or something that will be on-going?

J.   (Laughing) I think it's more appropriate to say: Do I see *men* lovers as a phase or on-going! Because I think being with women is definitely on-going. It's not a phase. Now that I can be close, in a sexual way if I want to, I think that all my life, if there's a woman who wants me close sexually as *well* as emotionally and mentally, or whatever the relationship is, I'd feel like those options are there, that now I *can* relate in as many ways as possible with a woman.

R.   And so that would be your primary thing?

J.   *That's* the thing. Like I don't know if it'll be primary, but that I know that's how it will be for the rest of my life, now, with women. Now, I don't *know* what it's going to be like with men.

R.   Because, you know, I'm still hung up about . . . I don't know. I still am interested in men, right now. If there was an exciting man around that was available that I was turned on to, I would like to be sleeping with him. And I'd always ask a woman that considered herself bisexual, that label, if she'd always had woman lovers at the time she had men lovers. You know, I wonder if some women do that, somehow as a balance for their own sexuality, because it might be too threatening to them to be involved or in love with a woman lover only. What made you explore your sexuality with women?

J.   I had to find out what my feelings were about and finally had the guts to do it.

R.   One of the things I'm aware of when I'm talking with women is around family, and non-monogamous kinds of things. I'm finding out the people I'm meeting are non-monogomous. What do you see yourself doing in terms of family and monogamous relationships?

J.   What do you mean — family?

R.   Do you think of yourself as having a family eventually, or living in an alterative family?

J.   I live collectively, now, and I like it, and I think I always will. I might take time off to live by myself for a few months, but I'll usually go back to group living, which to me can involve a family situation. I don't think I want to be part of a traditional small nuclear family. I've always liked to be around a lot of people, and feel the support and stimulation of other people. I like kids, and I've never had a thing particularly about wanting to have my own, but there might be a time, in a few years. I decided that when I'm 35, I'll have to make a decision. And I might adopt a few, maybe nine or ten year olds or whatever. And a lot of that depends on my life-style; I've always worked with kids and there's a definite thing about kids that I really dig. But "family" to me is a group of people, whether they're related or not, who feel a liking and support of each other. Which doesn't always happen in traditional quote American families.

R.   Right.

J.   So, my sense of family is there, but it's not traditional.

R.   Yes. I still have the fantasy of the traditional family. I think sometimes, I wish I could get married and then get divorced. And I would still like to live with a man in a big house for a year.

J.   I know what that is. Like, you could go through it, and then people won't bother you any more. And you've been through it and you can say: "Well I did it and I know what that's about."

R.   I am more concerned about my own feelings in this case. I don't want to bother myself. I keep on telling myself, why worry about marriage? Just live now. But what's going to happen when you're older, are you always going to be alone? And I do want some kind of family, but I don't know what that would be.

J.   Well, okay. The thing that I found out, in the community here, the gay subculture, is first of all, the subculture's fairly small. When you narrow it down to the kinds of interests you have as a person, most of the people I know are professionally oriented. A lot of them are Jewish, which was not a choice that I made.

R.   Yes, isn't that incredible!

J.   It just happens that that's the people I've met. So, the gay community is small, number one. So your choice of partners is narrow; although probably no narrower than if I were heterosexually oriented and looking for a single guy. But, then my own personal interests, being in the women's movement and geared to women in a professional sense, and I mean professional in the sense that I don't just hang around, or bum around, there are certain interests and academic kinds of interests and mental stimulations that I *want* from another person. So, those kinds of interests narrow things. I found a lot of the people in the Bay Area have been here for years and one person might, in the last ten years, might have been involved with three or four different lovers, who are all in this area. The people I know in this one house — there's a couple living together and an ex-lover of one of them, who's involved with somebody else now. And that's the sense of community and family that you don't get in many places. Once a couple breaks up, there may be a lot of hard feelings at first, but after a few months, you see each other again. There isn't the jealousy and the back-biting and the anger that you see in the straight community.

R. That's what I'm finding out in the commune, too. They're more heterosexually focused, though there's experimentation with bisexuality. Most of the people in the house have been lovers. There's a sense of community. Other groups are doing that, it isn't necessarily just within the gay community.

J. And it's less of a possession thing. You're not *mine*, you know, and I'm not so-and-so's possession. Women have been men's possessions for so long, they just went along with the house and the kids. And now you go up and down in primary and secondary relationships, and it's just nicer, because you're closer with a lot more people.

R. But the part that I find frustrating is that, with all these people, well, but you're saying a different thing. I'm finding out that a lot of these people, the people in the commune, and there are people that I've known in the gay community, are non-monogamous. And that, to me, I find, well maybe it's a separate issue, but, that's very difficult.

J. Okay, that's a different issue. We can talk about non-monogamous and monogamous relationships, because I know people who are doing both. Like, people in this house are both. And I can't handle more than one relationship at a time. I get very confused when there's more than one at a time. Or at least, one primary one. I can envision, if I were in a long-term relationship with someone, and I know couples like this, who, they might have an affair with the same person. They might do a threesome. But once you start having side relationships and they don't include the other person, there's much more of a chance that those side, secondary ones, will then become primary, and the couple's going to split. As far as monogamous itself, I think that's really a personal preference. If you *try* both monogamous and non-monogamous, then you find out where your head's at. And I just personally don't have enough energy. My focus is not people all the time. I like to have my own time and do projects and stuff. So I find that if I have one person, that's enough for me to handle.

R.   Earlier you were saying that a lot of women in the women's movement and gay community were strong women, and professional. That's why I've gotten off on the women's movement the most. In Washington, often the women I knew criticized me because I was too pushy on the job, too aggressive, but here I found that there's a commitment to work on the part of women. I mean, they take their work seriously, whatever they choose to be and I find that so exciting.

J.   Well, but I think there's a definite thing. If you have made a commitment that your life is going to be towards women. . . .

R.   This is gay?

J.   This is like, gay or being a feminist. Like women like Jane who is a psychologist and who won't marry again. Her primary focus in life is not men, she relates to men, but it's

243

not primary at all. Then you're *free*. You're free to do what you have to do as your life work, 'cause number one you've got to support yourself. You're not going to have somebody supporting you. I mean, there aren't the roles of wife and husband. And you're free to loosen all that energy to really concentrate on creating and being a person in yourself.

R.   Loosen what energy and from where?

J.   Well, like the energy women constantly use creating the home environment, kissing up to some guy and making *his* life comfortable, rather than doing whatever they want to do, and that's something I hadn't thought about in a while. I just have been feeling it, the last few months. And I said: "Just a second! I'm not waiting any more! Now, for thirty years I've been doing this: 'Well, I can't really be serious about anything, because I'm waiting.' "

R.   To get married to *him?*

J.   Yeah. I'm waiting to get married and have somebody support me.

R.   I haven't resolved that in myself. I sometimes still would like to be supported. I mean, I feel like I've worked really hard for ten years, like in this social change stuff, and in some ways, I mean I'm suddenly coming to the realization that I've always loved working, it's been really important to me and I lamented the fact that I couldn't find many other women that were committed and interested in their work. But suddenly it's dawned on me, not only is it convenient that I love it, but I might *have to do it* the rest of my life! That bothers me because I hate "shoulds." I mean, I hate *having* to do anything.

J.   Well, but that's how we're conditioned, though, as little

244

girls, that when we grow up we would be supported even if we went to college and got a career started, it'll only be until we got married.

R. I guess that's what I've been accepting in myself, that I'm always going to have to work, and I really don't want to. But I hear what you're saying, that a lot of women are working 'cause it's part of taking a stand for themselves, part of what the movement encourages. And they realize too they're going to have to support themselves, if they are not going to depend on men. But what I've found out here, I don't know what's causing it, but there are so many women just much more committed to their work. That's just very important to me. That I should see such a commitment.

J. A lot of people feel, being in the women's movement, that they've finally found their cause. I know I feel like I've finally found something that's *my* cause. I mean, I'm not a child, so I can't really fight for children like I was, and I'm not a black, so I can't fight for blacks, but I'm a *woman*, and I feel all the kinds of things that women are saying, that they are discriminated against. So it's something that's real, that can be mine all of my life.

R. I guess what I'm trying to say is the women that I have met here, tend to be more aggressive. Maybe they're just coming out, as a friend would say. I mean, I kept on saying I am grateful to be in California, that I've found some women that I feel are like me. I thought that I was going to start teaching myself to accept myself more, but still I'm looking for other models, or other people who are like me, so it's easier, I guess, to see other people like me.

J. The ones you worked with in D.C., were they married, or

single, or . . .?

R. Some of them were single and professional; some had their doctorates. And when I went back to D.C. this last time, one of the women was angry at me, but at least she came clean about it. She's married. She said: "You're just so damned assertive and I can't be." You know, she was honest about something she wants to do. This at least is what my friend was trying to say to me, that because of the women's movement, women are coming *out*. By 'coming out' I mean coming out in terms of their strengths. In fact, when I did go back to Washington I found a few women who started becoming stronger and more adamant. My friend's point is that women were *always* there, they just never came out. But somehow, there are a lot of strong women in the Bay Area. It's very exciting to me. I don't know if the women's movement has given them permission to be stronger, or what.

J. I think for a lot of them, it has. But I think any of the lesbian women that you meet, or gay women, who are really committed to women discovered that long ago. That they're going to have to survive and they can survive only if they support themselves.

R. I don't know, maybe they're just stronger people. I can't figure that part out. I mean Sara, she's married, she doesn't see herself as gay or anything, but I find her a very strong woman. I didn't find this kind of woman — heterosexual, bisexual or whatever you want to call her — in Washington.

J. Okay, well part of it could have been the circles you were in. That there aren't a whole lot of women who *are*. I mean, we've been so conditioned not to be.

R. Strong.

246

J. Yeah, so that you're not going to find a whole lot, anyway. I mean, you just happened to fall in with them here.

R. We've talked about *work*, we've talked about *sexuality*, and we've talked about *family*. Most of the women that I am interviewing, that are dealing with their sexuality in terms of other women, are into a *strong work* thing. There is a different kind of commitment than I knew previously with women about their work. I'm curious about what they're going to do about family. Because I think we're talking about an alternative structure, too, in living. I mean, it'll be curious to see where we're going to go. I still want to be with a man, and I don't know what form that's going to take. I'm also concerned about my work and how I'm going to do that. I can't stand the shit that you have to go through in a bureaucracy so I'm looking for a new form of work. The people I'm talking to also seem to be looking. I mean, we're reaching a certain phase in our lives where some of these things, some of these questions, are asked by lots of women at the same time. Are you getting tired?

J. Yes, let's stop.

Each Interview is an Event

For three solid hours Julia and I talked. All else in the world seemed to cease to exist. There was only Julia and me and we went down a deep dark tunnel. It took me days to recover. Julia said that she too was spaced for days. I woke up the next morning thinking that she may have been angry at me. We had exposed so much. We didn't know each other that well. This talk was really the beginning of our friendship.

247

TRACY

TRACY and I had dinner, wine and brandy with candles in the evening at her house. During one part of the interview she rubbed my foot, which was lying against the couch near her. We both looked at each other affectionately and there seemed to be an awareness between us of how the tape recorder could not pick up our physical closeness. The "keeping it" from the tape recorder made our affection feel special. The energy flowed between us and I felt very warmed.

July 12, 1973

Ruth.   I sort of hate doing this formal like, because it takes away from the way we were talking.

Tracy.   Oh no, we'll get it on.

R.   Do you care about the tape recorder?

T.   Uh uh.

R.   You don't want to hear my spiel about that it will be confidential?

T.   I trust you!

R.   What were you saying before? I am really interested in what you said about the differences between women and men lovers.

T.   I have more empathy with and really respect women. You know, they're less mysterious and hence less threatening. You know, more deserving of consideration.

R.   Why?

T.   Hmm. Partly because I think the affair takes place more in the head than in the loins.

R.   You mean, more in the heart? Or do you mean more in the head?

T.   Head and heart. But for me the fulfillments are more aesthetic, you know, more intellectual, ummm, less, I mean, the excitement is partly, the courage that you've broken the taboo, and . . . But also, you see, I just know what it feels like to be hurt, and I won't inflict that on somebody else who knows.

R.   You don't think a man knows what it's like to be hurt?

T.   Ah, sure they do, but it's a kind of, I perceive men as being lots less vulnerable than women. Just because in my

252

opinion that's not so much where they are. You know, that's not where they really stake their identities, in the emotional realm, as much as in the rational achievement-oriented realm. But I think that *I*, as a woman, really do . . . I mean sort of the field of my prowess and my interest and where I'm engaged is in love. You know. Being a lover and. . . .

R.   But.

T.   Being a wise lover.

R.   A wise lover.

T.   Uh huh.

R.   I mean, that's where you see your prowess and your main being is to be a wise lover? Not to be a great writer?

T.   Well, I think that the two things can enhance each other. I am interested in writers like myself, who have dealt with women. Lately I've been on an Isak Dinesen kick, and I'd like the illumination, the insight, she has into that.

R.   Will you say her name again.

T.   Isak Dinesen. She's a fascinating woman. She was a Danish baroness whose husband laid a case of the clap on her, but who lived on past him. I guess they separated. She managed a coffee plantation in Africa and, I'm not sure if her first book was the *Gothic Tales* or *Out of Africa,* but she's just got a *brilliant* psychology of relationships. Very insightful. She's a true romantic, and a Gothic romantic. I mean, her *Gothic Tales* always have a kind of touch of death about them. You know, it sort of rounds out the life/death thing. Anyway, obviously she was quite a woman, quite a lover. I can't imagine her having, those perceptions from one side without having many deep love experiences. But even with the writing and, you know, a certain amount of talent . . . the real fascinations of my life are people, ideas.

R.   Yeah. I feel myself that because I still haven't made it yet in a very long-term kind of relationship, you know, I wonder if I'd ever be satisfied with any of my achievements. I mean that the main thing that's missing that almost negates some of my other things, is the lack of an enduring relationship.

T.   Hmmmm. That's a shame. Even though you are successful.

R.   Or something that's more long-term than a year or so.

T.   Yeah. Interesting.

R.   When I got into Harvard I was really depressed. You know, I was *alone*. I mean, big bullshit. No, I don't mean it that way, but . . .

T.   But you know, it is kind of — Harvard! My God!

R.   That's right. Isn't that supposed to be *it*?

T.   Yeah. How can you not be satisfied when, you know. . . .

R.   'Cause you're damn lonely!

T.   Yeah. How can we not be satisfied!

R.   Right. I mean, that's like when you were talking, tonight, you made me sort of sad. So much of what you're saying, I have a whole bunch in me. Once one of my friends that I first met when I came here said, "You're crazy. You're bright!" On and on. You know — but I'm still not happy.

T.   Yeah, some ways I think that to complete the two agendas of being a successful woman, you know, getting through Harvard and getting your degree and doing brilliantly *and* having that relationship with some kind of continuity . . . Maybe it is impossible, or maybe "too difficult!"

R.   But men have it! Men are successful and have women lovers. They have wives, though one could certainly question the quality of their relationships.

T.   Well, they also have the society organized to fulfill those goals for them, too. I mean, it's not like you can just go to a corporation and then become a management trainee. Because most likely, even with the Equal Opportunity Commission, you'll be given a typing test! And the man will be put in the training program, so insofar as succeeding in the realm of men's achievements, you've got one strike against you. And then, if you do get your foot in the door for a job that doesn't drive you crazy, to go find a man that would do something like move to another town if you got promoted!

R.   And maybe not be threatened by you?

T.   Yeah. Even just not being threatened by you is going to be quite an achievement!

R.   Does it make you feel lonely?

T.   Yeah. I . . . lonely in the most fundamental way, of just questioning my sanity. How can I ever just really get cooled out when I've got several sets of goals and only a, you know only a limited chance of achieving any of them?

R.   What were your different goals?

T.   Well, being a great novelist, and I've already had one fling at that. I've been sort of disappointed, and it's going to be a while before I really feel good about writing fiction or just, you know, writing. I like writing about environment and population, I think I'm passable at it. But it all gets back to love. I'd really like to be able to write well about love.

R.   Me too. I wonder why.

T.   'Cause it's the key to happiness!

R.   Why do we want to write about it? I want to write about it, too. And I don't know that I can capture any of the feelings or be able to ask the questions to capture the feelings.

T.   Well, 'cause it's the only game in town. You know, as far
as we're concerned, I can presume that about you. I mean, it's
a hell of a lot more interesting than actuarial tables or, you
know, how to build a better Chrysler, or even the goddamned
environment. Sewage treatment, man (giggle), I'd much
rather talk about love than sewage treatment!

R.   You're sure, now (laughing)?

T.   I'm positive! I mean, that's why I wound up writing a
novel about a woman who was bisexual, instead of a critique of
the environment movement. Just much more interesting. I
was involved in an affair with a woman, and I just thought that
was the most fascinating and relevant thing going on. So I preferred to write about that. I thought a novel about that would
somehow illuminate the environment thing, too.

R.   How?

T.   Well, more by example than by explanation. But, I
guess, part of the thing that stimulated me was the idea that
there can be an ecology of relationships. At that time, I had
the faith. You know, that a number of different relationships
could really co-exist and feed each other insights and satis-
factions. You know, it made perfectly good sense to have this
artist in the novel, to have these two lovers, that were sort of
in the same realm of public affairs. But coming at their chores
from completely different perspectives. And ecology being
the integrative principle 'cause that's what an ecology is, you
know, sort of overall perception of an interacting system.

R.   And how do you see that relates to having an affair with a
woman?

T.   I guess because having affairs with both men and women sort of diversifies your life, and at the time that I was working on the book, I was so charged by the affair with the woman that it was really, giving me energy to take into the other much more sporadic affairs with men. And so. . . .

R.   You mean, it was like a base for you, a primary kind of commitment type of thing?

T.   Yeah. Well, I don't know how much of a commitment it actually amounted to be, at the time, but when Gale and I got off on it, both of us were between men. Between men, I say advisedly. I mean, neither of us *admitted* that at the time, but we were. We were seeking refuge in each other, you know, and also kind of . . . I was definitely admitting to this seduction that had been going on, and the, sort of less acknowledged seducing that I've been doing.

R.   You seduced her and she seduced you — is that what you're saying?

T.   Well, sure, it sort of did mean a come-on, but I maintained the kind of attractive, it seemed to me, superior role and this may be doing an injustice to her perceptions but I was a couple of years older and I was sort of idolized and, of course, I dug it. I mean, nothing like it! But while we were in school I didn't want to take the risk.

R.   You knew each other in school?

T.   Yeah, you know, Gale just took a shine to me, and I to her, but not quite as intensely, I think. Again, I just don't know how much of my ego is entering into this, but we began flirtations and sort of leading physical teases, but nothing . . . I knew what was being offered and suggested, but. . . .

R.   Had she slept with women before?

T.   No.

R. Was she consciously thinking of sleeping with you?

T. Yes.

R. Were you consciously thinking of sleeping with her?

T. I was thinking about it and just thought no — no, because at the time I was a senior in college and I thought, I think this would be a little heavy on my head, right about now, you know, I'm about to graduate and I have these other love affairs that I'm trying to hold together. And I just don't know if I could cope with being a lesbian — because that was what it amounted to.

R. You felt that it would amount to being a lesbian?

T. Yes. Because at the time I was unaware of bisexuality as a state of being. I just thought it was either you were heterosexual or you were a lesbian.

R. Were you at that time involved with men?

T. Oh, yeah.

R. As lovers?

T. Yeah.

R. But the mere fact of being attracted to women would mean that you were a lesbian?

T. Well, I think the fact of sleeping with a woman would have meant I was a lesbian.

R. It would negate the relationships with men?

T. I don't even think I carried the train of thought that far. It was just the standard dread of being a lesbian meant being attracted to women. So, it seemed to me a kind of scary proposition. After graduation, I hemmed and hawed around, for another year, and then one weekend in New York and we were both at a meeting and just surrounded by men and they were kind of flirting with us and all that, but Gale was infinitely the most attractive and complex being around and I just suddenly turned on with lust, to her, until we made love and it. . . .

R.   Did you ever talk about making love before you did?

T.   Yeah.

R.   Oh, you had?

T.   Yeah. We had. We had talked about it and, I think I was just off-putting, and she was delicious about it, she was infinitely patient.

R.   You said you felt you were what? Off?

T.   I just put it off. I said I don't think I can handle it. Which was true.

R.   Well, I think that was good. I *forced* myself. I had to know. It was an issue for me. It was real painful. It sounds like your first experience was nice. Was it?

T.   Oh, it was lovely. It was the very obvious thing to do.

R.   How lucky.

T.   Yes, it was wonderful. It was like a revelation. We were at the Village Gate, listening to Mose Allison. And had gone down with a group of people from this meeting, and she was justly clearly the most appealing person there on the grounds of all the appointments of . . . just in her own physical beauty and the attraction. It was obvious (laughter). And it got very, you know, sort of nervous-making, cause there we were just making overwhelming passes at each other, on that wavelength.

R.   That was fun, I bet.

T.   Oh, it was beautiful!

R.   Was it threatening? Or anxiety provoking?

T.   If it was anything that was not perfect, it was kind of humorous. You know, just the standard first night fumble, and it"s not just "oh, gee, it's a brand new body,' it's like *a brand new body*, a woman's body, and what do you do to make love? And so you kind of fake it. I was having my period so she really didn't know what to do with me and my cunt and I said: "Sorry." You know that's a funny thing, menstruation.

R.   Why?

T.   Well, just 'cause of the taboo.

R.   You mean, you don't make love when you're having your period?

T.   Well, a lot of religions have maintained that, and also whether or not you can forge ahead through the ascetic considerations. It's okay, but it takes. . . .

R.   That was an issue, too? That was as much of an issue as making love to a woman — making love and having your period?

T.   Yes. The overall shyness, you know. Another woman, Susan, I made love with just did mind giving head.

R.   Giving head?

T.   Eating.

R.   Oh, yeah.

T.   So I ate her, but she just sort of fingered me. It was like "Well, yes, I can dig that you don't like to give head" but also thinking it's really neat. Wish she would get on to it!

R.   Right.

T.   But knowing that kind of reluctance and shyness. It's really, I just feel immensely more sensitive with women. There is just more sensitivity about the whole encounter. You know what pleases you and you know how sensitive you are to things that are sort of mildly not pleasing, and so you come with those two perspectives on making love to another woman. Your own sensitivities and, sort of, you do those things that follow the golden rule! But then there's also, I always feel, a little kind of trepidation, like I don't want to really come on too strongly, or do something she's unprepared for, and might be embarrassed about 'cause for some reason there's that kind of stuff in sex, you know. Some people don't do things that others do. Out of three women I've slept with, only one out of three has really felt comfortable performing cunnilingus. Eating me.

R.   It's that they're new to making love with a woman.

T.   I expect so, and I expect maybe having some just general shyness about cunts which we all have, 'cause we don't know much about them!

R.   Are you in that relationship with Susan now? Do you consider it an ongoing relationship?

T.   Well, I think that was a very rare occasion between us. I can imagine us sleeping together again, but I think that the unstated purpose was to make it a physical covenant between us, and it has been done.

R.   What do you mean by physical covenant?

T.   Well, it's just the old biblical thing of *knowing* another person through sex. Now we're very easy with each other's bodies. And Susan is just sort of a recent lover. We've been friends for ages. We've known each other since high school but we only slept together just recently and I don't think that that's the mainstay of our relationship.

R.   In terms of Susan, well, and then Gale too, since it sounds like you were long-term friends before you were lovers, did the sexual intimacy have any effect on your friendship?

T.   In a funny way, I think that the sexual intimacy with Gale, since it is more of an ongoing thing, rounds out the friendship, because there are a lot of points where our personalities don't mesh very well.

R.   What do you mean by 'rounding out?'

T.   It just sort of fulfills some of the spaces that are left by the incomplete meshing.

R.   Can you give me a sense of what you mean by incomplete?

T.   Well, I think, you know, it can be summed up in just how comfortable you are with another person. Sometimes I just really disapprove of her and for strictly style reasons. I think since our relation started out as being kind of hierarchical and me being a senior and her being a sophomore. Her sort of idolizing me. I've had a hard time accepting the. . . .

R.   Equality?

T.   Well, I don't know if we've really gotten to equality. I don't think you ever get equality. I think what you get is sort of a series of concessions, you know, where you say that this is your prowess and this is my prowess, and this is yours and this is mine. I mean, that sounds like a negative number but the positive aspect of it is that she does this and this and this incredibly well and I really admire her. And I do these things and. . . .

R.   That's what you mean by equality? I thought equality had to do with control. Who is in control of the relationship? Who is the dependent person? Before you talked about it as a hierarchical relationship. It sounded like you would be more in control, and that's why I asked the question about being equal.

T.   Well, I guess I was thinking in terms of equal capacity and sort of equal qualities. But the thing that was weird is that we went through some upheavals, Gale and I, but after I finally succumbed to the notion that we were lovers I got into it and became very passionate and fawning to an extent. There's a whole chapter in the book that's about this.

R.   Would it be okay if I read it sometime?

T.   Sure.

R.   Do you consider your relationship with Gale, as an on-going thing?

T.   Yes. Ongoing and slightly problematic. There's no way around it.

R.   What kind of problems are you experiencing?

T.   Who's got the power and who's taking the initiative.

R.   So. That's control. Because I want my relationships to be equal I certainly have had my difficulties with some men. I remember with Larry, just fighting that he should use a rubber and half the time I would use a diaphragm. I mean, it's got to be equal. And hoping, or just thinking. . . I could have an equal relationship with a woman, because those kinds of, you know, who's supposed to be dominant, isn't built in. There are no roles. And with one of my very close friends who I just love dearly, we seemed to be able to share being in control and if one of us was upset the other person would be in charge. I think we've talked about that. I mean, there wasn't an issue of who was in charge and who wasn't and we were never lovers. But I was aware that that the struggles I was having with Larry at the time, I didn't have with her. And she was as important to me. My hope with women is that we won't have this control issue. But that is probably naive. I think I'll probably find that people are people.

T.   Well, I think control is sort of always an issue in love, because maybe security is always an issue and to have security, there has got to be a certain amount of control going on.

R.   How do you, to change the subject a little, what do you think of yourself sexually, I mean, your identity?

T.   Hmm. Well, lately (giggle), I'm *confused!* There was a time when I really thought I was a red hot mamma and I was screwing a lot. I was probably trying to prove something, most likely. Now I don't think of myself, I mean I just don't have a fixed opinion of myself sexually. I try to please. I think in some senses with men I probably capitulate and wind up unsatisfied when I ought to be saying, you know, I ought to develop a way of saying, "It would be just even more marvelous if you'd do this; slow down."

R.   Slow down!

T.   Yeah. With women, I aims to please! You know, I really want to be a fantastic lover.

R.   Why?

T.   'Cause women deserve it! (both laugh) And also because in a way it's a mode of, I suppose, competing with all the men in the world. You know, if I can really drive this woman crazy with pleasure, far out! Because how often do I get driven crazy with pleasure by a man? Not very often. You know, it takes a hell of a lot of sensitivity and cooperation and commitment to do good sex, I think. It's marvelous! I really like it. And in a sense I suppose it's power to do good sex. I mean to be a fantastic lover is powerful.

264

R.   Power in what sense?

T.   Well, it gets back to "the service of the Lord is perfect freedom." I mean when you're really. . . .

R. I don't understand.

T.   When you really, when you *really* submit to a sexual act, I mean this is all hypothesis, then you have incredible orgasms, because your mind is all at peace, and you're not thinking about the drip on the faucet in the kitchen, or any of the innumerable other things that can kind of distract you.

R.   When your mind's what??

T.   When your mind is really devoted to sex. You know, *the* sex act that's going on at the moment. Then you can really have total orgasms. But again, that in some ways, that's hearsay. Those exclusive climaxes are rarer in my experience. I don't have terrific orgasms every time I make love. I have some kind of orgasms almost every time, but the real transcendant moments are about as rare as you'd expect transcendant moments to be.

R.   I don't know if I completely understand. Now I know my orgasms aren't even as good as they used to be and I think I'm supposed to reach my prime now, right, thirty? I don't know.

T.   Yes.

R.   And around the control issue with orgasms, which I got into with men, around intercourse, when I first just made love with a man and we were just masturbating each other there was no problem. I enjoyed orgasms, but when I was supposed to have an orgasm with my nice Jewish boy during intercourse, Jesus, I couldn't get off, and I really got up tight, you know, 'cause I was *supposed* to. Now when I make love with a man, it's sort of like, well, I should hurry up and have

265

this orgasm, he'll get tired. Or, I'm *supposed* to, and I can't do it. I hear you saying that if you concentrate on a sex act, you won't hear the dripping faucet. But if you're so up tight about whether you're going to come or not, I don't know if that's an issue. I just can't do it.

T.   I, well, you know it *is*. I mean, that's a kind of distraction that really keeps you away from it. I don't know. Again I say it's hypothetical, because I really have a very Western mind and a lot of the notions that I admire philosophically and practically are more Zen type trips. But I *imagine* that it must be possible to just stop concentrating consciously, and just pay attention to what you're doing instead of noticing a million other things and hassling your strange relationship with this person and other things you may not altogether know.

R.   You mean, just focus on how you're feeling? Not what you're supposed to be doing, but just on the pleasure? That's hard for me.

T.   Yeah. A good friend who's a sex counselor described an exercise that he prescribes to some of his patients. He and his women friend counsel couples. Anyway, what they try to do at first is have couples discover all the ways that they can pleasure each other and achieve intimacy without intercourse. They prescribe evenings where one person just sits back and enjoys, while the other person totally concentrates on giving and pleasuring. And they say what usually happens in this system where somebody's absolutely passive and the other is very active is that the active party really gets off, you know.

R.   Right!

T.   Because you don't even get the slightest conflict in your

266

situation, because you're not saying: "I'm giving and I'm not getting." You know, and those. . . .

R. Because it's already set.

T. *You're* giving. You know, And they're getting.

R. That's that part about the role being set.

T. Um hm. Um hmm. And it's perfectly clear. And suddenly I guess you discover the pleasure of giving. You know, it's a good thing to do, a pleasurable thing to do, in addition to receiving pleasure.

R. Giving is a pleasurable thing to do?

T. Yeah. Sexual giving. And it's a wonderful, you know, complex pleasure, because it is in a sense exercising a certain power over the other person's body. The old cliche of, you know, playing the Strativarius. Making love.

R. You mean, you see it as a power thing over another person's body?

T. To an extent.

R. Why? Giving them an orgasm you mean?

T. Yeah. It's just sort of witnessing another person's abandon, and knowing that you're responsible for it.

R. How are you responsible?

T. In the sense that you've got them to a place where they give themselves over to pleasure. And they've got you to the place where you want to give to them. I mean, it's reciprocal, but subtle. Sometimes the love-making I've done with women has been sort of alternating who's taking the initiative. And this is like two solos, one woman doing the other woman.

R. Yeah.

T. Partly because the physical part of it's really more comfortable. I mean if you're not both into giving head then

267

love making requires like spraining your shoulder to masturbate the other woman.

R.   I think I'm lost.

T.   Just thinking in terms of. . . .

R.   We're talking about. . . .

T.   Sort of trading off the aggressive.

R.   Roles.

T.   Roles in bed. The only way I figure, I mean, say the most fulfilling and even symmetrical way for women to come together is by giving each other head simultaneously. But the alternatives to that involve basically masturbation . . . and I find it's just that old problem of having two arms when you're a lover, you know, one of them is getting in the way!

R.   Right!

T.   You can be reaching around and under and it gets awkward. I like love-making to be graceful, 'cause I think that's part of the essence of it.

R.   We were talking about control, and then you got into that with women you take turns.

T.   Um hmm.

R.   Do you mean taking turns being in control? Because we were talking about control and orgasm.

T.   Yeah. Take turns making love. I don't know if that's anyway near control.

R.   Somehow we were talking about orgasm, and how that had to do with control. It's sort of a thing that I deal with, because sometimes I feel myself being afraid to have an orgasm with a man because my feeling is — this is not a rational thing — but that he would be in control. I would be weak to his power. I like to have orgasms, and he can give me

268

an orgasm, and then I'll be under his control, 'cause I'll crave him.

T.   Well, I think it's really an acolade, you know, to a man or a woman to have an orgasm thanks to them. It really, it does say, you know, I surrendered.

R.   You think so?

T.   I, yeah, I mean.

R.   Cause there're all these books now, that say you give yourself your own orgasm. You set the atmosphere for yourself. You are in control.

T.   Well, I don't know. I have so little control over my own head that I could no more control my orgasm. I mean things like set and setting are really important to me in sex . . . say here I am in bed with this guy and he's kind of crude and stupid, you know, and I. . . .

R.   What are you doing in bed with him?

T.   Right! But can I give myself an orgasm?

R.   No.

T.   I don't think so. And I do, I don't know. Maybe it's corny to believe that there's such a thing as a skilled lover or that there are optimum situations, but. . . .

R.   Do you think women lovers are better? Or are men lovers better? Or is it more depending on the person?

T.   Well, I haven't had nearly as many women lovers as I have men.

R.   You've had three women lovers, right?

T.   Yeah, I don't, ummmm, maybe this is a cop-out, but I just don't think there's that much comparison. 'Cause of all the just totally divergent emotional content of the two.

R.   There's not that much comparison. You mean, that

they're so different?

T.   Yeah, indeed. Very different.

R.   How are they different?

T.   Well, 'cause of the emotional involvement with women being different.

R.   How is it different?

T.   How is it different. Hmmmm. . . more sensitive and subtle and complex and identical. You know, it's really golden rule time with a woman. Whereas with men I feel like, that I am in a way put upon by them because I've just walked into a lot of lions' dens out of curiosity in my love life, and have been burned an appropriate number of times.

R.   Appropriate! Is there a limit?

T.   And felt resentful! You know, just the whole cycle of going out and finding a disappointment. So I, in a way, I feel like men owe me some . . . men as a race owe me something because I've been hurt a few times.

R.   You've never been hurt by a woman?

T.   I've been hurt, but I guess I have more insight into the motivations.

R.   Of why?

T.   Plus the big hurt with Gale finally got worked out, for better or worse. I really do feel it's a fifty/fifty proposition. We're just in this one for the long haul.

R.   That's neat!

T.   And we're going to be in each other's lives. . . .

R.   I'm jealous!

T.   I don't know. In some ways I feel an obligation to see it through. And it's got its beautiful super moments and it's got its awful moments, but. . . .

270

R.   That's all relationships.

T.   Yeah.

R.   I mean . . . when I asked you what you thought of yourself sexually, and I had a sort of another answer in mind and
then you said you thought of yourself as a red hot mamma
sometimes? Is that what you said? You mean, you were just
sexually hot for people?

T.   Yeah. Yeah.

R.   I wondered, I mean the person I interviewed the other
day told me to try to stay out of categories, but for the record
do you think of yourself as bisexual, homosexual, heterosexual, sexual? What do you think? Do you have an identity
thing?

T.   More and more I think of myself as primarily sexual and
then bisexual. I am so delighted by women that I just don't
see, not ever, you know, ever excluding that experience for
any reason.

R.   Do you ever think of excluding relationshps with men for
any reason?

T.   No.

R.   Why do you stick with them if you complain so much
about them? You could ask me the same question.

T.   Alcohol hurts your liver, but it sure feels good.
Cigarettes wreck your life. . . .

R.   So there's a part of them you like?

T.   Oh, yeah.

R.   What?

T.   What do I like about men? Well I suppose it has something to do with the age-old affinity of sperm and ovum.

R.   Come on! A little bit more specific.

271

T.   A little more specific? Well, what I like about men? They have penises. And they're different from me. They're different from us. Harder. Stronger, physically sometimes. They have more accomplishments. More worldly accomplishments. Clearly distinguished.

R.   They have more worldly accomplishments?

T.   Yeah.

R.   Hmmmm.

T.   But it's the sex thing and it's the fact that there's something about a man's mind and a woman's mind — they're complimentary in a way.

R.   Do you find men's minds different?

T.   Somehow I find, it's very hard to express, but. . . .

R.   Many people feel that there is a big difference and mystery between men and women minds. Maybe I just repress it. I don't recognize that difference. When I get it on with a woman and am feeling close with her, I don't know if I feel differently than when I feel close with a man. I'm not sure. You definitely feel a difference?

T.   Well, I assume a difference, you know.

R.   We've been taught there is supposed to be, or is there a difference?

T.   Well, I don't know. That's really a ten year long question or answer, 'cause I just assume it so readily that I've never really bothered to investigate it. I don't know. I just regard men as a whole different; I really do have a double standard, I guess. I approach them differently.

R.   Is your standard less high for men than for women?

T.   In what sense? Oh, yeah. It's a lot more sexual for men than it is for women in a directer way. Foremost in my mind with a man, at some point in my encounters with any man I consider them sexually, you know: "Are we going to make love?" And with women I take in the aesthetics and the vibrations but making love is not as oppresive a question. Maybe because lovemaking with women is less threatening to the pride. Sometimes making love with a woman like Amy, my most recent lover, I feel a little threatened by the responsibility of the undertaking.

R.   Because it was her first time?

T.   Yeah. Yeah. And 'cause — no way am I going to — do I want to — trifle with a women's affections. Because I've been through a slight trifling by a woman and I have been through multiple triflings by men.

R.   Oh, yeah.

T.   And it's just nothing I want to do to somebody else without incredibly pressing reasons. So in that sense, the relationship with Amy is threatening because for me it implies a lot of follow through. I can't conceive of a one-night stand with women, although that may happen later on. I just haven't encountered that many sexually active bisexuals. But men are a sort of a challenge in a way. I mentioned before having a kind of a playboy philosophy. I think I'm into conquest a lot.

R.   With men or women? Both?

T.   With men.

R.   In the beginning you're saying men are more threatening to you or women are more threatening to you?

T.   Threatening in two different ways. With a woman I guess the threat is: don't want to hurt, do want to satisfy her, you know. Just don't want to be trivial with a woman. And with a

273

man the threat is: if he doesn't respond to my come-on, then there's something wrong with me.

R. What if a woman doesn't respond to your come-on? She's straight?

T. Ah, it's never happened. Again, you know, my total bisexual experience consists of three women, but so far I've just never spent a whole lot of time coming on to women. Partly because it's a serious enough commitment at this point in my mind that it's not the kind of thing you'd get into flirting about. Whereas with men, I feel for one thing, there is an identifiable game with identified rules. And, you know, sex with women is just up for grabs.

R. It's new. Yeah. We don't know.

T. There are no manners or morality or ethics.

R. In fact, when I first met this crowd of women, I didn't know why they were coming on to me. Just because they liked me as a friend, or were there sexual interests? I didn't know what they wanted. Work? It was confusing.

T. Yeah, it is. It's a really, it's a mixed blessing 'cause you get a sense that this was maybe what relationships were like before stereotypes, and then you just sort of supply your own rules as you go along.

R. You were talking earlier about how with women some-times you take turns making love. When I interviewed a woman yesterday, she was saying that that bothered her. It was something I had never thought about. With a man she felt she always got it on together at the same time. Orgasms.

T. The big O!

R. Right. And I don't know if she meant that necessarily she had an orgasm, but with a woman you take turns a lot. I mean

274

she said that she can't concentrate on having her orgasm or giving one if someone else is stimulating her, and she prefers to take turns, but that sometimes she feels it's more organically natural to have sex at the same time.

T.   I think that's entirely possible.

R.   What's entirely possible?

T.   That it's, it's maybe more organically sound to have sex, you know simultaneous orgasms with men. I don't discount evolution in a lot of this. The reason there are two sexes is to propagate the species. And whether or not you believe in instinct, I mean there's just such a phenomenal amount of conditioning for males and females to get together and procreate, or procreate and then stop it with contraception. We have just come to accept the heterosexual as norm.

R.   But I mean, do you in your own sex pleasure, do you find in your own love-making that you miss not doing it the same time? It sounds like you do sometimes.

T.   Once with Gale we got into a real soixante-neuf and we really just . . . it was glorious!

R.   Far out!

T.   Came right on together! You know, and it was. . . .

R.   But is it. . . .

T.   It wasn't a premeditated thing, it just happened that way.

R.   But is it, it doesn't sound like it's an issue with you, whether you take turns pleasuring, or whether you come at the same time.

T.   It's not. I mean, I find that the sex between us, it's still ceremonial, which is fine, you know.

R.   What do you mean, ceremonial?

T.   Sex between Gale and I signals a commitment and a very

deep sharing and trust. So it's not just homosexual significance, but also sort of original significance, which is neat, because sex should be meaningful. And you sometimes can exhaust those possibilities with men really fast, when you go through your first fifteen passionate affairs, and. . . .

R.   (Laughs) That never work out!

T.   To come out of them just like you've been on the roller-coaster for ten years.

R.   Do you ever think of yourself as being homosexual, now?

T.   No. In a way it would be about as much security as I've got, because. . . .

R.   If you thought you were homosexual?

T.   Yeah. If I knew which side of the fence, because. . . .

R.   Why do you have to choose?

T.   Well, just because choosing narrows down all the miserable possibilities that you have to decide — miserable, wonderful possibilities. My favorite Pogo quote, and my favorite quote altogether, is "We are confronted by insurmountable opportunities." There's just no real significant good without some interesting bad tacked on. And the good/bad of being bisexual — it really expands your realm, you know, a lot, but it gives you that much more wisdom, which is to say that the grass is just not greener on one side of the fence. The number I ran at the beginning with Gale was that: "Well, I've been disappointed in love many times by men. Now I'm in love with a woman. She will not disappoint me."

R.   Ah, right. She'll be perfect.

T.   Right. And, you know, there I was lying on the cot with a terrible cold, while she and Dick were balling away in the next room.

R.   Hurts just as much!

T.   No man had ever put me through a hurt like that! Because I'd had my guard up, with men, and I just "let it all down with this woman."

R.   I guess it has a lot to do with just being human beings, whether it be a man/woman thing or not. I don't know. I'm beginning to learn that a lot of difficulties I have in getting in close relationships is a problem around intimacy, and so . . . that sometimes I lament that, "God, I've increased my probability right! I've been making everyone possible to be lovers!" That still doesn't mean I have more lovers. It's more how I'm feeling. And, you know, a fear of getting really close —those same relationship problems happen with a man or a woman — it doesn't decrease some problems.

T.   I know.

R.   Do you see yourself going in any direction, sexually? Do you see yourself taking a bisexual mode of life? Or whatever that means?

T.   I've never heard that! Wooosh! Ummm. I really don't. . . . I mean, the only tendency I see in the past year or so is me becoming more selective, sexually. I hope, you know, I have hopes for a long and rich sex life, and I imagine that I will go through a lot of phases. One overall desire I have is to be less preoccupied and more just "at the moment" in sex with men and women. But I, intend to be sexual with men and women throughout.

R.   Well, how do you see yourself then in terms of family? What do you envision? Earlier we talked about marriage.

T.   Do I want a family?

R. Yeah. How do you envision yourself living happily ever after?

T. I'm going to marry a rich man who travels!

R. Me, too! (Laughter)

T. That's my job description. I could dig it! I like doing a lot of those household things; I like cooking. I don't think I'd ever want to raise kids, 'cause I just don't dig 'em that much.

R. But his travels would allow you to have the other lovers you want?

T. Uh huh. Well, I would assume there just would be no way to find a man that would interest me who wouldn't have other lovers.

R. Would you have other lovers out of defense?

T. Well, I would just have other lovers because that's the way I am. But I think — this is strictly hypothetical — that the thing that marriage would do in a relationship would be to provide minimal reassurance that you had a primary commitment to each other and that these other relationships had their own importance. But not the lifetime importance that marriage symbolizes. That's simply a fantasy.

R. It sounds like you're basically non-monogamous. The fantasy is non-monogamous.

T. Yeah, I think that it has got to be, because who can you be monogamous with? Who? Each of us is just so complex and so spoiled and so rare, and a . . . good/bad mixed bag of qualities. How can you expect all of that to be fulfilled? I mean, like Jim is an incredibly lush lover to be involved with because he is wonderful physically; he's just a neat intellect, and we really have good interaction at that level, which I prize 'cause I guess that is sort of the quest of every bright

278

woman — to find a person that she can think with. He is fun to travel with and all that, and yet there is a whole area of life which I cherish, which has to do with sophistication, finesse, and all those kinds of Fred Astaire, Ginger Roger qualities and not only does he not enjoy, he really takes a positive pleasure in not knowing about. And I cannot live without that — I'd make him live with these comparisons. So what do I do? I find a lover who can do those things, and once in a while I'd do those things with that lover, and it kind of rounds out the picture. But I don't know how well that all works. I mean, lately I've been so beset by jealousy, I just really feel at the mercy of that emotion. And, at the same time, I feel like it is very weak of me to do that, you know, to sort of succumb.

R. That bothers me a lot. That is one reason why I moved from the East Coast to the West Coast — the rhetoric of non-monogamous relationships and that we don't possess another person and that we can share and that you love more than one person. I mean, jealousy is a real emotion, it is real. All I hear people talking about is "I'm hung up," "I'm jealous. I shouldn't be." You know, goddamn it, that's a real emotion and all the 'shoulds' don't take away the pain. And I don't know what to do about that one, either.

What Do Your Old Friends Think?

R.   What did you old friends think? Did you tell them about
your involvement with women?

J.   Aaaah, I think there's only two that I've told among my
old friends, and one of them said, "Well, that's what you were
going to be doing anyway." She just saw it as a part of me. She
wasn't surprised about it, but this person's not surprised
about much at all!

R.   Did she accept it?

J.   Yes. And the other friend did too. There really aren't any
other old friends that I've talked with at length.

R.   I've just been away a year and I've told some of my single
friends. But the one woman I adore, who I loved when we
were roommates and couldn't touch, and just absolutely
craved. I was really turned on to her! I still haven't been able
to tell her what I've done with my love feelings for women, or
about this book, and that's the hardest thing for me. I guess
my love for her is really strong but I'm still afraid of being
rejected for what I'm doing now.

That's what I said about Anne in the interviews with Julia
and Tracy and yet I realized almost at the same time that I was
afraid to deal with our feelings for each other face to face. I
wrote a few months later in my journal:

I was reluctant to tell her about the book not so much
because I thought that she would reject me but because if I
told her what I was doing it would mean that the feelings between us would have to be dealt with. I was not at all sure that

I was ready to deal with my feelings for Anne face to face.

It has been my habit to tell someone something that I want to tell them just before we are about to part, so scarey for me is the telling. I had traveled with Mandy in France for three or four weeks and had planned to tell her about myself all through the trip. Dr. Tilbet kept on urging me to make love to her or to kiss her, but only when we had two days left of our vacation did I say something. This was also the case with Anne this last trip in D.C. I waited until I was practically on the airplane before I talked to her about the feelings I felt for her and asked her about the letter she had sent me telling me feelings that she said that she had for me. We were literally on the main road to Dulles Airport before I was able to utter a word to her and that word was barely audible. As I wrote this I realized that I also had trouble saying things, I always had placed our lack of communication on the fact that she couldn't stand me expressing my feelings, it always seemed to be so painful for her.

I brought up the letter that she had sent to me and Anne said what letter? Did I send you a letter? And then began the slow painful process of dealing with our feelings face to face. I said I wished we could have shared our feelings earlier. Why did she have to wait until we were 3,000 miles apart — and I was two years out of D.C.? She said "Don't you understand it was threatening to me to let myself say or know that I loved you." We talked about how our friendship was strained those last two years before she married Eric and that we really became more relaxed after her marriage as there was a sense of us feeling safe.

Letter from Anne
July 10, 1973

Ruth how is your book coming? We're all anxious to see it — and as I said on the phone — Kate wants to use it for her book club. Ruth don't ever fear that I, or any of us, will reject you for any reason whatever.

Do you think that our friendship is so shallow that it can't tolerate our different life styles? You do with your life whatever you want and I'll always love you. Just as long as you don't infringe on my life which needless to say would be difficult. You live 3,000 miles away and even if you lived here you wouldn't anyway. So just live your life the way you want to — the most important thing is to be happy. There are so many times I wish you lived here still — so many little things to talk about and to share. That's life.

Broadway

In the early days of my fascination with the California people whose lives I came to know and share, I spent an incredible evening on a motorcycle whipping through the heavy summer fog of San Francisco. I was out having dinner with two of my women friends, Jan and Cecila, who were lovers. Jan was married and she and Cecila began arguing about Jan's relationship with her husband, how it affected their relationship. In a moment of quick talk and harsh words, Jan walked off, leaving Cecila and I in the restaurant.

Shortly after Cecila and I left the restaurant to find Jan. As we walked up Broadway, I spotted a friend in the crowd, Alex Bloom, who was also a close friend of Jan's husband. I waved him over. I liked him and hadn't seen him in a while. But in a moment Cecila was screaming at him for interfering with her relationship with Jan.

At that moment under the flashing lights of Broadway enter the irate husband, who apparently was walking down Broadway to meet Alex for a drink. He began screaming at Cecila, "I don't give a damn what you think." Alex turned to me and asked, "What do you think?" I couldn't even begin to comprehend it all, the intricacies of their relationships were so complicated and ambiguous.

Cecila and I walked off to her motorbike and began an incredible search through the fog — with me on her bike jumping off at various Broadway bars to look for Jan. I remember as I rode sitting on the back of her bike wishing I had a notebook or tape recorder to get it all down — what little of it I could grasp.

It was incredible and unquestionably good material for a book in its heightened form, the husband and the wife's woman lover screaming at each other in the middle of a Friday night crowd on Broadway, the lights of neon flashing, the traffic bumper to bumper and the excitement in the air. Definitely the opening or closing of a late 70's movie on Feminism á la *Bob Carol Ted and Alice* or á la *Bloom in Love*.

I have one other scene for my screen play which best can be written by my friends storming the bastille of liberal institutions for their discriminatory treatment of woman.

Their role playing scene with the head of an institution clearly depicts a new and strong way that women are interacting with men, and could be quite funny. My opening scene is of course the three women in bed — trying to understand their feelings for women and what to do with it all.

When I told a close male friend about the Broadway scene he was not at all amused. He got angry. What is so funny about a man hurting? It's strange how all the movies with the "husband, the wife and the other woman" were okay, and sometimes considered quite comical. But they don't seem quite so funny on the other foot — when the situation shows two women choosing each other at the time rather than the man.

After Cecila and I found Jan, I split. I was invited into their ensuing discussion but I felt I should leave them alone. I am a coward when it comes to sitting in on other peoples' fights. I had had enough. I felt lonely as I drove home through the city, along Broadway, stopping the last block before getting on the Bay Bridge to Berkeley at a phone booth to call Jan to see if she was okay. I was half hoping I would be invited back. It was lonely in the car after all that intensity. And that scene before my eyes and no one with whom to share it.

I returned to Berkeley angry. The next day was the 4th of July. I spent it mostly alone, only leaving the house for a long walk up through Tilden Park. I was going through some of my holiday feelings, feeling blue. I very much wanted Jan and Cecila's lives to work out. I wanted it possible to be married and have a woman lover. And it wasn't working out.

284

GRETA

I MET Greta through Ginger. She had been one of Ginger's lovers. I was particularly interested in interviewing her because she lived with a man and had had woman lovers. When I first went to interview her she was making chocolate chip cookies. We talked for awhile and then went downstairs to her darkroom where I learned what cropping pictures was all about. It was fun to watch her developing photographs. As we chatted I had the sense it was best to do a formal interview with the tape recorder another time. During our conversation Greta asked me what I was going to do about my sexuality. She was angry. She thought I was doing a strictly intellectual trip disconnected from my own life. She had recently been interviewed about her sexuality by a woman doing a scientific study, and she felt ripped off — violated. She had thought I was into the same intellectual voyeuristic trip, and was pleased and surprised that I was sharing my personal process and that I was actually exploring my own sexuality with women.

When I interviewed Greta formally, we had difficulty getting down and talking in any depth at first. I soon found that she thought I would be disappointed since she did not currently have a woman lover. I explained why I was fascinated to know her. At that time I thought I wanted to be living with a man and also having women lovers, and I wanted to know how this structure worked in her life. Once we got through this tension, we relaxed and had a good time. The interview went fine.

August 2, 1973

Greta: I feel that we're not getting into any depth, but I don't know that we can because I don't feel that I'm where you . . . I'm not sure that I'm at the point that you need some-body to interview. I've got an old man, and I'm very happy living with him.

Ruth: Yeah.

G.   And, you know, women are *friends* for me right now. It's not sexual. I don't know if that's what you're looking for or not.

R: Umm. . .

G.   I feel like I'm a disappointment for you.

R.   Really?

G.   Because of that, yeah.

R.   No, I just think it's really neat that you, I don't know, I wish I had a man right now. And I would like to be into men and into women. I mean, I see your situation and I really ad-mire the way you're living with Mark. And, you know, the fact that you're not involved with a woman right now doesn't mean that you're not bisexual, does it?

G.   No.

R.   So, why do. . . .

G.   I feel like I'm a disappointment for you because I think you're looking for someone who's more deeply involved with women sexually now than I am.

R.   I don't feel that.

G.   Oh! Good! Okay! You know, being bisexual right now isn't that big a part of my life. I'm still attracted to women, I still look at women, but I think a lot of women do that. You know, I feel frustrated about the interview.

R.   Well, maybe I'll just ask a few more questions and then we can stop. Maybe we can try another time.

G.   Okay.

R.   I was really looking forward to interviewing you. I wanted to get to know you. I've interviewed two women. One of them is with only women right now. And the other one has had a long on-going relationship with a man. She's non-monogamous, and has a lot of different relationships, including relationships with women, and yet, you're the third and you're the only one that's living with a man. I thought that was particularly interesting 'cause I would like to work out something like that.

G.   That's nice. You know, I don't see loving women, like you say as a reaction to men.

R.   Oh?

G.   It's something totally unrelated. It's such a totally different thing, you know. Why is it a reaction to hating men? It's really not for me. No, it's totally different.

R.   That's how I feel about it too, completely.

G.   Yeah, and people say: "Do you like making love with men or women better?" That's a totally impossible question!

R.   Why?

G.   Because it's *different*.

R.   How's it different?

G.   Ah. It's different in the way it feels, different in my feelings, and it's different in the way society looks at it. Society says it's a "no no" to make love with women, and therefore, you know, that makes it exciting.

R.   That makes it exciting?

G.   Yeah!

R.   Breaking that taboo?

G.   Right, right! And I don't like that, but I still know that that's a factor involved in making love with women. The fact that you're doing something that you *know* is "wrong." That you know is against society, you know, is a little bit of rebellion.

R.   That's interesting.

G.   I have a lot of feelings toward women. I really enjoy walking down the street and looking at pretty women. I really enjoy that.

R.   I caught myself just now, when I was walking here. I saw a couple walking, and this time I flashed at the man, and I said to myself: "See! You flashed at the man, you're still attracted to men too." But you know, that's how secure I'm feeling today!

G.   You're all right! I went through that about a year ago, of just noticing the women, and I got very worried about myself. That's not normal, right? And I would consciously look for a man that I liked. But, I don't know. I've gotten over that I think. And you know, I mostly notice women rather than men.

R.   Right.

G.   And that's that.

R.   One of the women that I interviewed was saying — I think it's really far out the way she said it — you know, look it's Madison Avenue. I mean, they've sold women as the aesthetic beauty, and we *all* like them. They are beautiful!

G.   I just flashed on something. I think it's very easy for me to be bisexual because of the friends I have, because of the kind of circle that I'm in. I'm in a very middle to upper class liberal intellectual circle, circuit, and my friends are the type who would understand. And I just realized that it would probably be very hard to be bisexual in Kentucky. Out here we have the pick-up bar scene but you know even up on Union Street, it would also be impossible to be bisexual.

R.   Why?

G.   Because I think that people see things one way, you know. You're either heterosexual or you're homosexual.

R.   Right.

G.   And there's no middle ground. There's no role model for that. I mean, who do you know who's bisexual, if you're in that circuit?

R.   If you're in which circuit?

G.   If you're in that Union Street one?

R.   I've never been there.

G.   Secretarial, Market Street, Montgomery Street straight area. Those women we saw at Vidal Sassoon?

R.   Yes?

G.   They have no role model for that. That sort of carryings on.

R.   Washington was so difficult. I mean it was really painful just coming to accept the feelings that I had, and knowing that they were okay. Knowing no one that was bisexual, *no one*, not even knowing a Lesbian until the last year when I opened my eyes, and you know, and propositioned her!

G.   Right.

R.   I asked you before if you were non-monogamous, if you see yourself as non-monogamous. I was wondering if bisexual women just because they like both men and women might find themselves being non-monogamous, being with both. I mean, I guess I was thinking of that for myself.

G.   I'm being monogamous now. But, in the past I haven't been.

R.   Yeah.

G.   But I've been monogamous only in the sense that I haven't made it with other men.

R.   Yeah.

G.   And that for a long time that's where Mark was at. He wasn't threatened by women. And he felt that as long as I was with women I wasn't "stepping out on him."

R.   Right.

G.   And that was sort of a way of saying women aren't quite as good as men, you know, therefore of course you can go out with them.

R.   How do you feel about that?

G.   (whistling, sighing exclamation) Uh, how do I feel about it now?

R.   Or him feeling that way?

G.   I still feel the same way. You know, but I also, at this point, I don't want him to be threatened. You know, 'cause it's not good for him to be threatened. He's not happy when he's threatened, and so it's okay that he feels that way. But it's also kind of a bummer.

R.   Yeah.

G.   For *me*. You know, because it's like I said it's sort of saying women aren't as good.

R.   Right. In some ways I feel he should almost be more threatened, 'cause at times it gets more intense with a woman than with a man. I don't know. That's sometimes how I feel it might be. I'm more into fantasy. I've never had a woman and a man at the same time.

G.   Oh, neither have I! Sounds nice!

R.   I mean, in the same time period of my life.

G.   Oh.

R.   Haven't you ever made love with a woman and a man at the same time?

G.   Uh ah. (negative).

R.   Ginger told me, I think, that she'd made love with you and another man.

G.   Oh, that's right! Oh my god! Totally blocked that out!

R.   Uh huh.

G.   And it was totally accidental, it was really neat.

R.   It must have been nice.

G.   He came back after his billfold, which it turned out he had lost. He came back looking for it and Ginger and I were in bed, and we were just terrifically turned on. He hopped into bed with us. It wasn't planned at all. I liked it.

R.   I did that once with one of my very good friends and her husband, and that was really nice. We were breaking so many taboos at the same time! It was pretty heavy! But it was also a way for me to touch another woman, by having a man there, you know, to hold onto to. . . .

G.   To make it okay!

R.   Yeah.

G.   Mark and I made it with another couple once. And it was interesting. There were very strict lines which developed. Like Mark could not really make it with the other guy. Mark really couldn't even touch the other guy. The other guy couldn't touch Mark. I seemed to be the only free one in the room!

R.   Yeah, right. How did you feel about that?

G.   Ah, it was nice at the time, but afterwards it didn't work 'cause I was getting extremely jealous. Mark was getting jealous. The other woman was getting jealous, the other man was getting jealous.

R.   Oh.

G.   Also, I really didn't like it because I felt like my energies were going so many places. There were so many places for it to go!

R.   How did you get involved with a woman? Why did you or how did that happen?

G.   I had always been interested in other women, and I had always been attracted to other women, but I had never done anything about it. So the first time it was really experimentation. And it happened to be with someone I liked, and that was it. It was just the one time. And nothing else ever happened with a woman for probably three or four years. Then I started having all these fantasy trips about what women were like, and what it would be like to make love with a woman, and how I was really going to go crazy, I was going to love it. I knew I was a dyke, and I was never going to like men again. And Mark said, "For God's sake, get it out of your system! Do something about it." You know, call up the information lady, and find out where the gay bars are. Do something about it!

R.   Far out! This was when you were with Mark?

G.   Yeah.

R.   He was so supportive about it? That's terrific!

G.   Yeah! And so I had a friend come up from Los Angeles

who was an acknowledged Lesbian. She took me in hand. Now this is really insane. She's about 20, maybe 19 and I'm 28. We went to Mabe's and had this absolutely awful, horrendous experience with all these heavy dyky ladies standing around being very tough — cigarettes rolled up in their shirtsleeves. I knew that wasn't me. But I went back again by myself, getting very brave. Mark was out of town or something for the night. I went back again, and met this very heavy duty dyke lady. Motorcycle jacket, boots and leather, you know, the whole number. I figured out later that the reason I did that was because it kept the sex roles so straight for me. I mean it was very obvious who was male, and who was female. It was not threatening at all. And so that went on for about a month. And didn't work. She became very threatened by anyone even *trying* to get close to her. Not succeeding, but even trying! Even wanting to. Totally freaked her out, and she couldn't handle it. And so when I happened to go to Santa Cruz I decided that I would pick myself up a woman.

R.   Why didn't you ever get it on with your friend? The one who was helping you out?

G.   Because she was living with another woman.

R.   Oh.

G.   You know, she was safe. She was very safe for me. So when I went down to Santa Cruz I decided that I was going to pick myself up a woman, and went to the bars down there for five nights in a row, got absolutely nowhere.

R.   Oh wow.

G.   And came away convinced that I was probably the homliest dyke in existence!

R.   (laughs)

G.   And that was the reason I couldn't score at the bars. So I came back from Santa Cruz with a guy. Mark was gone.

R.   With a guy!!

G.   Yeah! A guy I had just met, and who was a friend of a friend, and he was driving back to San Francisco. So I came back with him, and he and I made it! And I thought: "Well I guess that's were it's at for me!" The next day this woman from Santa Cruz called and said, "I'm totally hot for your body! I'm coming down!" I *couldn't* believe it!

R.   Where did you meet her? At the bar?

G.   Yeah, I met her at the bar. And so she came down and we made it one night, and you know, since then I've just decided that combing the bar scene is not for me. It just doesn't work for me.

R.   Me too. Homosexual, heterosexual or bisexual I just don't like the bar trip.

G.   Right. It just doesn't work for me. And since then I've sort of gotten straightened out a little bit. For me, sex with a woman was not sex with a woman friend. It was sex with a sex object, who happened to be a woman.

R.   I see.

G.   Since then, I have figured sex with women is sex with friends! And you know, it was something that had to be kept very separate from my life. I mean, this leather lady that I met was very separate from my life here. It was totally a different thing and the two never crossed. But it's not that way anymore.

R.   In what way do you do it now?

G.   Sex is not a big part of my relationship with women now. But the women that I'm interested in, I bring home. You know, they're my friends. Like Barbara who's also a good friend of Mark's, and, that's basically it! They're a part of my life now. It's not something over on the other side, over in another place.

R. You're making it more of a total relationship. You're integrating the sex and the friendship.

G. Yeah, right. And sex is very definitely taking second seat.

R. You mentioned that there are some women friends you would like to make love with, but it's not really that important. You want to make love with them but you don't?

G. Yeah, right.

R. How about Barbara? That's someone you said you had made love with for a time, and then your friendship evolved.

G. Yeah, to a different level, and she's making it with men now, and with women. I'm going to go see her tonight. Mark will probably come later. I'm going to a party with her. But . . . we're not having a sexual . . . We're having a sexual relationship, but we don't fuck! Does that make any sense? Like we touch and we kiss and we hold hands and I hug her and she hugs me, I sit on her feet but. . . .

R. Do you get turned on?

G. Yeah, very turned on. Yeah. But it would take so much energy to make love with her now that I don't.

R. Why?

G. I don't like to just make love with someone and then split. I don't like quickies. I like to spend the night. And I don't want to spend the night away from Mark, that's one thing it boils down to and that's just not where Barbara and I are now.

298

R.   I love the way you describe that. Exploring my bisexuality gave me permission to touch women, and then somehow I've gotten to the point where I just *love* being turned on! And I can sit in a room and just get pleasure from that.

G.   Yeah, right.

R.   You know, I have a roommate that I just really like. I love touching her. I don't think I get turned on anymore, but exploring my sexuality with women got me to the point that I can easily be affectionate and I really get pleasure from touching.

If you were close friends with some of the women that you had sex with, did that have any effect on the intimacy of your relationship? Did you become closer? What did the sex do?

G.   Yeah. We became closer. It's not monopolized the relationship and it's not made it, you know, cosmically important. I have other women friends that I've not had sex with that I am as close to. But it's given a degree of intimacy and importance to the relationship for me.

R.   How is making love with a woman different from making love with a man? One of my friends said she thought it was more sensuous and warm. Does that feel right to you?

G.   Yeah, yeah. Also, I really dig knowing how it feels, how what I'm doing feels. I don't have any idea what it feels like to have a cock. To have a cock stroked, or sucked, or have hair run over a cock which destroys Mark totally. I have no *idea* what that's like! And yet, when I make love with a woman, I know what that feels like. I know what it feels like to have your breast stroked. I know what that feels like for me.

R.   Yeah, it turns me on sometimes when I feel the woman

respond 'cause I know how I would respond.

G. Right, right.

R. Do you ever have that sense of mirror image?

G. Oh yeah, sure. Like you can feel the juices start to flow. I'm more sensitive to women.

R. Right.

G. And you know where the woman's at. You know how far along she is, you know what you can do from that point on. And that's a real ego trip for me with women.

R. Why? What do you mean? Can you explain?

G. Ah . . . I enjoy giving pleasure to women more than I do to men.

R. Why?

G. That's what it boils down to. This is a real revelation. I don't know. I really don't know.

R. That's interesting.

G. It has to do with being a little more detached with women.

R. Detached?

G. Yeah. Because when I'm fucking with a man, I'm so involved with the whole thing that I really don't get detached enough.

R. With a man?

G. Yeah, with a man. Because I'm so involved that it's impossible to get that objectivity.

R. You mean because you're fucking. I mean, you're both fucking each other at the same time?

G. Yeah, right, yeah. It's impossible to get objective.

R. Haven't you ever just pleasured Mark? Just made love to him while he lays back?

G.   I have, yeah. But it's not the ego trip that it is with a woman for me.

R.   Can you explain more about how you feel about that? I don't know what you mean by the ego trip exactly.

G.   I feel really good, and powerful, and successful, and pleased with myself when a woman comes and comes and comes, and says, "Oh that feels so good, don't stop!" You know, that whole number. And I feel, well when I'm with a man, you know, it's hard to be objective. It's hard to sort of step back and take that compliment.

R.   When he comes.

G.   When he comes, yeah.

R.   'Cause you don't feel like you've done anything. I mean he just gets off in your cunt.

G.   That's sort of it, yeah! Yeah!

R.   That's interesting.

G.   That's right. And yet with a woman I do a lot more active participation. It's a lot more "because of me," "because of what I'm doing," "because of where I'm putting my fingers," because of, you know, all that sort of thing, whereas with a man, it's not that way.

R.   You see him being more active and you more passive?

G.   Yeah.

R.   So you have more of a passive role.

G.   That's something really important that I never knew!

R.   That's nice! That makes me feel better! (pause) One of the things that sometimes bothered one of the woman I interviewed about making love with a woman was that you took turns. How do you feel about that?

G.   I really like taking turns. I really like that. You know one woman I made love with was an exceptionally good lover. She was really good. She taught me about taking turns and about how a woman's body responds. But also I got the feeling that she was good in that she knows a lot of techniques.

R. Yeah.

G. And that's not all being a good lover is . . . you know. . . .

R. Right. What else is it?

G. It's getting involved with someone . . . it's really caring about someone . . . it's caring about them beyond caring about their body. Mark is a good lover. Not because he's got a lot of techniques, but because he doesn't perform, we're very real with each other, cause we laugh a lot in bed, and you know, for reasons totally different from the reasons Roberta was a good lover.

R. What are the reasons you think she was a good lover?

G. Because she knew a lot of techniques! Because she knows where women, especially me, like to be touched. She knows how to do it, she knows how hard, how soft, she's very sensitive to what I wanted at a particular time — you know, the beginning and the end, what I wanted when, she was very good in those ways, and she's taught me a lot in that respect. Just an awful lot. But being a lover is also outside of bed! And you know, outside of bed she was lousy. She didn't care about me or wanting to be close.

R. That must have been very painful relating to her . . . Do you have any clues to why you acted out your bisexuality, most people act out just their heterosexual feelings?

G. Because I got tired of fantasizing about it. It was taking up so much time and energy!

R.   Me too, me too.

G.   I decided it was just time . . . I decided, and Mark decided, it was just time to. . . .

R.   Uh, I really love that. I love your reason. Do you feel better about yourself 'cause you made love with a woman?

G.   Yeah! Because I had a fantasy, and instead of running away from the fantasy and feeling guilty, and horrible, and psychotic that I was a homosexual, I dealt with it! Which is a pretty courageous thing to do.

R.   Yes.

G.   It makes me feel better about myself. Makes me a better bread-winner, and a better photographer, a better human being all around! I'll tell you the biggest argument against being with a woman, that I know of.

R.   Yeah?

G.   And it is, you may think I'm kidding! This is absolutely true, it's walking down the street with a woman and not being able to hold her hand.

R.   How does that make you feel?

G.   It makes me feel shitty!

R.   Why?

G.   Because I'm letting society tell me what to do! And I don't like that!

R.   Are there any things that you don't like about sleeping with a man, that you don't find with a woman? Or visa versa?

G.   Men burp and snore, and most women don't.

R.   How about sexually?

G.   I like the smell of women a lot better than I like the smell of men. For me it's very practical things.

R.   Like?

G.   Like snoring. And women generally weigh less. And I like that. And they're smaller. You know. That's what I like about women, you know but the fact that Mark is a hairy, heavy human being, I also really like that!

R.   Do you discover things about yourself in a relationship with a woman lover?

G.   Yeah. I've discovered I like making my own decisions, making decisions for myself. I would decide when I'd spend the night with Ginger, or Roberta; I went to find a woman lover for myself. Totally by myself; Mark had nothing to do with it!

R.   He was supportive.

G.   He was supportive at first but later on, he would become vaguely jealous and say: "I don't want you to spend the night away from me." And I would say: "Look, this is something I really want to do." And He'd say: "Okay." And I knew he wasn't really serious, 'cause if he was really serious, he'd say: "Look, don't go! I really need you here tonight."

R.   Has being with a woman lover helped you to take better care of yourself?

G.   Yeah. It's made me a stronger person. I feel so much better about myself and I am so much happier.

Avocado Sandwich
Was like a
Fleeting delight.

I was having such a wonderful time with Ginger. She seemed to get a lot of joy from showing me things, from being in charge and showing me the ropes. It was the same feeling that I sometimes experienced with Nita that I felt Gloria experienced with me — wanting to treat another woman. Treat her to dinner, show her things that she hasn't yet experienced, whether it be some special restaurant or some kind of perfect dessert.

It could be a mothering thing or something that my aunts would do for me. It was that same feeling I had when my mother or my father took me some place special they thought I would like.

Sometime immediately after Big Sur, after a wonderful night of love-making, Ginger took me on an errand with her, to get her laundry. On the way we stopped for a sandwich at a corner store. Ginger announced that this would be one of the most wonderful sandwiches I ever had. She bought the sandwiches and brought them back to the car with soda and dessert. I just loved all this attention! Then she decided that she wanted to show me a beautiful San Francisco place most people don't know about. We drove there to eat . . . Fort Hunt was underneath the Golden Gate Bridge where the water splashes on the cars if the bay is rough. An old fisherman stood by our car fishing, catching the spray on his raincoat. I gobbled down my sandwich. It was delicious! Ginger was

306

right, I have never been able to find an avocado sandwich as good with those big chunky onions. But I had been to Fort Hunt before. I was taken there by an old Aberfoyle roommate Kate when I first came to San Francisco eight years ago. Kate didn't miss showing me a thing then, but I never thought that the next time I would be there would be with a woman lover! I remember as Ginger and I drove back through the cypress trees she gave me a kiss. I was watching two boys riding bicycles. Ginger said "Don't worry. Most people don't think about what we're doing. Lots of women kiss." I wasn't worried. I was just watching the boys climb that steep hill, wondering how they did it.

As I write about Fort Hunt, I think about the other day when I was tap dancing above the Pierce Street Annex. I had also been there with Kate eight years ago and never dreamed that later I would be doing the old huff and shuffle above the Annex with good friends. Life is just like that.

ELLEN

ELLEN was a woman active in the educational reform movement, whom I met at Dragon's Eye, a Berkeley Commune. She is now living on the east coast. When she came to visit the commune I thought it would be wonderful to interview her. We had talked to each other over the years about our work at NIMH but we had never taken the time to know each other.

August 18, 1973

Ruth: Why is being bisexual supposed to be a cop-out?
Ellen: Okay, there are two issues: one is political and one is personal. And the question of bisexuality as a cop-out is part of the political issue.
R.   Right.
E.   I think it primarily depends on how you define yourself, and whether it matters whether you define yourself. In a particularly strong lesbian community, first of all, you'll get hassled from one side if you call yourself bisexual. Often, people may call themselves lesbian but still operate in a whole variety of ways. I'm sure there are some women who hate men and will have nothing to do with them — avoid contact, etcetera. There are others who still have men friends, maybe gay men friends, and others who will be very much bisexual in terms of their sexual involvements and friendships and relationships. So I think the question of a cop-out is primarily a political issue. And it really came home to me very strongly when someone in a group setting asked people to define themselves, in other words, to arrange themselves around the room — "Women who identified themselves as lesbians over here, bisexuals here and straight over here." I was sitting at the back of the room, which was the bisexual place, and I just stayed there. And I realized that, in that group, I had not come to terms with my need for confidentiality and professional considerations and so forth, and that I wouldn't — I had not come to a point where I was going to say, "OK! I'm a lesbian!" And that also the definitions are very unclear. But I realized that that was an okay place to be — I mean in

the bisexual group in anybody's eyes. Because I still had, you know, half of me was still on the "right" side of the line. I mean, it's easy to chalk it up as a passing phase, all kinds of things like that. So that's a political issue. Basically I avoid labelling myself. In terms of personal issues, I feel personally very much bisexual. I love both men and women and I enjoy making love with both men and women. The thing that I would like to make clear to young women who are really unsure about where their sexuality lies, is that it's not so much a matter of who you're relating to in terms of what sex they are. It's a matter of individual considerations and that you're going to run into the *same* problems relating to women as you are relating to men in terms of intimacy. Having been with women periodically and with men in a variety of different kinds of relationships, what becomes critically *clear* to me — what becomes critical is my own sense of self as an independent person. I mean, regardless of the relationships I'm in, and almost regardless of the work I'm doing, but not totally.

R.   I agree with you — having a sense of self is critical. But I want to get back a little bit to being a lesbian. It's been a big threat to me. And sometimes, being bisexual, you know, if I watch myself and monitor myself from outside, like you say, it's sort of easier, you know: 'Whew! I'm bisexual.' Then that's okay, 'cause I still like men. But the fact is, that I *am* bisexual, and I *do* like both, you know. When I'm feeling very secure, then I know that's where I am. It is a personal issue. On the other hand I hope, as I go through this year and I talk to more and more women, and as I live my own personal life, that to fear being lesbian is going to be ridiculous. But, I think, maybe this thing that you said the last time, that if you choose to be lesbian you could get cut out of the goodies in this society, is a very real and a very political issue!

E.   What I was going to say is bisexuality can imply a lesbian who also sleeps with men, or can imply, perhaps, a woman who is primarily with men and also sleeps with women, both ways. Particularly if it's the former; she's a lesbian who also sleeps with men, she still, if she's ultimately lesbian and does not want to be dependent on men, she has to be financially independent. And I think there's a growing awareness among women in general, that, ultimately, you want to be financially independent, and the way to be financially independent is by being into your work. I *know* that my own personal independence, regardless of the money situation, has to do with defining myself by me and by the work that I do. I would like to make a side comment on relationships with men and independence.

A lot of men, are getting out of school and are getting into professional trips and into their work things who have picked up wives along the way. They probably are the men we'd be most interested in seeing, right now. The ones who are *not,* are the ones we would not want to see. What you begin to do, is meet the divorcees, who have lots of problems, themselves, you know, they're probably going to have to work through so I figure, well, maybe I'll meet some of them in three years. Men who've been divorced for three or four years and they've gone through the kinds of things that I've gone through — because their world was shattered. I feel often that my world was shattered.

R.   How was your world shattered?

314

E.   By the fact that I was brought up in a certain way, and that suddenly, that way was not going to be appropriate for me.

R.   How were you brought up?

E.   I'm sure that I vaguely expected to work until I got married and then I'd eventually . . . I mean, I never thought about it . . . but the expectation was that I would not define myself until I was married, and then once I was established with someone, then I could go and do my own thing. Anyway eventually I'm going to meet some men who are going to be in similar positions.

R.   Why do you think they'll be in similar positions? I don't see. . . .

E.   Well, some of it's optimism. . . .

R.   In what way will they be in a similar position?

E.   Where they are not dependent on a woman to be dependent on them and to support them. They'll be the individual person, who still has room for relationships, and is willing to work it through.

R.   Ah, where they're not having a woman being dependent on them. . . .

E.   But they in themselves are also independent people, in the sense that I feel I like to be an independent person.

R.   I hope so but that might be a long time in coming! I would like to change the subject a little. The last woman I interviewed, I asked what she would like to ask other bisexual women and what she would want from this dialogue that we are having and she said: "I want to know how other women deal with their parents." That was the main thing, which I guess surprised me. Is that a concern for you?

315

E.   I feel I can think about that in a couple of ways. One is, to think that I can work it through with my parents and that that would be okay; the other is, that they would be very, very hurt. I don't want to hurt my parents; I've avoided doing that, successfully, for some time. They may, I mean, they could sort of surmise lots of stuff from the kinds of things that I've done, and how I talk, and the work that I do. But we never feel free to talk about it, in which case, you know, if it did come out in the open, it would probably be something like, "Yes, I thought so," or whatever. But if I talked with my parents I would make very clear to them that I do very strongly consider myself bisexual. That, sure, I may end up with a woman for a period of time, or for a great length of time, or whatever, but that does *not* mean that I don't like men; it may mean that I'm choosey in terms of the men that I spend my time with. But it may also mean that I am not necessarily inclined toward, you know, getting married and "living happily ever after."

R.   Which has nothing to do with whether you're bisexual or not.

E.   Right. I think today counting on any relationship to last for any tremendous length of time just becomes more and more difficult. But at the same time, I'm sure people still struggle for it. Dealing with that sense of impermanency, it's just incredibly hard, I think.

R.   How did you get involved with your first woman lover? Had you been attracted to women for a long time?

E.   It wasn't until I was 23, when I was with the women's project — there were a lot of us on a camp trip, sleeping together in the same room. Two of us who had known each

other before started making out and eventually slept together. And then suddenly we realized — neither of us had
slept with a woman before — we suddenly realized that:
"Look at what we did! What are we going to do with it now?"
It was easier for me, because we lived in different cities, so
that there wasn't a question of what does that mean? We were
also both up tight, obviously, and there was a lot to learn. I
mean, you're scared, and you're afraid you don't know what
you're doing and it's sometimes hard to talk about it.

And I know that I was — I think that I was afraid, almost from
the beginning, of having someone dependent on me because
I'd never been in that position, and I still don't know how to
handle it. I've avoided men like that, partly because they
were often weaker than the kind of men I'm attracted to. And
suddenly, to be in a power position just really freaked me.
The reason I think that I was open to that kind of experience
in the first place was that a woman friend of mine, whom I
didn't know very well at the time, but who I saw as a role
model and I respected, and she was doing work that I liked,
and so forth, turned out to be a lesbian! And what it meant
was that, here's a woman that I respect tremendously and
suddenly you put a "lesbian" label on her! You add that to the
whole thing, and what it meant was that in some ways it legitimized lesbianism for me.

R.   What was so admirable about her for you as a role model.

E.   I liked the way, I liked the way her life was. I mean, she
was doing the kind of work that I wanted to be doing, coun-
selling and working with people, and she seemed to have a
good head on her shoulders, and I liked her style.

R.   So it just happened for you?

317

E.   Okay. For me first of all, I think I had just started masturbating the year before that happened.

R.   When you were 22?

E.   Right. And that I think also opened up the possibility. You begin to know what's pleasurable for you, and then therefore you obviously know what's going to be pleasurable for another woman, too. I mean, at least the gross details. And then sort of all that happening over a period of about a year or so, made it much more possible, mentally, to get into it. But I'd certainly never thought about sleeping with a woman before.

R.   It was never an issue for you when you were younger?

E.   No, no. And it didn't bother me that other women were. In some ways, I feel a lot easier about sleeping with women because I'm not moving out of fear. I'm not moving out of feeling that I can't make it with men.

R.   What are you moving out of?

E.   The fact that it's *nice!*

R.   How's it nice?

E.   That it's nice to be able to act on feelings towards other people, sexually. I think the other thing that makes me feel good, at the same time, is that, okay, you meet a woman. And, instead of very quickly going through a sexual "Well, what's going to happen here?" which is what typically happens with a guy, you've got a lot more space and a lot more choices in terms of the kinds of relationship you can have.

R.   With a woman?

E.   With a woman. You can have a casual relationship where occasionally you might run into each other, or you might be working at the same place, in different offices or something, and say: "Hey, how about lunch today?" You could be living relatively nearby a friend and you could call her up, maybe once a month, and just *talk* I mean, there's a woman I do that with. You know, maybe you regularly spend time with a friend and go to meetings together or you play tennis together, or whatever. A nice friendship. Or you may have a good, close, solid friend, that if you've got a problem, you could go talk to her anytime.

R.   Hm Hmm. You don't find those options with men?

E.   Well, they're much harder to find, but I'm beginning to. Also the fact that I'm beginning to find those options with men, having those choices — both sexually intimate, and close friendships and casual friendships, and all of that makes me feel a lot happier — especially in conjunction with my feelings of being an independent, strong person. Let me finish the whole thing about women. Obviously, you can also have a sexual relationship. That can be casually sexual but I still don't know how to handle that.

R.   Me neither.

E.   Or it can be part of a growing, intimate relationship. It can be total infatuation, it can be friends, where that's, where it seems like the appropriate thing to do, and so forth.

R.   Is it true that you did not think about having sexual relationships with women before you actually got involved with a woman sexually? It wasn't something you pre-thought; it just happened?

E.   I have no idea how I would have reacted if it had become an intellectual thing for me. I just have no idea. I'm just so glad it happened.

R.   It just happened.

E.   Watching women, now, going through these intellectual trips, it's really hard. Because I sympathize tremendously. At the same time, I don't want to walk in and be a guinea pig for them so they can get it over with. You know, it's like a virginity trip again. It's really strange.

R.   Women coming to you and asking you to sleep with them?

E.   Yes.

R.   What do your friends think of your having women lovers? What do you tell them?

E.   When I first slept with a woman, I eventually told my role model, you know, the woman that I found out was a lesbian and she was very supportive, and very delighted about that. Probably because she feels very strongly that that's a good place to be. I told a few other people, periodically. The first woman I had slept with had been part of the community where she had been, for a while, so those people knew about both of us, and that was okay. I've vacillated in terms of my connections with other people, and some of it has to do with my own personal strengths. I often feel chameleon-like. If I'm feeling very strong, have a personal core, I can do that *well*, in terms of being with heterosexual people, and being with lesbians, and being with a strong women's community, and then, you know, turning 'round and going to my work situation, which is very different. And if I, if I lose that sense of myself, then those switchings just go haywire. But none of my friends said: "Oh, dear Ellen! How could you!"

R.   Were there any friends you were afriad to tell?

E.   It's not a matter of afraid to tell. I think it's a matter of timing. A combination of whether they want to know, and that's *my* judgment, obviously, and whether that's going to change our relationship, in way I don't want it to change. Or whether it's necessary. And also whether I trust them. You know, whether they're close enough to me, whether I feel there's going to be the possibility of an understanding of confidentiality. I mean, it's illegal in many ways. It's also that, professionally, I can be bothered. And I'm still young. I don't choose to cut off my options, professionally, right now. I'm *not* about to go and say "Hey, look, I love women!" and choke on it.

R.   If you were close friends with a woman previously, what effect did your sexual intimacy have, if you made love with them. Did it change the friendship?

E.   Well, the women I've been lovers with I have not known them well. It was. . . .

R.   It sounds like you have a heterosexual head, to use one of my friend's terms. I mean, you got to know the women first sexually.

E.   Yeah. Well, you see, there are a lot of women friends that I've made during this past year that I feel really close to. But at the moment with most of them, I wouldn't want to get into a sexual thing, because that would be too threatening to those kinds of friendships.

R.   Right, right.

E.   But the one woman that I was sleeping with this year, I'm sure I did have a choice, but I didn't choose to see it. You know, she's the one person I've been very, very strongly attracted to. The one woman. And, you know, sure if she'd drawn back, in terms of the sexual thing we wouldn't have gotten involved right away. But she didn't. And we encouraged each other, and it was just incredibly fine to get together. I mean, I haven't felt that in years, even with men.

R.   What did you feel?

E.   As though I really wanted to be with her all the time. And it was just obviously a sexual kind of physical attraction, as well as wanting to talk for hours. And once it was okay to touch her, and to touch each other obviously, we weren't going to stop anything from happening. We didn't intellectually sit down and say, well now, do we sleep together or don't we sleep together? We just did that. And I'm leary of that because of my infatuation tendencies. Because I really think that I can't really trust that.

R.   Why. Do you go out of control?

E.   Yeah. I just lose control and I lose perspective and I lose my own sense of self.

R.   And so it was an intense infatuation.

E.   Absolutely! Yes! But in some ways you take a lot of chances. I mean the possibility of it working out into a long-term relationship, is much smaller than if it was a friendship that builds up over time, and where you add sex to it because it's nice to sleep with your friends. Another thing, I think, is that there are certain sorts of sexual dances that you go through with men, and you know those patterns.

R.   Yes, right.

E.   And when you suddenly open up that with a woman! I know that at times, I can get very uptight, and if I'm not feeling *okay* about it — like, I'm just afraid that things are going to be *awkward*, that it's going to mess up the friendship — why bother a thing that's good?

322

R.   Right.

E.   And so, that's something that I know over the time I'm going to have to learn.

R.   How do you handle sex with a woman. Do you talk about it or do you just sort of avoid it?

E.   Oh. no! I mean, I talk about it. I sort of checked it out with one woman friend. Sort of, because I wasn't quite sure what the first signals were, and I would say, you know "What are you saying?" and she said, you know "Don't worry! I'm not putting out things you're not seeing. Don't worry about it." So that we sort of re-affirmed our friendship and said "Gee, that's nice," and we hugged each other.

R.   But you didn't want to do a sexual thing?

E.   Yes. We didn't want to sleep together.

R.   With one of my friends, when I left her house I went to kiss her goodbye. I don't know whether this is the dance of the women, but the last time, she went to kiss me on the lips and I went to kiss her on the cheek, and *this* time, I went to kiss her on the lips and she went to kiss me on the cheek; it was very awkward.

E.   There was a guy, we'd been in the same circles and stuff, and we ran into each other in the company of other people, and so he came up to me, and I realized he had his hand out, to give me a handshake, and my tendency would be to put my arm half around him and give him a hug. But then he reciprocated by sort of coming up and kissing me on the cheek; it was very awkward.

R.   The same situation.

E.   It was the same sort of situation. With lots of people, you're two individual people who aren't quite sure of what's happening between you. The thing is, I really like to give women, men, anyone, half hugs, because that saves people's personal space. I mean, they can choose to do what they want with it.

R. What do you find the same with your male and female lovers?

E. This last relationship I had with a woman, the intensity of the feelings were the same — it could have been with a man. There was very little difference there, in terms of both the hassles and the joys. And I felt the same way, I really wanted to spend time with her. I called her — we called each other a lot. In terms of beginning to get together, and feeling the same shyness, and a whole lot of stuff — it could have been with a man in that respect.

R. What do you mean, shyness.

E. Checking — making sure that the feelings are shared, and being afraid that they're not. Sexually speaking, just physical sex — there were all kinds of things that were the same.

R. Did you like her to do the same things to you that a man would?

E. Yeah. Obviously, the major difference is that a woman cannot penetrate you in the same way that that a man can. And my sense is that is something different.

R. In my experience a woman can use her hand it can be the same experience.

E. Okay. And if you want to say what women have — another woman has breasts, she's much softer, and feels different, and that those two things are probably the greatest differences. Relating to a woman has this whole, kind of, what

324

she feels like and that kind of thing to it.

R.   What do you mean?

E.   I'm trying to say that there are some things that are possible with a woman that are not possible with a man, and some things possible with a man that aren't possible with a woman.

R.   Yes, but let's see if we can go through those and make them clear. The samenesses, you are saying, are the intensity of the relationship and the hassles of worrying about being close or not. These are still there with a woman, the same as with a man?

E.   Yes. The other thing, okay, is that it's very difficult for me to have an orgasm when a man is inside me. Practically impossible. Due to my physiology. My anatomy.

R.   Yeah.

E.   Therefore, my orgasms are very similar, because I usually arrive at them the same way, which is manually.

R.   Does he usually touch you after intercourse?

E.   Before.

R.   Before? And then you have intercourse?

E.   Yeah. I prefer that, in some ways, probably because he's, you know . . . wiped out . . . (laughs)

R.   He's usually wiped out afterwards. Yeah, and then they won't touch you afterwards! A male bisexual I interviewed said the same thing about making love with a man — they get wiped out and tired after making love.

E.   What I realized, particularly not having slept with men for a while, then when I started sleeping with men again, there's just something that's a whole different thing about the sex act. It's penetration, and all the pleasures that come from that and a very different set of feelings.

R. What different kinds of pleasures?

E. They're *not* orgasmic. It's just that, I mean, obviously, your vaginal area has feelings and all kinds of things. My ultimate goal is not necessarily to always have an orgasm. I mean, it's nice just to have a man inside of me.

R. Right.

E. It's also — I mean one of the things I learned when I started masturbating — is the selfish pleasure of having total concentration on yourself and your own pleasure. And that's certainly possible with two women.

R. Why isn't that possible with a man?

E. It's also possible with a man, but I sometimes feel like, I'm more in touch with how *she* feels. I mean, I know — okay, I can feel that way and I know that I can make her feel that way, and it's very clear. I know that. I'm not always as clear as to what's going to make *him* feel as good as I feel. It took me a long time to accept the way I am — to accept my anatomy, and that I was not probably going to come with him in me and it was okay. You know, this is just the way I am. This is what I need and/or, this is what makes me feel good. And I know that with two women, penetration isn't a focus. There's no question about asking for something or taking turns, or coming together, or any of that, I mean, it's all, because of the sameness. But I do think being with women and being able to sort of share and figure out what makes each other pleasurable, and so forth, and being able to *ask* for it, has legitimized my being able to talk more and more with men and say — "Look!" This is what I need and this is how I am!" "Or lets take turns pleasuring each other!"

R. I felt uncomfortable with the man I lived with for a year

326

saying what I wanted. He felt that there was something wrong with me because I couldn't come with him inside me. Then I read in *Our Bodies, Ourselves* that there's no such thing as a "vaginal orgasm," right?

E.   Yeah. But the other thing, like, it depends on the place of your clitoris! There was a woman I knew who was doing push-ups when she was in high school. And she had an orgasm. That's just pressure.

R.   Sort of where your clitoris is located?

E.   Yeah, I mean, just pressure on the floor. Well, I mean, obviously, it's not very localized. She can come just touching, you know, all kinds of places. And okay, so that's the way she's built. That's not the way *I'm* built. And the other thing, of course, is in terms of the placement of your clitoris. If your clitoris is away from your vaginal opening, there's very little that a guy can do to stimulate it with his penis. You know, if indeed you need direct pressure on your clitoris to come, and I'm not the only woman who does, then it won't work.

R.   Right. I just want to see if I understand what you were saying about female lovers and male lovers.

E.   The thing is, okay, let me say it again. What's the same is that it's a closeness and a warmth and all the other things that just feel good. Secondly, sure, if orgasm comes into it, that's nice, to have orgasm with someone. Sometimes it's also nice to have them by yourself. Thirdly, it's like one of the closest unions you can have with someone. And regardless of what you do, I mean, with one man, there may be, I mean, he may really enjoy oral sex, you know, taking it or giving it. But with another man, I would never do that. They're individual differences.

327

R. By people rather than by sex.

E. Right, and I feel that way.

R. Interesting. Some of the women that I've talked to say that being with a woman can be more sensuous and warm, and the lovemaking is longer; you know, that it's not so focused on fucking.

E. Well, to me, that depends on the person. I'm sure that men who make love for a long time and who do not focus only on intercourse are very rare to find. But when you do find one, it's just as nice. But I can understand their feelings. . . . You see for the very same reason that *men* like women, I like women, too. They're soft, they're not hairy, in terms of beards. It's sort of allowing *all* of your feelings of cuddling and closeness and warmth and touching, without getting into a whole penetration thing, which I sometimes really enjoy. Being able to have that kind of nonpenetration experience with a man is nice, but as I said it is rare. What I would like to be able to do is put that out more comfortably with, I suppose with both men and women — my wanting to cuddle and to hold and be held. And some of that is assuming responsibility and power, you know — taking power situation, that's regardless of whom you relate to. It is hard; women aren't used to initiating . . . you know often I felt, particularly in college, that if a guy got turned on, when he was with me, that I was responsible for that, I mean, I had to do something with it — that's another thing I'm beginning to learn. There was a guy I spent some time with this past year who I'd cuddle with. I knew he was excited, but he enjoyed making out and I'd leave him in that state, and that was okay. Because I knew that, well, first of all, I no longer took all the responsibility, and he was certainly never going to put it on me. I appreciated that because it's nice to cuddle! . . . and especially after being with women, I really love to do that with a woman or a man I care for.

Redefining My Sexuality

When I began my exploration on women loving women, I thought in terms of my bisexuality rather than my overall sexuality. Though I was determined to develop a new perspective in redefining my sexuality, in the early interviews I used the labels homosexual, lesbian and heterosexual. Later I learned to drop these terms. What I have attempted here is to show the thinking and feeling processes I went through in this part of my journey.

There are aspects of this process that I wish I had not gone through. But I did. For instance my need to define myself and my sexuality by allowing for a man in my life. In later sections of the book I will explore some of the reasons for this and their political implications.

I had interviewed Julia and Tracy within two days of each other. I was exhausted. After that I decided to allow more time between interviews — to recover, absorb the material and to be reflective.

As I continued the interviews I began to realize that I had a fantasy about how I wanted bisexual women to be — bright, good-looking, committed to their work, aggressive but gentle and so forth. I somehow thought bisexual women were more fully evolved than either heterosexual or homosexual people. I saw bisexuality as a higher level of relating. I felt that it must be easier to love only women or only men than to recognize emotional and sexual feelings for both men and women in oneself. But I realized all bisexuals weren't going to be fantastic people. People who are bisexual are like any other kind of people.

I began to see how I had been defining myself from the outside. I wanted my first woman lover to be intelligent and attractive, have long hair, and be bisexual. I wanted her to reflect me back to me. If she had all these characteristics, then so would I. The fact that my first woman lover defined herself as a lesbian was very threatening to me because the way I defined myself from the outside meant that I would be a lesbian too. I must have thought that if I slept with a woman who loved only women I too must love only women. If I slept with a woman who loved both men and women it was somehow less threatening, because she was how I wanted to define myself. I was also afraid to have only a woman lover because of the taboos around being a lesbian.

When I began my exploration I thought in monolithic

hierarchial terms. If a person had evolved to be "bisexual" they were bound to be a more superior person in general. I had looked up to many of the friends I loved back East, and now I was confused. Who was superior? I soon realized that I could no longer judge a person as either "up" and "down" and that we all had different qualities, different strengths. Though one person may have openly dealt with her feelings for both men and women it didn't mean that she could necessarily relate more intimately to other people or handle other issues in her life more effectively. I was beginning to stop seeing the world in hierarchies, to stop making either, or judgments. My view of bisexuality was very threatening to me at first because I was putting myself above people that I had admired for years — I was invested in seeing them as people who knew how to handle their lives better than I.

As I began interviewing the first woman I realized that I was in a sense dealing with whether I was okay. Though I could continue interviewing other women for the content of the book, I had to begin to deal with myself and look inward at who I was, to start remaking my own judgments about myself and my okayness. I tried to discover what and how I felt about these issues around sexuality separate from the interviews. I knew how these women felt but I wanted to be more clear with myself about how I felt.

I tried to be aware of the difference between how I felt and how society decreed I was supposed to feel. It was in the places I felt conflict that I had negative feelings toward myself. I spent hours on the floor doing breathing exercises trying to figure out how I felt. Through therapy I had discovered I had a great resistance in myself to look directly at myself and who I was — a running rabbit. Sometimes relaxing exercises helped me look at myself more clearly. It was through my feelings rather than by using my intellect, which often folded back on itself, that clarity came. I was beginning to define my sexuality from the inside.

At first I had defined myself, my sexuality, from the outside by defining a bisexual as one who would have both a male and a woman lover at the same time to balance her sexuality. That is why by definition I felt a bisexual person was non-monogamous, because loving both men and women would require having more than one lover. It took me three or four interviews to integrate this knowledge into my being — that one could have one lover (be monogamous) and be bisexual. And that one's lover could be a woman. That is if one defined oneself from the inside — from one's feelings rather than by objects outside oneself, i.e. the sex of one's lover. One could have sexual and emotional feelings for both men and women, fall in love with one person, a women or a man, and chose to be monogamous — to have one lover. And ideally it would be nice to choose people by who they were and not by their sex.

It took me several months to get the idea out of my head that being bisexual did not necessarily mean being non-monogamous. One didn't have to have a female and a male lover at the same time. It was so threatening. You mean that one could be bisexual and spend the rest of her life with a woman? How awful, how sad. I didn't want any part of that. I was invested in the notion that all bisexuals were non-monogamous. That way I could have a man in my life.

I found so many levels of feelings in myself around this

333

issue. As I spent time with myself asking myself how I felt I saw that I definitely had feelings for both men and women. Instead of running for fear that I might have feelings for women I decided to face my feelings straight on. I was afraid my feelings for women ruled out my feelings for men. The society seemed to say that you were either heterosexual or homosexual. So I asked myself, what were my feelings, not what society would say or do. Did I have feelings for both men and women? The answer was yes. The closer I listened to myself, the stronger and more sure I began to feel about myself. I no longer had to worry about whether I was with a male lover or a woman lover to define who I was.

About this time I went to a conference on bisexuality. At first I feared that the academicians would have completed the work I had begun, and experienced a sense of relief mixed with anger when I saw the inadequacy of their content and the bias of their research. I thought at least they were going to give me some answers, some new insights. I had expounded on being your own authority in health matters at NIMH but I still had not yet incorporated this philosophy into my own being. Why was I still so tied to these people in academia — to their world of the "outside authority?" I knew the type of research they conducted from my work at NIMH.

And when researchers talked of their "subjects" in the lesbian community as if they were special creatures I got a pit in my stomach. I was even more angry and ashamed of myself for still having been tied to the academic community.

So I had to be my own authority. I was breaking new ground. I had no "authorities" to go to anymore. I and the other women I interviewed were going to be my authorities.

I began to try to learn to drop labels and to talk more in terms of overall sexuality rather than bisexuality. I feel that everyone is ultimately bisexual. By definition sexuality encompasses bisexuality. So bisexuality is really a compartmentalization of sexuality.

Because I was learning to redefine sexuality I often slipped back and used the concept "bisexuality." It took me a long time to stop thinking in terms of labels.

By the time I interviewed Greta I learned to broaden my definition of sexuality further. We have so compartmentalized sexuality in this society that to many people it means just sex — intercourse. It does not mean hugging, or caring, or emotional or spiritual or intellectual involvement. We have separated our sexuality from our total being. Greata said she and Barbara have a sexual relationship. They are turned on to each other and they hug and kiss. They don't make love. They are very close friends emotionally, intellectually and spiritually. I suggest that sexuality is part of our total being and that hugging and kissing someone is indeed part of sexuality.

Many women do not express "affection" toward other women, like hugging, kissing and touching because it would imply something sexual (it may mean that they "like women"). It does. Sexuality is a part of one's total being. There are various degrees of expressing sexuality. Being turned on to a friend is part of my sexuality, hugging a friend is another part and making love still another. It now seems easier to me to think that I have different choices or ways of expressing my sexuality rather than worrying whether touch-

335

ing my close women friends is sexual or not and what that could mean.

It is a matter of how close or intimate we want to be with another person that may determine how we wish to express our sexuality.

There are many different degrees of expressing sexuality. I know that I and other women have often felt uncomfortable touching men and/or women because of what it could imply and what expectations were put on us. The more I get into my own power, particularly with men, the more I realize that I can determine how I will express my sexuality with another person and that because I hug someone and am warm does not mean we have to make love. It does not commit me to going beyond my own feelings. Ellen learned to say she wanted just to cuddle with a man without feeling she had to make love.

Julia said we sometimes don't show affection to men because of the expectations that go with touching — somehow it means we are expected to make love and we want to avoid that hassle later in the evening. That same non-touching idea some of us carry over to women — because we have connected it to sex as men did when we were being affectionate!

There is so much pressure in this society on sex that it is sometimes difficult to be held and comforted. I talked to one close male friend about this and he responded "You know men have the same problem. Sometimes I find it difficult to ask to be held without feeling I must make love to my partner."

336

What I have attempted to do is broaden my definition of sexuality. To have it be more encompassing rather than to be a small element in my life. To me sexuality does not mean only making love. Also I have eliminated social categories which don't fit my feelings. This way I don't have to be homosexual, heterosexual, bisexual, lesbian or straight. As a human being I am a sexual being, not a series of labels.

What is so difficult about defining myself is that it is sometimes hard to distinguish whether the voice inside of me is how I feel or society's voice that I have been taught. For years I did not have orgasms during intercourse, though I had orgasms when I was stimulated clitorally before or after intercourse. Sometimes I thought something was wrong with me because I did not have an orgasm during intercourse, "a vaginal orgasm." Then I read in *Our Bodies Ourselves* about Masters and Johnson's research and their discovery that there is only one female orgasm — a clitoral orgasm. The clitoris is where all female orgasms are based. I had to read those sentences over and over to believe it. Sometimes even now I feel that somehow I should have an orgasm during intercourse, so strong is the social voice within me. As women, we have defined our own sexuality through our interactions with men. The men I made love with also felt there was something wrong with me for not having an orgasm during intercourse. And some of them did not hesitate to express these feelings (see interview with Ellen for further discussion). Men have been taught that they are supposed to know how to make love to a women and to focus on intercourse and orgasm.

337

I talked to a friend about the difficulties women sometimes experience having orgasm when they make love with
men. We talked about why even when we ask some men to
touch us the way we want we sometimes still don't experience
orgasm. However we can easily come to climax when we masturbate or make love to women.

My friend says what is wrong with sexual manuals and
therapies like Masters and Johnson is that though they tell us
how to touch they do not take into account the feelings,
tensions and expectations females and males bring to bed with
them which effect love-making. The attitudes men have in
this society towards women do not allow for easy open trusting relationships.*

---

* The societal attitude often in lovemaking is sexual intercourse and the
focus is orgasm. Sex is seen in terms of stages — foreplay, intercourse
and afterplay with the first and last stages being necessary but "not the
true essence of lovemaking." With this attitude men and women often
focus on performance and worry whether what they are doing is right or
wrong, instead of focusing on pleasure and sharing.

Through exploring my sexuality with women I've learned about pleasuring and taking turns. I see lovemaking without goals, a total body
orientation — each partner exploring intimacy and pleasure. There are
many pleasurable aspects of lovemaking — orgasm is one of them. There
are no hierarchies in sex play. I enjoy all the sensations I experience in
my body.

BECKY

BECKY was a woman that I met through Julia. She was a professional woman who had become very active in the women's movement in graduate school. Through her ongoing contacts with other women in the movement she found herself in love with a woman. She has been living with her woman lover for over a year now.

Last Christmas I was feeling a bit lonely and needed to get away. The book was going slowly and I needed a break. Julia suggested that I take a vacation with Becky, an old friend of hers, was looking to get away too. I had enjoyed meeting Becky and looked forward to talking to her on our vacation. We chose to go to Puerto Vallarta. I was quite excited as I had enjoyed myself so much there before. Becky and I spent many long hours in Puerta Vallarta talking about relationships, the women's movement and our work. When I returned from there I decided I wanted to interview her and spent one evening before the interview talking to her and her woman lover. I liked her perspective and the types of issues that interested her concerning relationships between women.

January 29, 1974

Ruth: You once said there's more risk-taking involved in a relationship with a woman, because when two women share feelings each woman knows exactly how the other feels. Sometimes, with Jessica and Alan, I experienced this. I told Jessica that I'd found this incredible thing in therapy, about something in me, something that was very profound to me. I could tell her and there would really be meaning. I could tell Alan and it just wouldn't mean anything. She could really relate to it.

Becky.   Yeah, I think that's true. Exposure means more, because the woman is more apt to really understand that it *is* an exposure. I found that is a difference between men and women in relationships, that if I'd done something that I felt really was a big deal, and made me really vulnerable, and a man didn't get it, you know, just didn't see it at all, I just didn't take it as an exposure. It's kind of like a relief: "Ah, you didn't understand!" But the woman is more apt to understand, so the risk quality is different. I'm not sure it's a matter of being more vulnerable with a woman, I think it's just a matter of having a different quality about it.

R.   Yeah. What quality?

B.   Well, I think it's a different quality because she understands more. I don't know, maybe there's more interaction over it; maybe she shares it in a way that's very similar to my reactions.

R.   You feel she shares it in a way similar to your reactions because she's a woman, or, do you feel there could be some men that could share it similarly? I've found some men who feel similar to the way I do.

B.   Well, I suppose it's possible, but from where I'm coming from, you know, the way most men are socialized and raised, I would think it's unusual. And also, I suppose I don't know that many very sensitive men. That may be it, too.

R.   What is it like relating to another woman without defined roles and patterns.

B.   I've been thinking about how women relate to men, how women automatically do something because it's their role — without even thinking about it — and how all the tiny assumptions, about how you run your life suddenly disappear when you relate to a woman. When Virginia and I started this relationship, it was really funny, because neither of us had really been an initiator before, and so here you had two non-initiators — really! Like, not just shy, but really having never been initiators — only knowing how to maybe passively initiate, giving clues and hints, but here you can't do that to each other, right?

R.   Yeah — (laughter) — what was it like?

B.   It was like dancing around; it was like dancing around and being about 14 years old. It was very funny.

R.   What happened.

B.   Well, like not knowing how to initiate physical intimacy — that was really the thing. We had a fairly good relationship, so some of it came automatically. Umm . . . really, just not knowing how to initiate physical intimacy. And I was petrified, because I didn't want to do anything that would be repulsed, or would offend, or that the other person didn't want or, you know, all those things. And then I'm stuck with this not very good ability to express it verbally. I couldn't say,

"Do you want me to do this?" or "Are you ready for that?" — not having the confidence to do that — and maybe even being a little bit romantic, and not wanting to have this little checklist — are you ready for this or that! And this made it really a . . . fumbling around . . . it was kind of cute. . . .

R.   It sounds kind of exciting, too, in a way. I don't understand though — because to me, initiating would be just to go kiss a woman on the mouth — that would be easy. . . .

B.   Okay, so when you've got past that step, doing that — then what would happen?

R.   I figure if you can do that, then it's okay . . . (laughter)

B.   Well, let's say you got to that, but then you don't know. . . .

R.   If it's all right to go further?

B.   Yeah!

R.   I hate being rejected — I guess what I have done — I've kissed Jessica, now okay — that's right — then I got to the point where I felt she didn't want to go any further . . . and yet you know, sometimes, when men would push it, you'd be glad . . . you know, you wouldn't want them to, but then, once you really got into it, you were glad it happened . . . And to have to do that pushing — and then, knowing how it feels *not* to want it. . . .

B.   Yeah and then also we were living in the same house. Now, if you have a date sort of structure it might be a little easier. One goes to the other's house, and you start kissing and then you sort of lay down and it's. . . .

R.   How come you didn't just talk about it? "Do we want to make love, or get physically intimate?"

B.   I don't remember talking about it. We must have a little

345

bit. I have found that I feel much more relaxed, sexually, with a woman. I enjoy it much more. I find orgasm much easier to attain, and I am *more* comfortable asking for things but I'm *still* not comfortable asking for things.

R.　Ellen, the woman I interviewed back in August who is from the east, has been dealing with bisexuality and the women's movement. She kept on saying that the one thing she wanted to see stated in this book, is that relationships are no easier with women than they are with men. She questioned what would happen when all these women who are angry with men and turn to women for love, find the same problems? What's going to happen when they feel they have no place to go? She really felt strongly about that. She wanted the book to say, you know, it's no easier.

B.　Well, I disagree. I think that it is easier. It isn't *easy*, but it's easier. I think that, ah well, unfortunately, I feel I'll start repeating what I said earlier. What I *have* been saying is that it's easier. There's more understanding, and less tension, and less hostility. In other words, there's more potential there for an intimate relationship. I'm saying that it's easier to have an intimate relationship with someone who's the *same* than to struggle through a lot of differences. For instance — I think this is true in other ways, too — I find that it's easier for people who come from the same religious background, because they have similar cultural patterns in their background, in the way they were raised. It's easier for people from the same geographical area, I mean, say, the differences between the East and the South.

R.　There are two different levels. I've found the same thing that Ellen found. I thought if I worked out my feelings around women, I would be able to get in a close relationship with women or men. And that the way to get into intimate relationships was to find out what it was all about, in terms of my feelings for women. And I've tried to get into long-term relationships with women, to find out whatever my fears are. It's intimacy, for me, it's not whether it would be with a man or a woman, because I repeat the same patterns. I chose women who have other lovers, like I did with men. I have the same problems around being close to someone and saying what I want. Maybe it's like you say, it's easier for me to take a risk with a women, in some ways, to say what I want, because she'll be more accepting, maybe, than a man. But it's still hard, it may be easier, but some of the problems are the same.

B.   Yeah, but I see a lot of differences, too. I mean, I don't see that being able to be close to a woman means that I have to be close to men. It may, and it may not. One thing, that isn't one of my goals. Like, I really don't see. . . .

R.   My goal isn't to be close to men, but my goal is to be in a relationship that's really intimate and that carries over a long period of time. And I'm not in one. That would be my goal; I don't care who the person is.

B.   You see, Ellen's statement angers me. I disagree with it completely. I don't like the bit about 'angry women!' I mean of course women are angry, but to me that sounds like "See how these women are screwed up!" and "Now they're turning to women, but they're so screwed up, that isn't going to help, and what are we going to do with all these screwed-up, messed-up women, when they find that *that* won't work, either?"

347

R.   I don't feel that's what she was saying. I mean, I thought that what she was really saying was that, when you really got down to relating, the problems around relating, around being close, are the same hard problems with men or women, that being close to a person is really difficult.

B.   Well, that's true. I think that traditionally, in intimate relationships between men and women, women have been more of the nurturer; they've been more the emotional glue in the relationship. They bring out the tensions in the relationship, they resolve, they pacify, they smooth over, they do all those things that help keep a relationship together. Well, what happens when you have two women, you know, two women struggling in a relationship, they have to *share* that role. . . .

R.   The nurturing role?

B.   Yeah. So already, you have a difference, because already you've broken one of the patterns. Not completely, of course, because women have absorbed that role to different degrees, and there are all kinds of other things happening.

R.   But if two people are more willing to do that nurturing, and focusing on whatever's going on within the relationship, that is wonderful!

B.   Right! So there's a difference right there.

R.   True. It has to do with patterning.

B.   I think that men are more interested in taking from a relationship than giving. So what do you have when you have two givers?

R.   Do those people have trouble receiving?

B.   Right. They have to learn to receive.

R.   Have you had trouble receiving?

348

B.   Yeah, I think I do have trouble receiving. But it's been a very warm experience for me to receive, very nice; something I never experienced with men. And I'm learning, I mean, that is something that is coming into my life.

R.   To let someone do something for you?

B.   Right.

R.   What about power? How do you think about power in a relationship? How does that come into play?

B.   Well, the major power is the power to be able to terminate the relationship, or, you know, change it drastically. I think my feeling is often that the other person has the power. That's because I tend to be pretty passive.

R.   Does it bother you, that they have the power?

B.   Well, no. I really give it, in the sense that I'm passive, so it doesn't bother me that much. But I'm more of a reactor than an actor and I rarely end relationships, for instance. And power, to me, seems to be an issue in a relationship when things aren't going that well. I usually don't see power as a big issue when things are all right, then it seems to be pretty equally divided. Except that I've felt, you know, a number of power frustrations with men that come from the whole politics of it all. I mean, men have a potential power, even if they're not in a place where they're exercising it.

R.   How do they have potential power?

B.   They have the social assets, the economic assets. I'm trying to think of something that someone said the other day, I don't think it was you, a woman was telling me about some couple in which the woman was supporting him, and the usual roles were reversed. We were talking about why she was so miserable, or why she was under this man's control.

349

And the reason was that *he* could change the relationship at any time. He was acquiescing to not working, and he had the power, because if he decided to assume the role of the strong one, he could. Men always have that option.

R.   Physically strong?

B.   Physically strong, economically strong, going places. It's easier for a man to go places than for a woman. I think it's a little easier for a man to meet people, all kinds of advantages.

R.   Right. I guess I'm talking about power in terms of control, and I guess you are too, but control within a relationship.

B.   Well, those things make a tremendous difference. I really think so.

R.   I think you are absolutely right. We had a discussion about women who get involved with women, and we defined four types, four ways. Do you want to talk about it?

B.   Yes. Maybe you've got everything I've had to say about it, but it's something that I'm interested in, and I'm constantly exploring.

R.   Yeah. I would like it to come in your words, but I'll go over my notes. Okay, one type, the first type was Julia and me, who had it in our heads for a real long time to love women, had always liked women, sort of feared it and didn't know what to do. We were involved with men. It took us ten years to act on it. The second type was like you and Ellen who have been involved only with men during your lives. Women were your friends. Ellen got involved in the movement, and one day at a weekend workshop she found herself making love to a woman. She hadn't thought about loving women before. I assume your relationships were like that at first.

B.   Yes, my thing was losing contact with men for negative

reasons, because I didn't like this and I didn't like that, and getting closer to women, and then falling in love with a woman. But not thinking, "well, I'm going to be a lesbian and maybe find somebody," but I really became attracted to a woman I grew very close to.

R. You weren't aware of having sexual feelings for women when you were younger and wondering about yourself? You were probably so busy with your work (laughing) you wouldn't even know if you had those feelings. I know you now, I know how your kind works. I've always envied people like you. Now I understand (both laughing). Like, I kept on asking my friend Mandy, did she ever have any of those feelings for women? And she'd just push them back, and never get to a place where she could deal with them.

B. Maybe that's what happens.

R. And there were two other types we talked about.

B. Well, the third type was the woman who always related to women, and has always related to women sexually. The pattern I see is that, occasionally, they relate to men, but often at the urging of a psychiatrist or parent, or to show or prove to themselves that they don't like men, and to try it. . . .

R. They just knew that they would fall in love with women. They just wanted women. And the fourth type was the mode that I don't feel comfortable with. When you sleep with other women as a statement of the movement — women who are into an intellectual — ideological trip. I do doubt, however, that there are many women like that. I am also uncomfortable with women who sleep with other women because "bisexuality is in."

I wanted to ask you if you feared you were a lesbian? Ellen said she freaked *after* she slept with a woman, like, OmiGod! How did you feel after you slept with a woman?

B.   I didn't get freaky, of course I'd been primed too. I mean, a lot of people were doing it at that time, and so I had been in a fair number of discussions about reactions to women sleeping with women, and things like that. So I had time to think about it. But I just felt this tremendous surge of freedom. I had this tremendous high!

R.   Why?

B.   I always thought it was a barrier. I had thought that, I mean, it never dawned on me before, but when I was getting closer to women, and lesbianism was becoming an issue for me, I always thought, well I might like women a lot, but all my inhibitions, all my socialization! I could never sleep with them; I just wouldn't be comfortable. It wouldn't be a plea-sure to me; it would just be, I couldn't do it! That was my feel-ing. I just couldn't do it. And I didn't want to do it; why should I want to do it? But what I got was freedom! I could do it! You know, half the human race is opened up to me. It was very positive. And I was really happy because I had been mostly socializing with women, and now there were all these new vistas; I could relate to them in different ways. And also what was important was that I got to fulfill my sexual needs with women, because I was beginning to worry a little about my sexual needs and where I was going to get them fulfilled.

R.   You said it was like a relief. You had an alternative, while your other women friends were dealing with where they were going to find a good man. You had found your alternative. Were you ever worried about whether you were okay because

352

you slept with women?

B.   No, because I was pretty well politicized by then. I had always been very liberal toward homosexuality. And I grew up in an era when, well, obviously, there were some negative connotations, but while I was in college, homosexuals were studied, their subcultures were studied, but it wasn't like there was any heavy negative judgment trip.

R.   Now you're taking on the label of lesbian; is that political too?

B.   Well, I'm not sure what else I'd call myself.

R.   Well, actually, in a sense, your sexuality is . . . you know, you've been involved sexually as much with men. In fact, in that article that I showed you on female orgasm they were talking about people not knowing the definition of bisexuality. But I think it's the awareness of having feelings for both sexes, physically and emotionally, whether they are expressed or not. It's really who you are, not who you sleep with. Whether you express it or not. Did you ever have any feelings that you — negative feelings that you were sort of masculine? I used to feel masculine and aggressive.

B.   Oh yeah. Oh yeah. I mean, because I've been a high achiever and in a man's world, I've always been made to feel that somehow I was too aggressive. I was just a little too masculine. It was never in relation to my looks or things like that, but how I behaved. I was a little uppity.

R.   Did you feel ugly? How did you feel?

B.   It was usually in a relationship. I tended to be in relationships, so that's a cushion. Because if you have a relationship, if I had a relationship going, I didn't feel weird, you know, because I could make it both ways. That's the way I

353

liked to think about myself.

R.   You could be aggressive, but you could still have your relationships?

B.   Yeah. I could be feminine and great and fill all those roles, and I could be aggressive and outgoing and achieving too.

R.   I was in a relationship, too, but I would still feel ugly. When I lived with Larry and went to work every day and would have to fight with some of those men to get something done, sometimes I felt ugly.

B.   Well, I have never felt that I was unattractive. I've never felt that I was especially ugly. I have felt that I was sort of average-looking, and sometimes I looked better than others, but I never had a real heavy 'I hate my looks' thing.

R.   Are you sure you're Jewish? (laughing) What did you learn from being with other women?

B.   Your questions are good about giving and receiving. We talked about a lot of that. Things about passivity and activity. A lot of those ideas have been really good.

R.   Tracy said she put less focus on orgasm, more focus on pleasuring, just a more total perspective.

B.   Oh, yeah. I have a lot more extended love-making, although probably not *that* extended, but extended for *me*. Affection, much more into affection.

R.   Isn't that delightful? That's one thing that came out with all the women, that they felt that one of the main things they learned was all different degrees of affection.

B.   And also the ability to be more childlike, because I guess with men, I really repressed that, because there was too much of the child-father thing, and I really stayed away from

354

that, anything like that bothered me.

R.   Acting child-like with a man?

B.   With a man, yes. But with a woman, I've very comfortable doing that, and so that's been another thing that's opened up for me.

R.   Yeah, I think I've always been playful, sort of childlike. How about mothering? Phyllis Chesler points out that female children usually don't get nurtured or mothered in this culture as often as male children. I always like to be touched and have women hug me, or just stroke me on the head. I just love that affection now.

B.   Well, I'm afraid of all the things that I said — I wasn't craving affection from anybody. I didn't have these feelings towards women.

R.   But if you're receiving, that child-like thing is just really nice to have. You weren't aware that you even wanted that?

B.   I was aware of wanting it, but I just never let myself do it with men.

R.   Being child-like, you mean, and letting men mother you?

B.   Yeah.

R.   When one of my old male friends asked me why I wasn't married about two years ago, I said that I thought I liked women. At the time he went through this whole thing about how he saw me as really wanting to be taken care of, which shocked me, because I was into my heavy independent trip. I was just touched, because I really did want to be taken care of. He could see that. And he then went on to say he didn't mean this as a put-down of women, that men responded over a continuum and I could find a man who would be mothering and nurturing as a woman, which I do believe is true.

B.   Well, I think that everyone wants to be taken care of, and some people know how to touch that nerve.

R.   You mean, to get it, or to ask for it?

B.   Well, to even know that: "Oh, you want to be taken care of!" Because no one wants to grow up, and everybody wants to be a child and to be taken care of. Everybody likes that feeling. I don't think that was any very big revelation.

R.   Well, I was shocked, because I've always been playing this real independent trip, and it's just now that I'm really very strongly aware that I can even admit to myself that I want to be taken care of. I mean, I want that, and I also want to take care of somebody.

B.   I'd like to be taken care of, but only in a sort of superficial kind of way. If somebody *really* starts to take care of me, then they probably take care of my independence, which I also treasure.

R.   I like my friendship with Thomas. I mean, that's been the most incredible kind of friendship that I've had. You know, the way he picked me up at your house and asked if I felt like I wanted to stay longer? I didn't even think about it. He just said: "Are you sure you want to leave right away?" and he said: "Well, call me back in ten minutes." I finally said I didn't want to leave. I mean, he's just supportive, he just takes care of me, and is aware of how I'm feeling.

B.   Well, that's sensitivity, waiting until you're ready to go.

R.   I really appreciate that kind of taking care of, I just love that. We all should learn to share that nurturing mother role — both men and women!

R.   Do you ever feel a sense of tension about being a lesbian or being bisexual? What do you do with your feelings towards

356

men? Do you have any sexual feelings towards men?

B.   Oh, I feel much better towards men since I started relating sexually to women. Because they aren't threatening. Because before, they were the only alternative. If I didn't find men that I could relate to, then I wouldn't have a relationship. I wouldn't have any sexual relationships, that's for sure.

R.   Right.

B.   But once I started relating to women, then men were much less of a hassle, because I felt more comfortable. I didn't need them anymore, so I wasn't threatened by them, and I felt much better. I don't think they've changed, but it's just that I don't have to be quite as defensive.

R.   Ellen was saying that one day they'll change too. They won't need some woman to need them. And they won't need to play the roles that they have been playing. Maybe eventually we'll all come to a solution. I had found that because I was putting much more emphasis on my relationships with a woman, that women were become in a sense the "enemy." I was uncomfortable with women that I really craved; I just couldn't relax. Finally I decided I just tried too hard and made them too important. And that I had the same situation that I had had when men were so important. You see what I mean? Let's quit.

Being Happier and Closer to my Core

When I was in Puerto Vallarta with Becky I was feeling very badly on the inside, and yet when I looked at myself in

357

the mirror I was quite surprised to see that I looked lovely. Usually when I felt badly and ugly inside, I looked ugly in the mirror. But something was slowly beginning to happen to me, the stronger and better I felt about myself. I was just feeling better in general and so even though I hurt a lot inside, my outside just refused to go with the usual signals. It was a period when I began to let go and let things be okay. I was becoming more connected to myself. The strong professional woman in the suede jumper who scared me was not connected to me. The more I connected my inside feelings with my outside the more I could see myself clearly and the softer and lovelier I felt.

In the mirror I look soft and beautiful. Inside I feel hard, detached and torn in pain. It is hard to imagine that my body belongs to the person who smiles softly out at me. She looks more beautiful and fine each month. It is a strange paradox. I begin to see myself as beautiful when I look into the mirror, yet I feel more and more removed from myself at the same time. There are two of me. Maybe I am building a center from the outside in.

I was depressed before I left for Puerto Vallarta. My panic was a caricature of myself. My body was rebelling one more last time. I was reaching a place where I finally was going to let myself be happy.

I want to be wild, feel
every nerve in my body
catch every breath there
is to be

I wrote in my journal:

It is a strange thing that I have discovered here in California. Coming all that way through all that turmoil I tried to leave behind in Washington, D.C. The closer I get to my core, the more calm and controlled I've become, the happier and younger I feel. Inside/outside paradoxes. I feel younger in my maturity. In California I feel younger when I am over 30 than I did in D.C. when I was 21. I feel so much less in turmoil and so much stronger. In those days I was frightened to death. So young and frail. I thought I could easily break. I had no idea how strong I was or that indeed I am strong.

I feel a sense of rebirth. I certainly have more fun now. Partially, I've reabsorbed my life this past year, withdrawing from the active world, getting to know myself. I am emerging anew, refreshed and quite excited. I am still not used to being so happy and having my life so settled.

HOW IT FEELS TO BE CLOSE

(for J. S.

People don't talk about how it feels to be close. The gentleness and awe of being in love, the awe of discovering each other's bodies. Smells and sensuous feelings are rarely mentioned.

THIS is the place I put the feelings I wanted to see in a book about women sharing their feelings. It is a record of some of my feelings from my relationships with other women. Its flow is like a narrative. I would recommend it to be read like poetry. It may be too intense to be read in one sitting. The narrative itself resumes on page 414.

I have also included some writings by other women and excerpts from the interviews.

Ruth

Journal
January 1973

The long tender warm close nights

silk hair, firm bodies underneath

cool sheets

Jessica being soft, her hair hanging and lovely

January 1973
Journal

who will be my primary love

who will hold me, love me, stroke me

crave me the long long nights of my life.

We had gone horse-back riding that day up the winding hills of Marin. The two of us on our horses — Jessica on Nepenthe with his head always lurking forward and me on Shadow his firm body as calm as his brown-toned skin. We had ridden up the ridge above the trees. It was all very romantic. We came home to Jessica's house and took a long hot shower as our bodies melted against the driving hot water. Sore muscles relaxed with such pleasure that I barely had the energy to move from the shower.

We held each other closely and felt the warm coolness of our long nude bodies. Fresh bodies exhilarated by our closeness and the sweet tiredness of exhausted relaxed muscles. We kissed and I lay on top of her feeling her silky body against me as she stroked my back slowly with her finger tips. Her smell was sweet as I lifted myself to look at her breasts and face. We just smiled deeply and hugged again tightly. I told her I saw her as a gift and she echoed my feelings.

Then there was a long silence and she said when Michael comes we wouldn't be able to hold each other again. And I felt in my ecstasy that it would be a crime against the universe if we no longer were able to hold each other and feel our silken bodies and pounding hearts.

Journal
November 1972

                         Ruth
                       ╱
Mirror Image
                       ╲
                         Jessica

mirror image

I compete with you

and you with me

We show each other

we are beautiful

don't we know it

without the reflection

I didn't know it without the reflection

Journal
February 1, 1973

Jessica she gave me gifts

   of her

   of me

Lisa said Yvonne loved her

in part because she was a

woman and wanted to make love

to a woman. She added

I know she loved me too.

Another memory of running up the hill at Muir Beach
by Jessica

I remember the scents — the moist earth, the pungent
chapparal I've never smelled anywhere but California and the
brisk, clean after-the-rain salt air from the ocean below, blowing up so strong it seemed to fill my lungs without my even
taking a breath.

I remember feeling we were so special that day — you
and I — so alive and full of energy and having such fun!
Everyone else seemed so lethargic by comparison and I
almost felt impatient that no one had the energy you and I
did. At one point I told myself I was being "adolescent"
gamboling about and that I should grow up and calm down!
But I couldn't contain my joy. I felt like a kid in love turning
cartwheels. I loved you, I loved Alan, I loved these people we
worked with, I loved this special place. It was one of those
rare moments when everything, but everything was all right.

Julia

"In the beginning we would hug

goodbye, things like that and then

that sort of stopped . . . I forget

that that's really a sign that

things are *too* intense a lot

of times."

Stroking my head

I had begun to learn to ask for what I wanted. I shyly asked her to touch my head. I had always felt that if someone stroked your head that meant a special kind of caring.

I love it when she pulls my hair off my neck with her hand and rubs my neck. The pulling of my hair back always feels so motherly to me and warm.

Nurturing

Late last night I went over to Brooke's house. When I
arrived she was in bed reading an autobiography about
Thomas Jefferson. The room was very warm and two small
lamps indirectly lit it. I washed up and got into bed and
curled up beside her. That comfort, that nurturing, the light
in her room and the wind going through on a summer evening
was bliss for me as her hand went gently through my hair
while she read. I felt comforted and reassured, such a simple
pleasure. Why I deprive myself I do not know. I fell asleep
cuddling myself against her body, listening to her turn the
pages of her book.

I remember that sound when I took my naps while my
mother was reading. I felt like a child. Before I fell asleep
Brooke talked about a description in Lillian Hellman's book,
Unfinished Woman, about a friendship between two women
. . . "Two strong talented women . . . I think that is the way
she phrased it. She said it is the first description she had read
of such a friendship. It was rare.

378

Anais Nin, *The Diary of Anais Nin*

A flippant evening. . . . June and I sink into this need of warmth and love. Gifts, praise, words, admiration, incense, flowers, perfume. . . .

We need each other. We do not know, at times, which one is the child, which one the mother; which one the sister, which one the older wiser friend; which one dependent, which one protective. We maintain a maddening oscillation, and we do not know what we want of each other.

Tonight it is June who says "I want to dance with you." It is June who leads me, she heavy and I light and willowy. We glide on the last beat of a jazz piece which is descending and gasping and dying. The men, in stiff evening shirts, stiffen even more in their chairs. The women close their lips tightly. The musicians smile, benign and malicious, rejoicing in the spectacle, which has the effect of a slap in the face of the pompous diners. They cannot help exclaiming that we are beautiful together. June dark, secret under the brim of her Greta Garbo felt hat, heavy-caped, tragic and pale, and I a contrast to her in every way. The musicians grin. The men feel insulted. At the table a waiter is waiting to tell us we cannot dance again. Then I call for the bill like a grand seigneur and we leave. I have the acrid taste of rebellion on my lips. We got to the Cabaret Fetiche. There the men and women were unmasked, at ease. We are not outcasts. Men struggle to catch our attention. June responds. I bristle with jealousy.

Marion N. Fay

"Woman shall . . ." she said, her words
descending among seaweed tangles where I soul-
diving search the inward aches buried hardened
beneath my former excavations, tears iced in
dank crustacean cold.

"From within . . ." she spoke again
reaching depth terrain, her sun-lustrous words
warming the stone cold shell and dark interiors,
softened, open luminous, my tears no longer
frozen like snow melt now flow.

Greta and Barbara

"We have a sexual relationship with each other. We hug and kiss and are turned on to each other. We sit on each other's feet. We don't fuck, we don't make love."

Tracy

"And we went to sleep and woke up the next morning and we got stoned and drank some coffee, and made love. It was incredible! It was just gorgeous. She is ravishingly beautiful, and that knocks me out — all the time — I just . . . worry about the fact that I'm so overwhelmed by her beauty, because it's sort of a nonfeminist thing to be, but she's just lovely. Her face was made for viewing at six inches — it's just exciting. And she's a very sexual woman. So, we made love, and it was like a continuous high for me, never an orgasm, but just that kind of wonderful plateau of ecstasy."

The fire roars and its light dances on the ceiling. Carol King plays in the background. Lying in Ginger's arms making delicious love I remembered the times I heard those very same songs and had wished that I had a lover. That made being with her even more delicious.

Journal
April 1973

Earlier this evening

Ginger walked clear across

an empty room to give

me a hug

She seemed so open and exposed

I felt that she was so brave

there was no question she was

walking directly to me

to hug me.

Journal
March 1973

She is not ashamed to

ask for what she wants

She is strong and

does not have asking for what she

needs as a conflict

with her strength —

it is her strength

tame me

teach me

not to be afraid

to be close

April 1973

She was upset about her work and some of her relationships that night. She was lying on the floor of her room, very upset and withdrawn. I tried to comfort her by stroking her gently. It was like stroking a piece of glass. Once she turned and smiled at me. After that we made no more connection.

She had removed herself from me shortly after we had returned from our trip to Big Sur. There were difficulties at work and there were all the other relationships she had to deal with here in the city. I tried to regain the closeness we had shared and some of the excitement that I had experienced with her the first few weeks after our trip. I wrote her a letter/ poem in my journal which I read to her on the phone. It was entitled I don't want "no package deals." I wanted more than just a weekend relationship. We saw each other a few times after that when it was good. Then it was all downhill. She withdrew from me.

April 1974
San Francisco

I wonder if it is weird to observe someones clothing, recognize a tee shirt and remember how it was to touch someone's body — remember touching her breast and a feeling of
sensuality running through my body. I find some comfort in
working in this room as once it held some comfort for me and
so much excitement.

The excitement: at the moment of its intensity feeling
high and turned on having spent a few hours drinking at a
neighborhood bar on Broadway and then driving home, following her in her car, stopping for some chocolate before
riding home — like one gallops over the plains — over the
hills of San Francisco. Anticipation. Coming home and lying
on the floor, lights dim, music on. She gets undressed. I just
lay in the dark waiting and feeling. My body lying in the dark
aware of her changing; why doesn't she just lie beside me?
Does she have to get undressed right away? And then she lies
beside me and I lie across the rug diagonally . . . only my
head near her and she said "why do you run away . . . did you
forget?" And then she gently pulls me toward her and holds
me. I pull away and hide as she runs her sensuous touch over
my body, making me come so alive in my sexuality.
I respond with such excitement when I let myself be won
over. I lose myself in my bodily feelings. It is as if I were out
of control. I reveal my passion. She touches me all over my
leotard. My body riffs with excitement. It hungers for her
touch and adjusts itself so that it is exposed in its entirety and

each part can be easily touched by her hand. I hold her and my body responds with a passion hidden from myself — unawakened for years. She says you just crave to be touched, as my body jerks and stops and presses forward to her touch.

The event holds a sweetness for me now. As I read the words I have just written . . . a distant sweetness, something like the fire as it becomes different shapes of the disintegrating paper in her fireplace, a sweetness that I am drawn to . . . almost too precious to feel. Like when waterfalls become a flame that sweetness, and the hot coals of a Point Reyes fire became cold snow of the alps.

PASSION

Do I expose my passion? It is one thing for women to gently love each other; it is to me beautiful and romantic. But to show my raw passion before the world . . . to my friends I am not sure that I would be capable of such revelation. I am not sure. No, it is that people would see a part of myself that I am not at all sure I want to expose. Am I feeling uncomfortable with my passion and perhaps lust? Is it not sweet or romantic to me. Am I afraid that it will scare others away, that it will scare me away? Or that I have revealed my hunger for touch?

We touched very gently, her hand just barely touching the skin of my cheek and running down it like a wisp of hair

And my hand touching her cheek gently as we both kissed, so gently and slowly that tears just welled up in my eyes and flowed uncontrollably down my face.

At that moment it seemed that all my life I had wanted to be able to kiss a woman that I loved that much.

Sally

"Faith and I were very close. I just
loved her. We lived together for years.

When she would sit down next to
me and touch me,
I would feel uncomfortable and
move away."

We used to sit up late talking, Anne

on her bed and me propped up on a chair

with my feet across her bed. Sometimes

when I was feeling warm I would put

my foot next to hers

She would move her foot away

When I was hurting

Sometimes I used to feel that

I hurt too much to be touched

I wanted to be with her and made sure that I saw her before the holiday. When I went over to her house I was so unsure of myself that I almost wanted to leave before I sat but for a minute. We talked awhile and fell asleep in the sun together. She got cold and went into the house and fell asleep on her bed. I was still outside in the sun, when the phone rang and she had a long conversation. And then I felt like a fool being there, so I got ready to go. She said, "Oh, are you going already?" And I said yes and she walked me down the stairs. I was thinking to myself: "Did she want me to stay? Should I ask to stay longer?" Then she gave me a hug . . . real close, that scared me and made me unsure that she was really meaning to hug me so close. There we were the only two people in this huge room. I remember that she was wearing a long dark thick robe and that when I felt her against me, her body getting so close that she stepped/tripped on my feet, I felt: "Is this a mistake? Does she mean to hold me so close?" Now there was no one else in the room so it had to be me. I think I pulled away a little and felt my heart gulp/hurt slightly. I was scared she got so close.

"It is the life long problem of only children that they doubt all affection that is offered, even that which has been proved, and so, as the years passed, I told myself that Sigerist had been polite and kind to me, but that I had not gone back to see him because I was not needed or wanted. I only recognized the vanity behind my lack of vanity when his daughter published part of his diary in which there is proof of what he felt for me."
—Lillian Hellman, *Pentimento*

Seeing Imogene last night

I was shy and uptight.

And it was so difficult to be

myself.

My friend uses her eyes to talk

and I look and then I look away.

And when I look she looks away.

Intimacy

I was alone

it took me a long time to partake

(I once read in a magazine somewhere
that Greta Garbo said this about herself.)

Why was it so hard for me to get what I wanted?

I was thinking while lying in Ginger's arms

when it seemed so easy and so simple

Why

Thanksgiving Dinner with Jessica
November 1973

We hadn't seen each other for a long time. After Michael moved in with her and her affair with Alan became more intense she had no energy for anyone else.

The silence between us was painful and heavy. I wondered what she was thinking. I was thinking about her and the deep feeling that I had that was almost a sob. I made casual remarks — not relevant to the feelings between us. We were always shy and awkward with each other. We tried to talk. Before we parted Jessica wanted to hug goodbye. We held each other tightly, and I began to cry. I hugged her as close as I could and aligned my body to hers. I smelled her sweet smell — oil from the Body Shop. Her hand rubbed my head, she remembered what I liked. Our feelings were so intense. It lasted a minute. It was still all there, all our feelings, all our love.

I like to sleep with Melinda

She kisses my back like I like to kiss my lovers' back

and likes to put her arms

around me.

She is as affectionate as I am.

She gets close. I've never had someone
feel close into me. That was scary. It
wasn't so much that you would feel close
into her but its almost like she enters you.

Alone

you are spaced

so I go home

to give you space

and I am

alone

I didn't ask for what I wanted.

Journal
October 1973

Sometimes I just don't find men as beautiful

as women, and feel that they are lucky

when someone like Jessica makes love to them.

Closeness
January 1974

I just returned from a walk through the winter-spring air.
Everything is so clear and crisp. I looked at all the new buds
from the trees and bushes and took in all the flowers in bloom.
As I walked I held my body against the hedges along the side-
walk and got as close to them as possible. At one point I gazed
into the thick hedges and looked at the world within, with
tiny branches going every which way. It reminded me of
being in the redwoods and ferns and feeling the soothing
comfort of the moist filtered fresh air of that special world. I
ran my fingers down the bark of a tree and felt the many
bumps and then walked and walked and loved each flower I
saw, especially the one big yellow reddish rose on the top of a
stock looking ever so proud. And then I thought of my friend
and how I know now I can be very happy and comfort myself.
But that I have to let go of all that I am holding on to — that
foolish agony in my head. And then I thought of writing a letter to her or just plain writing about what I feel so that all is
not buried so deep inside. Yet I fear that by writing I will only
be repeating the pattern of obsession about her.

I enjoyed very much getting close to you on our trip. It
was a special kind of closeness I had not felt before. I never
had a woman put her hand on my shoulder while we drove to
the airport in a car full of people. It felt like a declaration of
our new friendship. I felt awkward but loved it. We really are
going to be buddies. On the plane when you put your face

into mine you were so warm I wanted to cry. I just loved it. When you laid down to rest after we talked for a while in the infinite night of the jet plane — broken only by little lights surrounded by people and yet focused so much on each other — I loved the closeness I experienced with you. I loved your head in my lap and your arm wrapped around my knee. I never had experienced anyone feeling so close to me.

As we talked I was learning to know you and how you felt — how you felt close to the people you loved and why you left one behind. In the airport you played with a little toy man who walked funny when you wound him up . . . all men seem to walk funny when they are wound up. Your little face so open, childlike and warm getting a kick out of the funny dance that the little toy was doing.

I returned home so happy and wrote in my journal I felt that something very special had happened between us and I wanted to hold on to it.

And then came the painful part of calling you and asking you to do things or just to say hello . . . at times you seemed so far away. Or maybe just not interested. But then I thought too hard and too much. The relationship seemed to dwell so much in my head.

I felt what you had shared with me about yourself was very special. No one before had showed me so much of their feelings about themselves. As we held each other in bed you talked about your sister, your mother, your family. You showed me your feelings and told me that before you came to California you felt that you had no family. That touched me. I felt you. Other people I have gotten to know and liked I had not experienced in quite the same way.

I liked Alison because

she could easily make love to a lot of people

I wish I could be more like that

I decided that I was going to begin to take more responsibility for my relationships and start saying what I wanted. I was not going to expect that the other woman would initiate or that she had it together more than I around relating intimately and sexually.

I told her after the long meeting that I wanted to sleep and hold her and we went back to our room. She showered and got ready for bed and I got brave enough to move the two twin beds together.

April 1974

I have begun to get used to the start and stop of friendships in my experiences in California. Though I don't think
that anyone can ever get used to that. I just simply have
become more philosophical about it. Yes, that was our
closeness way back in October. It was real when it happened;
it was a nice moment that we had. I had hoped that that
moment would continue but it didn't. Or those intense kisses
with Melinda and with other women that evening of the
dinner party when we kissed and shared and were close. That
happened and it was part of my life but that closeness in the
relationships is no more.

That was strange. I mean

that's the trouble with so

many people — you get that

warm little bit of experience

they'll share with you, then you

can't even touch them again

emotionally

Often I had savored those feelings of how it felt when I held you. That warm closeness. Often I fell asleep with my arm across my chest holding my shoulder like I held you.

YOU CAN'T MAKE IT HAPPEN
Perhaps you can *let* it happen

Thomas had finished his book and decided that he would resolve the tensions in his relationships by June and be living with this woman friend of his that he had been liking for a long time. He said "It would be just too much for me to have my book done and my woman lover." And I said "You mean the universe wouldn't let you have both — a woman lover and your work done?" I think that one can have some control over their work and get it done. I am sometimes not so sure how much control one can have over their relationships.

They are not the kind of things that you can plan and say at this point in your life We will be here. You can want the close relationship but I have found that the more I try to get a relationship to be the way that I want it the more unlikely it will happen.

I have been surprised by the number of times I haven't been trying and fate somehow brought me what I wanted. Often with the person that I was trying so hard to be close to. But it happens so often when the other person wants it to happen. When that person wants to be close, not when I am trying to get it. It doesn't exactly make sense; I am learning to get more of what I want from people that I love by asking for what I want.

With Jessica I used to try to be close. Now that I don't try in the same sense that I was trying then; she unendingly surprises me with gifts and things that I always wanted

411

from a woman that I loved. I don't have the urgency for them, and there they are. Sometimes I've had a hard time believing that this is happening to me. That my universe does include such wonderful things.

Jessica: our closeness isn't like my fantasy of closeness. On some levels it is not as romantic as I fantasized. Especially when we talk about where we are and how we feel about our process and our relationship. It is very practical. But then it's romantic when we have wine and then she says "Wait a toast," and says "To our love," and I smile shyly, not daring to look into the universe. I didn't even have the nerve to fantasize about that one and she gave it to me. Sometimes there is an unreality when she toasts to our love or when she gives me a gold chain and looks at me when I am leaning over her writing and she says "the chain looks just like I wanted it to look on you." It is hard for me to look at it straight in the eye, perhaps like Jessica's "looking a poppy straight in the eye."

I could say that on some levels I am afraid to let it all in, to let in all her love of me.

What do you do when you finally start getting the things you want after you have been invested so long in trying to get them?

D.C. '74

I left D.C. in 1972, but it took two years to leave officially.
In fact, I had to go back to find out that I had *left a*
long time ago.

I had left D.C., its power and intensity and work,
That's what I had left.

Last year before I began the second draft of the book I felt
that I needed to go back East to see my old friends. It was
time for a vacation, but more than that it was time for me to
come up for air after all the writing I had done that past year.
Before I withdrew from the world again to write I needed to
touch my past life in D.C. and to test my reality.

After the trip I came home feeling how sane my life is
here. Back East I was labeled "insane." There I was "insane,"

414

here I am sane. Here I love women and men, I am assertive, into my work, and not in a couple. I am 32 years old, I play a lot, and I don't work the traditional 9 to 5 shift. I am very comfortable with who I am. Here there are a lot of people like me to play and work with.

Back there among the people I was with I was an oddity. I did not live the proper life, and behave "right."

On Going East

I had flown to Boston first to visit with Mandy and Pam. I wanted to understand my relationships with my old friends. I thought perhaps I was not seeing what had been there for me, their affection, and that if I had clearly asked for what I wanted, I would have gotten more support and more strokes. Talking to Mandy and Pam, I learned I was wrong. It was then that Mandy had said that I should have left; I did not fit in, I was in the wrong place.

When I finally flew down to D.C. from Boston the pain of discussing old feelings with these friends was just too great. What was the point?

Once in D.C., Eric picked me up at the airport and brought me back to the house. Anne was waiting in the living room, sleeping on the floor. She had fallen asleep on the floor while watching TV. When I knocked on the door, I woke her up. The expression on her face, disoriented from just waking, was just like my mother's. The transference was complete.

The next day I visited with Anne until late afternoon. We had been talking about my book. I had given her the outline.

For the first time in a long while we were talking frankly to each other. Just as I felt that we had finally begun to open up to each other, I had to run off to a meeting. As she read the outline she said it is too bad you didn't know all these things before. We never really finished the conversation. I tried to bring it up again later, but it just didn't work. We did not talk again until that last ride to the airport when she told me she couldn't tell me she loved me because it was too threatening to let herself know.

I had a scheduled meeting in town with a friend I had funded when I was at NIMH, so I ran off to meet him. I drove through old Alexandria, then caught the drive along the Potomic to the Memorial Bridge, and into D.C.

It was on this ride into the city that I knew that I had left.

The streets reaked with

a thickness and a moisture

of heaviness.

A super — real reality one gets

only after one has left and returned

and only in the very second

the very instant

of the return.

The city was under construction. A subway is still being put in, and Connecticut Avenue was still being torn up. I rode over the boarded street as I looked at the new buildings. I had just passed the White House and the Executive Office Buildings down from the corner on Pennsylvania Avenue. One could not help be aware of the power, and the abuse of power, in this city. I felt it almost oozing from the new federal office buildings, from the very pores of their red bricks.

This was the city of Watergate. Living in Washington I sometimes had to fight from becoming so immersed in the city that I lost all distance, all perspective. This is just one of the spots on the earth, not the only spot, not all the important things in human existence happen here.

I parked my car in the garage at Florida and Connecticut Avenues and walked over to my friend's office. I passed the restaurant where I had lunch with my first boss in Washington — Arthur Peal from the American Friends Service Committee.

It was hot and humid and I was glad to reach the shady side of the street.

I was a bit excited and filled with anticipation as I entered the building, where Dan's youth project was located. I had been there before as another person, as a frantic person. I stopped in the ladies room to look at myself. I said to myself, pleased with my reflection, "You look lovely." Never before in all the years in D.C. racing to meetings did I tell myself that I was lovely or did I feel that I looked lovely. I had felt that I looked attractive, professional, competent, but never did I feel that I was soft and never was I so pleased.

I forgot that people in D.C. are very busy and often are late. I arrived at Dan's office to find that he had tried to get me earlier and that Jane the other person we were to meet was delayed. Dan had another appointment and asked if I would mind waiting for awhile. I was angry that I had interrupted my conversation with Anne. But I realized that I should have called and checked to see if he were running on time.

I went downstairs to wait. I wanted to be outside in the city with my new feelings. I sat on the steps and just looked up at the Hilton and then down Connecticut Avenue. I was so pleased that I had left and that indeed my life in D.C. was over.

When Dan came out of the building we walked and talked. He didn't look me in the eyes. He was going a mile a minute about the youth programs and projects. I said something about how glad I was to no longer be at NIMH. And how I used to run around this city so frantically. He reflected that he had the feeling, when he would call me at NIMH, that I was like a wound up top, and that if I let go I would go spinning down the hall. And he jokingly spun around on Connecticut Avenue as we walked under the trees while the Friday night rush hour whizzed by. The only trouble was that he was spinning more and more. We had changed places.

Upon returning to California I was elated. I wrote in my journal:

May, 1974

How lucky I am to be back. How lucky that I live here. How lucky that Berkeley exists. And that there is a thing called feminism!

THE CORE ISSUES

WHEN I began this book I wanted to write something beyond the pain. What are we going to do next? I felt that if women were going to take power we have to devise new perceptions and new ways so that we do not find ourselves like the men and the society we are trying to change.

In writing this book I wanted to teach myself to rely on my own experiences and feelings. To be my own authority for my life. These core issues are a summary of some of the things I have learned on my journey (from myself and from other women). I want to share with other women and encourage them to test my perceptions against their own.

The issues that I raise here are the major areas and questions I am working on in my own life. I had hoped to go into them much more deeply and have all the problems worked out in my life before I finished this book.

I remember once in the early stages of the book complaining to Tracy that I wanted a lover, and that I was trying to work out issues of intimacy for myself so I could go on with my writing. She said "If you wait to work out of these issues you will never get the book out. The things you are dealing with are the problems of a lifetime."

I hope others will continue to develop and explore these areas in their own journeys. What I have learned I feel will be useful in anyone's struggle toward independence and in developing their own power.

The core issues by their nature are overlapping. Many involve erasing the restrictions of sex role stereotypes. In writing the core issues I have tried to describe the process I went through to explore these areas.

THE PLEASURE OF BEING ALONE

VERY little do we hear about the pleasure of being alone with oneself. In California one of the wonderful things that I discovered was the pleasure I could give myself and the pleasure that I found being connected to the earth.

I was so afraid of being alone that I mostly thought of it in negative terms — loneliness, isolation, without a lover. The media talks of women alone — meaning a woman without a man — a single woman. For me exploring other meanings of being alone has been not only enriching but very nourishing. It is the only way that I could have completed a book of this intensity and one covering such a painful period of my life.

IN OUR SOCIETY WE DON'T KNOW THAT IT IS OKAY TO SPEND TIME ALONE.

We are always supposed to be part of a group or in a couple. Society says that it is not okay to be alone. In fact this society encourages people to spend time in groups, in couples, or to be with their family. Women especially are not encouraged to go off and be alone, or do what they want, let alone to go off and do their own work. We have been taught that is selfish. Society has raised women to nurture other people, not themselves or each other. And mothers most often nurture their sons, not their daughters.

When the bottom fell out of my life in Topeka my first year in California, when two of my closest friends, Jessica and Alan, moved away from me into a couple, I reached a place in my life where I began to realize my old ways of feeling better no longer worked. That I could no longer run to other people to fill my void — or make another relationship which would see me through a few more years. That was not healthy and what's more it didn't work. I was so torn apart no more reassurances could help. I had only what was left of me to rebuild myself with.

I realized in anger then that the only one that could help me was me. I wrote a series of poems in my journal:

I have

  no insides

I am alone

  no one

  can help me

No one can deal

   with the static

    frantic, pain

    that cycles out of my mouth

      where is my soul?

Will I last

Will I survive

Will I not self-destruct

and fly

fly off into pain

At what price

all those screaming painful

wars

at what price?

is there

a bottom?

is there a limit?

will there be an end

    to my pain?

it goes forever, you see

with no padding on either

side, it is just a shell which

holds my void, not even a strong

shell to hold a full and radiant

echo —

a tin echo of hell.

The container of my

    void is not yet healed

the intensity of the day leaves me raw

inside

outside

   emptiness

bleak.

All I am is me.

Oh I hurt so

   deeply

my only

salvation is in my

   solitude —

no "one to help me"

   hold me

and help me to fill the

   hollow empty

     space

It was during this period when I was hurting so much that I had a long talk with Jessica, who taught me so much about being alone and comforting myself. Jessica and I were having difficulty communicating when our relationship became very painful and intense particularly around Alan, so we asked a mutual friend, Jerry, who was a therapist, to sit and listen to us talk. Our tensions and anger over Alan were not resolved at this meeting but our friendship has survived that ordeal. What was most important to me was I began to learn another meaning for being alone.

Jerry and Jessica told me that I needed to spend more time alone and I yelled: "What do you mean I need to spend more time alone. I have spent lots of time alone! I came to California alone! I travelled to France alone! I ride my horse alone!" In fact I was sick of doing things alone. I had lived in D.C. my last year alone. Yes I could handle being alone competently and professionally but they were talking about *enjoying myself being alone*, comforting myself. That was a different thing than I thought being alone entailed. It never occurred to me to pleasure myself when I was upset. I never thought to hug myself or stroke myself gently.

Being alone was something I could do successfully. I had gone to Aspen alone for a week of skiing my very second year after college and had had a good time. I have travelled to Europe by myself, but these times alone for me were a strain. I had to push myself to go out and meet other people. I was never quite comfortable. Imagine a full day of skiing, home for a nap and then pushing myself to go out for a drink so that I could meet someone to go to dinner with, if I hadn't as yet met Mr. Right on the slopes. The tension of being alone was that I always had to put energy out to meet people.

BEING ALONE MEANT HAVING TO
MEET PEOPLE, NOT BEING WITH MYSELF.

How much easier it would have been had I learned to enjoy my own company and found myself as exciting as a favorite friend — or for that matter *just felt it was okay to be alone*. The pressure certainly wouldn't have been so great. In fact I would have been more relaxed.

"What's wrong with that girl. She is eating dinner alone!" When I was in my early 20's I would feel very ugly inside sitting eating dinner alone — wondering what people were thinking of me. I remember one time going out with the "nice Jewish boy of my life" for dinner and seeing a lady at the other table who was eating alone, on a Saturday night. "How sad and pitiful" I thought of her. What was really sad and pitiful was my relationship to Jared. I would have been better off eating dinner alone than being in that relationship with all that pain!

Jerry commented that he could never imagine me taking long hot baths and relaxing with candlelight. I could never slow down that much to relax. I was always so frantic that I would be alone. Jessica urged me to take care of myself first. She felt that was most important, to learn how to nurture myself. When I learned how to comfort and pleasure myself I began to feel very powerful.

I believe that my feeling that it was not okay to be alone contributed to my discomfort of being alone with myself and added to my franticness. I never allowed myself to sit still long enough to be with myself — consequently I rarely comforted myself. I could never settle into myself.

Let me explain this conflict more clearly. When I came to California my main goal in life was to have an intimate relationship with someone. I think I put it in terms of "an enduring relationship." I would say that even though my life had been filled with exciting times and successes, the main thing that was missing from it was an enduring relationship. So I was in constant battle with myself because often when I did enjoy being alone, reading and feeling close to myself, I would feel torn . . . Shouldn't I be out meeting and being with other people? If I kept constantly complaining that I didn't like being alone and wanted to be in a relationship, how could I expect to be in one unless I went out, met people and stopped spending so much time alone? A part of me was always thinking that I was missing out on a chance of finding a lover and therefore not being lonely.

And

Sometimes I was afraid I

would like being alone

so much that I would

always be alone.

The conflict: being alone, enjoying myself,

liking being alone but thinking I should

be with people because I felt so alone, and that

unless I were with people I couldn't meet someone to love.

I had no sense that being alone with myself would help me be closer to myself and that constantly going out to meet someone was going to do me no good. It was only much later that I realized my essential love — that primary lover I had searched for — had to be me. What was missing from my whole formula was me. The answer to my most basic question "Who will be my primary lover?" is me. I need to have myself before I can have anyone else.

When I felt painfully alone I had a hard time saying no . . . I want to be with myself. I always did what my mom told me. "Go darling! Through him you may be able to meet some other man that you care for." "If you are lonely don't sit home." Even if I enjoyed being with myself or a woman friend, which was often all the more pleasant.

I don't know that I actually ever heard my mother's voice verbalize those exact words, but she must have said similar lines in my youth. The voice I heard most often saying those things was society's. It was everywhere and had become so integrated in me that when I said no, I always felt maybe I should have said yes and gone out. It was not until I came to California that I actually felt the relief of saying no to a man without the after-taste of a slight pang of disquiet. (The relief of not having to spend time with men or giving them a chance because they are *men*, and I should get to know them, was wonderful!)

When I was living with Larry I would sometimes make an attempt to be alone, but would be so torn. I would say to myself: "What is wrong with me? I have someone I love dearly who wants to be with me often and now I want to be alone!" I would come home from an intense day at work and would want to relax or reflect on the day. Larry was always ready to do something, to have people over or go somewhere. When I indicated I wanted to be by myself for awhile, he would run off. Then I'd worry that he was off with another woman. So my time alone was hardly nourishing or free of distractions.

Inside/Outside

Because I was so focused on my feelings and the personal side of my life, I did not look outward enough to see that the negative messages I have in myself are something that the society is saying. "Don't spend so much time alone." "Don't sleep with other women." As I write this I think of a way I can work with my feelings. When I hear a conflict in myself and see that part of me wants to do something and the other part doesn't, I stop and look outward and ask what society says is the prescribed way of behavior. Then I go back inside myself and see how I feel about what I want to do. If the behavior in conflict is one of society's "shoulds" I try to be clear with myself and do what I want to do.

Often when I am in these conflicts it is because I want to do one thing and society has raised me to do another. Sometimes I tend to feel that these things are only my conflicts, that I am the only one with them, rather than looking outward, seeing them in terms of the total society and its messages. This is another level of the political.

I feel that since there are really few supports or societal messages for women to have our own space we must carefully guard our needs to be alone and stay connected to ourselves. It is even more difficult and perhaps more important to keep this space when one is relating in a couple, especially in a heterosexual couple.

Developing My Inner Core

After my talk with Jessica and Jerry I began to look at myself directly. I realized that I kept myself scattered and that I did not have a core.

Once Jessica, Alan and I were lying around talking and Alan or Jessica asked: "Where is your soul, your center?" My answer: "Outside in front of me." They said their soul was in their chest or in their head. I liked to think of myself as open and tried to keep everything out front. Mostly I was scattered and did not protect myself.

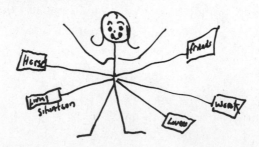

When I realized that I had no space within myself to go to for comfort, I started spending time with myself. I tried to get in touch with my feelings. I would spend hours with myself, taking long walks, reading, crying, hugging myself.

This time being alone was different than times before. I would listen to myself to see what I was feeling. I did not go for walks to distract myself but to feel my body move and to enjoy my feelings — to enjoy watching tall grass and flowers move with the wind.

If I were anxious instead of running frantically from activity to activity I would take time out to be still with myself, to get in touch with how I was feeling. Sometimes when I did, I found I was running from a lot of sad feelings. In Washington I would have never considered it legitimate to stay home from work to experience my feelings. I began to develop a core.

One of the first things I did being alone with myself was take that vacation to Puerto Vallarta, to recover and repair myself. Here for the first time I experienced the excitement and comfort with myself I usually got from a best friend. This time I had no interest in nor felt no pressure to be with other people.

The sheer delight of being alone after a full day of sun, sound, wind and foam rolling upon foam. A cool breeze through my room, a hot shower. Walking through my room nude, cool cream and then cool sheets. Reading, high-beamed ceiling with shingles interlaced. How can you do that with someone in your room? You can, but it's not the same and intimate.

I have gained a sense of power finding that I can give my-self some of the things I always wanted — strokes and comfort. That in itself is very nurturing.

I can make myself feel better. I don't have to go to other people for comfort. It is wonderful to get comfort from others, but it is also wonderful to discover you can comfort yourself.

Feelings

I began to explore the different ways that I could get in touch with my feelings to develop my inner core — my own inner space.

I found that I could get in touch with the different layers of my feelings through drawings. I am too much of a thinker and drawing not only allowed me to get out of my head but the process itself was very comforting and nourishing. As I described in the narrative I also used body and verbal therapies to get in touch with my feelings.

My journal too was and is a wonderful comfort! Writing in my journal freely and then reading my writings helped me to be closer to myself and understand my feelings. It is a wonderful way to learn to be with yourself.

I had a constant battle with myself trying to reconcile
my feelings and my intellect. It took me a long time
to accept that I didn't have to understand everything
I felt and did or that other women felt and did.

I learned to allow my feelings to emerge freely in me. And I allowed time for my feelings to make themselves clear to me. Doing this enabled me to trust myself more and to know myself. I consider my feelings another reality, as valid if not more so than rational reality.

If I am in a meeting with some people and feel they are uncomfortable or something is strange, though they say everything is fine, I always try to listen to my intuitions and feelings to understand what is happening between me and my friends and/or colleagues. Trusting my feelings has made me feel more powerful.

I discussed this pull between my intellect and my feelings with Jessica; she said: "Giving myself permission to listen to my gut and heart has allowed me to open up new powers. I feel much more intuitive and experience different kinds of sensory levels in addition to the rational. If I constantly feel I have to understand my feelings I distort them. Feelings are not rational and cannot be figured out in an intellectual way. Often when people try to figure out their feelings and can't, they feel bad and consider themselves "crazy." Right, we are

446

supposed to get it together in our heads. We are supposed to be cerebral and rational. Trying hard (pushing) to figure out our feelings can cut them off."

Structuring My Space

After I developed a sense of an inner core

and became aware that I needed to nourish myself,

I started looking at the way I

structured my outside space.

I drew little pictures to represent my

feelings and the way I envisioned my inside and outside

spaces

So very important to my sanity, a place to go to inside myself.

Doing what I want.

Tuning myself to my insides, developing an inner space,

a sanctuary.

447

Since I have learned to do this I have an inner space

that gets deeper and deeper and richer and richer.

Now I do not try always to catch the

bouncing ball at the right time.

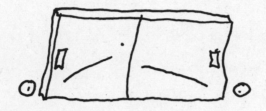

Structuring My Outside Space

Before, my outside space was linear

trying to catch each event as it occurred

rather than dimensional.

I missed the depth and joy of my inner world.

I lived by catching events rather than asking myself what I wanted to do in the universe. I had a sense that if I changed the way the cards came up I would miss something.

By trying to respond to every event and person that came along I allowed myself to be buffeted around by them.

Now I Try to Structure My Own Space

I control what goes in and out of my space and how I want events arranged.

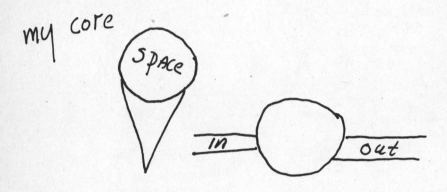

asking myself What I want to do? When do I want to do it?

Structuring my space from the inside not the outside.

I am taking responsibility and control of my space, taking control of my life.

In Washington I liked to let whatever happened in the day enter in rather than saying "No this is not good for me." It was like a game to see if I could fit all the events that popped up in one day into my life: tennis, a party, a meeting place, a day's work.

I have learned

and chose which events and people I want to see.

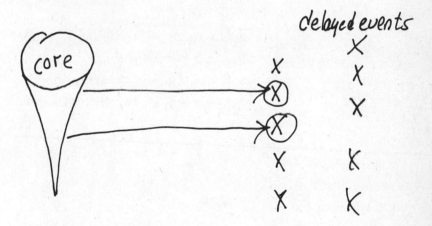

And I try to be sure that I have a balance of nourishing and pleasuable events in my life.

451

Seeing the way I dealt with my outside space in Washington made me aware of how I allowed myself to be scattered. By constantly running from one event to another I did not stay connected to myself nor did I take time to comfort and nourish myself. I discovered that when I would stand still I could derive more pleasure from myself.

I have found that responding from my core — doing what I want — helps me to do those things that are intrinsically important to me. I have found that if I listen very closely to what I want to do and do that I don't experience competitive feelings and am less apt to find myself in a competitive situation.

Nurturing Myself

When I decided I wanted to explore the meaning of being alone and nurturing myself further I decided to talk to Jessica again. Through our discussion it became very clear to us both that getting in touch with our feelings in and of itself was a particularly nurturing process.

An Inner Space
Developing this space is
nurturing yourself

What I want to emphasize here is something we both stressed. Jessica helped me get in touch with "being alone" with myself. But this past year she was involved in a relationship in which she did not take the space she needed for herself. A lot of factors affected her, but the point I wish to make is that we all go in and out of touch with enjoying being alone, being in touch with that inner space. In other words just because I *know* it is good to allow time to be with myself, and I have learned ways to nourish myself, doesn't mean I can always stay in that place. Sometimes I lose that sense and allow outside pressures and demands to swallow me up. It is difficult to keep in touch with that sense of being alone with yourself and maintaining your inner space. Writing down ways to deal with being along and nourishing yourself is one thing, dealing with it is an on-going struggle.

Each of us has or can discover our own ways to nourish ourselves. We have to find ways that will work best for us. Sometimes I find it easy to get in touch with my inner space and be still. Other times I am just too scattered or anxious to be able to comfort myself. No matter how long I sit or how deeply I breathe I just have to wait for whatever is going on in me to subside.

Nurturing

I discovered for myself that there are two different levels of nurturing. One level is the nurturing I do to comfort and protect myself when I am in pain. The other is the nurturing I do for myself to pleasure myself. They both can be the same activity but the distinction is important.

I learned about nurturing through my pain, but what has evolved for me now is treating myself well. Just enjoying doing good things for myself. I do not want to be doing good things for myself only as rewards or as comfort when I am in pain. I want pleasuring myself to be a part of my everyday life.

Ways that I have found to pleasure and nourish myself are:

Being with my horse, being outdoors, going for long walks, playing tennis, tap dancing, wearing clothes that make me happy, reading a comforting book, stroking myself and telling myself good things, going to a movie, playing with good friends, crying sometimes. Crying is very nurturing; it is not holding back feelings from myself. I even enjoy a long bath now! But I have found that by far the most nurturing thing is going to place inside myself, being with my feelings and being connected to myself.

What I am emphasizing here are the things we can do for ourselves alone.

On Monday after a very hectic and disturbing weekend I went up to the Berkeley Hills to my favorite spot in Tilden, the golf course, which is for me a very peaceful place that calms and stills me. And often its terrain with a stand of tall trees and green green grass reminds me of the east.

I sit there in the shade leaning against a lone bench beside a tree looking down over the golf course. I watch the people — their smallness emphasized by the gigantic vastness of the landscape and the tall trees surrounding them. Most people laugh about my visits to the golf course though few people once they have been there, haven't appreciated its fine beauty. The air is so clear that a fallen tree sticking up across the field seems as if it were in 3-D animation. Shadows, the cool breezes and the depth of field looking down and across the course is like I imagine an lsd trip to be.

The calm in the hills envelops me. I soon quiet my body to the ever present stillness. I sit on the ground with my knees folded up near my chest and my arms hugging them, occasionally my chin resting on my bare shoulders. I tell myself that I am so glad to be with myself. I love myself again. I had completely lost touch with myself this weekend. So much was happening which was so distracting. I became disconnected from myself. I just sit there very still, for three hours. I begin to feel soft, and to melt into myself.

When I returned to Berkeley to do an errand before going home I bumped into a friend who had been at my house this weekend. She said "My you always look pretty at the beginning of the week!" That is because I get Mondays to myself and relax and wait until I am in touch with myself before I begin my week's work.

Downstairs in the dining room the light of day peers through the windows. I can watch the trees and leaves and flowers of the Acacia shake and shimmy in the breeze. The light tones the chimneys on the big statuesque house across the way . . . leaves part of the chimneys bright yellow and other sides toned shadowed.

Receptive Mode

Another way that I have found to nurture myself is to listen to my own rhythm. And not push myself. Not being "a driven woman" was a hard lesson to learn. I used to always force myself to get my work done, or to do things I felt I should. Now that I ask myself what I want to do and try to follow my own flow, I find I have much more fun and more energy for my work.

It is a matter of learning how I am; not fighting myself.

Writing is a nurturing process for me. It has helped me to get more in touch with myself, to listen to my own rhythm. I have begun to think of myself as an instrument that I need to nourish and take care of so energy can easily flow from me. This is an entirely new mode for me. In Washington I always pushed myself. I did not have the easy sense of *letting* my energy flow.

I call my new mode the receptive mode.

It is this mode that I am trying to develop in my day to day life.

I ask myself what I want to do and try to get in touch with my feelings. I know I have a certain amount of work I want to get done. But I know if I push myself to do it — it is not going to happen very easily or creatively. This morning I awoke to a full day's writing schedule but I felt it was almost barbarian to bounce out of bed and begin right away. I felt like being outside, so I immediately left the house, did my errands and went for a long walk. I came back energized and ready to work. If I had sat at my desk the minute I got up, if I hadn't listened to myself, my energy would not have flowed. And I may have had a miserable day.

456

I see myself making sure I provide myself with enough time for pleasure. I treat myself in a way that things easily flow from me. I see myself nourishing the structure of my inner core,

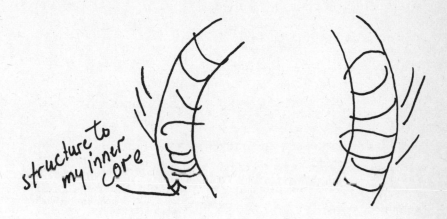

structure to my inner core

providing myself with good strokes so my energy flows.

I take care of this structure. I do not push it. I stroke it. The feeling is a sort of opening of myself; allowing me to emerge.

One of the ways I "stroke my structure" is to structure my space so it contains a balance of nourishing and pleasurable events. If I must do things that drain me, I try to make sure I put free spaces in between for pleasure, for being alone, to maintain a connection with my feelings. I try not to deal with too many heavy events in one day. I listen to my rhythm and see how much I can take. If it is better to deal with a heavy issue another day, I put it off. In D.C. I never would have thought of such a thing.

Alone

loneliness

Sometimes the loneliness of alone was

so intolerable for me that I used

to hope that I would become

so self-sufficient that I would

never need anyone again.

When I felt lonely I would get so frantic I would call a lot of people and talk. Now I can comfort myself or maybe spend time with friends or lovers, but sometimes the feelings of loneliness are still there. My friend Clara suggests it is best sometimes just to be still, hold your loneliness and feel it.

Being in a Couple and Intimacy

I had always felt if I were in a couple I wouldn't be lonely.

There is a fantasy about being in a couple that is taken on by people who see themselves as "single" and probably also taken on by people who see themselves in a couple; that they are not supposed to be lonely on the part of the couple: and on the part of the single person — that if they were in a couple they wouldn't be lonely.

During the period I lived in D.C. I thought I would be happy if I were only married or in a couple. I focused on having a man rather than being happy with myself.

I would feel supremely angry when I felt that I should be with someone. "How come there is no one in the universe for me to be a partner with? Help, help, I WANT A LOVER! And my anger turned into seething and tearful eyes. I just couldn't stand it any longer! I wanted someone for me. I wanted a lover." These feelings usually reached a crescendo around holiday time.

Sometimes I felt like a failure for
not having made it in a long term
relationship with a man.

Many of my women friends in D.C.
felt this same way. I saw
these same feelings expressed by other
women in *Our Bodies, Ourselves.*

It was particularly during the holidays that I often used my single women friends to reflect back to me that I was okay. If my friend was a single attractive woman — if she were pretty and unattached — it meant somehow that I was okay being single. I saw my okayness in her beauty. Having her exist and being with her was reassuring to me. She seemed fine to me and therefore I was fine. I did not look at myself directly.

I spoke with my friend Jessica about being in a couple and loneliness.

Jessica: I was just going to say that, for me anyway — while I don't generalize that all relationships are that lonely, I think that there are a lot of relationships in which people are not close. I think that what can definitely happen is that people can be more lonely in a relationship than they can alone. For me, I have found I can be more lonely in a relationship than when I'm with myself . . . my lover Michael and I played a role in structuring our loneliness, narrowly defining what we could be to each other. One of my goals now is to learn to be as real with other people as I can be with myself, alone. That'll never totally be true—but I'm striving toward being more real and centered "This is me. Here I am." with other people.

R. Instead of trying to conform to another's expectations.

J. Exactly! One of Michaels ways of closing the gap between us and trying to feel less lonely was sex. A lot of times making love for us was really good. Physically, it was probably the most satisfying sexual relationship I've ever had with a man. But a lot of other times it was a really alienating thing for me,

460

because I'd use it to try to get closer, when there was no way that sex was going to close the gap unless we were more real with each other.

Being in a couple is no
measure of intimacy
or
how close people are.
And is
no guarantee against loneliness.

Women who I have interviewed who are in intimate relationships with women have expressed these same feelings about loneliness and being in a couple. One woman jokingly stated: "People in a couple worrying about how the relationship is going and those who are single worrying about not being in a couple. It is not much fun!"

Space with Another Person

We close the doors
between us
for reasons of warmth
        Diane Fabric

When you like someone a lot it is difficult to keep your boundaries, your own space. I have found when I am close to someone it is more difficult for me to take the space I need for myself — to be alone or to do my own work. When I like someone I like to be with them often. But I have learned that if I don't listen to myself and provide the space I need for myself, I begin to resent the other person. I also start not liking myself because I haven't asserted my needs to get my work done, or to be alone. I tend to become jealous that the other person gets their work done or takes their needed space while I don't.

It is my responsibility to make sure I take care of my own space and choose people to be close to who are considerate of my need for space. Ideally what works best for me is to have the person I am close to be aware of my need for space and guard it as I do. I in turn try to be aware and responsible for her or his needs for space. This is difficult and it takes practice when you enjoy being with someone so much.

It has become easier for me to maintain my own space with another person since I have learned the importance of being alone and being with myself.

Once when Jessica and I had spent a long period of time together I suddenly wanted to be with myself. We had reached a place in our conversation which was very sensitive to me and I wanted to withdraw for awhile and be with myself and my feelings.

It wasn't that I didn't want to be with her or that I was rejecting her. I wanted to be with me. That is a hard thing to convey to another person, especially a lover. The energy is that I need just to be with myself; the force is not that I am trying to get away from her but that I need to be with me.

I told Phil my friend from Boston about this concept. He said it is still hard for him not to take his lover's need to be alone as a rejection of him. That is something we all need to work on. As I have come to recognize my own need for space it has been easier for me to recognize other people's and be supportive of them. And I am learning not to feel their moving to be with themselves as a rejection of me.

Men, Relationships and Space

In my relationship with Larry in D.C. and with other male lovers I have had difficulty maintaining my own space. Larry would demand a lot of my time and when *he wanted* it! If I said no — which I often tried to do — I was afraid I'd lose him. And if I decided to take time to be with myself or time to go elsewhere, when I did, I was afraid that I would lose him. I stayed around and became very resentful.

I have often been afraid if I got close to someone I would lose my independence — partly because they would make demands on my space and partly because I would want to be with them and would not take the space I needed.

I want to learn how to be close to someone without losing my independence. As I have become more grounded in myself and act more from my own feelings, rather than catching each event as it comes, this issue has begun to dissolve for me. I listen to what I want to do and do it. I do not lose myself with other people.

Because I have more of a sense of myself I don't experience the fear I did with Larry — that the other person will go away because I wasn't available when he wanted to be with me. I have experienced these feelings mostly with men.

With a man it was always harder for me to keep my space because I tended to drop everything when *he* called. At one time in my life having a man and a relationship was more important than taking care of me. I felt that relationships came first! My work and myself were second. My relationship with Larry at this point in my life seems so far away, but I feel the example is still relevant. I think it is much harder for women to maintain their space with men than with other women. Men tend not to respect a woman's need for space. Most men are still caught up in traditional sex roles and are very demanding of women's time. In my experience women are more supportive of each other's needs.

It is almost a cliche to state that in a heterosexual relationship women do most of the work to maintain the relationship, and usually play the nurturing and supportive role. Women have played this nurturing role so well that often we have lost our need to be with ourselves. I have read

new books recently which encourage women to develop and maintain this nurturing role, to support their man who is inherently much more active. So much for backlashes! In heterosexual relationships *both* partners need to learn to be nurturing. We all need to learn to "mother" each other.

I have had difficulty learning to keep my own space around other women I like a lot. But it is not so much that women are so demanding. It is more that I still need to learn when I like someone a lot to listen to my needs to be with myself.

Most often my favorite love-making is having someone hold me, someone to lean against while we sleep through the night. But sometimes my space with myself is more important than being held all night.

466

Men In The Night

Men often ride in the night after making love, while women turn over and go back to sleep. Last night I was with a close woman friend who I was having a wonderful time with, and thought to myself "If I weren't the man I wouldn't have to go home, I would be home." (For some reason because we were at her house I thought of myself in the role of the man.) Then I said to myself that I am a woman, that we both are women, but because we happen to be at her house I would have to ride home in the crisp air of night. And then I flashed how men usually have to ride home in the evening because they take the woman to her home, make out or make love and then return to their own abode. How many American men have developed the pattern of lovemaking and then riding in the cool of night?

When I made love with men in their homes usually I would leave in the morning. The men who made love with me in my home sometimes slept through till morning or would leave in the night. Sometimes when they would leave I wished they wouldn't but sometimes I was glad to have the space to myself and be able to start a new day by myself without a person from the day before.

Last night when I was with Clara we did not make love but this analogy seemed applicable to me. I was at her house, and after much closeness and intimacy, I had to go out in the cold of night. I did not have to go. I chose to. Clara had asked me to stay. We could have snuggled up in her bed and I could have gone home in the morning, but I wanted to start the new day fresh, and alone. I wanted the day for myself. I knew that I needed to be with myself and I wanted to have the choice of what I would do unencumbered by having to consider the wishes or wants of another person who happened to fit in my life from the night before.

When I first began thinking about this piece I was lying on the living room floor listening to music, and into my mind came the passage in *Patience* and *Sara* by Isabel Miller about boys being lucky because when they love a girl they can hold her hand and kiss her as they desire. I thought but boys have to walk home in the dead of night after being close and intimate and girls need only walk upstairs and go to bed, or if in bed, merely snuggle up under the covers.

I like Clara yet I did not want to be with her today, I wanted to be with me. This was one of the first times for me after being with someone I liked a lot that I was conscious of taking the space I needed. I don't want to be with someone if it means I escape being with myself and with feelings that are in me.

I was glad Clara did not ask to be with me today because that would have put pressure on me. I would have been able to say that I wanted to be alone but if she specifically requested to be with me I would have found that very difficult.

Working on this book has trained me to know the importance of being with myself. If I don't spend enough time with myself it is very difficult to write.

From my interview with Tracy, September 1973

Tracy: And she called me up and said she felt like a shit, and this and that, and — I was just in the state of, well, it's been about seven days since I've been alone, and I just cannot be with another person. But she wanted to be with me . . . and I sort of, you know, waited for her to invite herself, and she didn't and so we wound up being apart that day, and I sort of felt like it was a necessary choice, but incredibly hard for me. And, um, I've just sort of felt guilty about it, since, because she is as mysterious as I originally thought — but she's not as strong as I thought, and I'm very frightened by *any* dependence that she might develop on me, because I feel that — I'm a responsible person in relationships, but, no matter how true I am to this idea, I really do need time to myself. And — there come points where it's either him, her, or me this afternoon — and it had better be *me*, and that ain't the Christian choice!

R.   Would it make a difference — if Roger was putting that out? Saying I really want you here — I'm hurting today. How would you feel if *he* was doing that?

T.   I think I'd be more sympathetic just because I've been more brought up to accede to men's demands.

R.   We have to learn to stop doing that! The thing that I've been learning from my friend at work — that I had trouble practicing — is to take care of myself first — that's most important; then I'm going to be able to give to the other person more, too. We don't take care of ourselves enough; that is one of my biggest weaknesses.

469

Women need to learn to protect themselves
    We've been brought up to nourish others
      and be protected by men

It is important

that women learn

to spend time alone

with themselves.

Not in a Couple

When I told a friend about the different topics I was discussing in this book she was most excited about the Alone issue. By alone I meant being with myself and nurturing myself. By alone she meant being by herself and not in a couple. She told me to read an exciting section in *Our Bodies Our Selves* about this issue. I of course immediately did so and heard myself re-echo similar feelings expressed by other women in the article.

Since I came to California and became involved with feminists I no longer thought of myself as a single girl, or as single, but as a woman. This is a very important change for me. I hadn't realized until that incident that I had stopped dealing with whether it was okay to be single and stopped looking to other single women to reaffirm me.

Here in the Bay Area I have met independent women who didn't have as part of their primary identity being in a couple. And those women who were married didn't seem as if they were in a couple relationship at all.

The women in *Our Bodies Our Selves* spoke of having "varying degrees of intimacy with people, primarily women. None of them had a primary relationship that defined who they were." They stated "together we are trying to explore our independence and find positive identities for ourselves — not in isolation from other people, but outside of relationships that feel limiting or defining."

I had always lived my life in D.C. thinking of myself as a single person waiting for the time I would be living with a

man. The period in my life between adolescence and being in a couple or being married was "in between." It sort of didn't count.

I realized that I liked the way I lived now and began to explore what living "not in a couple meant" to me. I have many friends and live within a community of people I have found supportive. How absurd to look at this life which I actively chose as something before the "ultimate in my life" . . . being in a couple. Why should I look at this period in my life as a transition period — as something less than it actually is? I enjoy my life — it is very full!

When I first came to California I still aspired to be in a couple relationship with a man. I wanted to be married and be non-monogomous within a couple and have women lovers in my life or be in a triangle with a man and woman.

As I opened to my feelings for women and took my own power I wanted to be in *a couple* with a *man* or a *woman* — whomever I would become close to.

I was excited that I began to feel I didn't need a man in my life to be happy. If I could be in a relationship with a woman I felt I could be content. I was proud when I began to feel that I didn't want or need a man in my life to be able to be close to a woman or to — as I talked about in the Interviews Section — define my sexuality, "balance it," or define me.

When I wrote the final version of the process I went through in defining my sexuality I was surprised to see the contortions I had put myself through — including creating a definition for bisexuality so that a man was still in my life. I was still dependent on having a man to define myself. I was male identified rather than female identified.

473

It wasn't until much later that I realized the primary lover that I was looking for had to be me. That I could be content as long as I had a sense of myself — felt connected to myself.

I now see choosing to live "not in a couple" as a positive choice for me just as choosing to be in a couple can be a positive choice for others. I have intimate relationships with both women and men but do not have couple relationships with either.

I want my basic identity to be with myself, not as part of a couple or in a relationship. It was very exciting to discover the changes I had gone through in exploring my independence. I never before considered that not being in a couple could be a valid option in my life.

I see my goal as being an independent person, having intimate relationships but not being in a couple.

Being in a couple —
and not being in a couple —
both can be positive and both negative

Since I began my journey I have learned that I would prefer not to live with my lovers but to have my own separate space and live with my friends.

What is easier about exploring
not living in a couple and exploring
my independence is
living in a community of women
who give me support —
and living with three other women
Colette, Emma and Rhoda.

474

STRENGTH

At one moment we are children playing
and the next moment powerful women.
Our soft sides and strong sides at once.

W<small>HEN</small> I began my journey I wanted to teach myself a new perspective for looking at the world. We have been taught to compartmentalize things and I wanted to try and see the world more whole. I wanted to leave behind the perspective of seeing the world through straight Aristotelean thinking with its either/or logic . . . that things are either one way or the other — hard or soft, weak or strong, hot or cold, aggressive or passive, rather than both. I wanted to under- stand the concept that reality manifests itself in the guise of pairs of opposites — "that we live in a universe where sin- gle realities express themselves in two opposite polari- ties."* I wanted to learn to experience pairs of opposites simultaneously.

---

* Copyright © 1972 Andrew Weil, *The Natural Mind*, Houghton-Mifflin Co., Boston.

Sex role characteristics.

Female	*Male*
soft	hard
passive	aggressive
feeling	insensitive

Female and male roles have been defined in either/or logic; women and men are able only to express parts of themselves if they follow these strict sex role stereotypes. Most people have been raised by parents who followed these definitions and have gone to schools and worked in institutions where the standard sex role is the rule. We live in a society which supports these stereotypes, and penalizes those who have gone outside them. I want to be able to express all aspects of myself and not feel in conflict about being a woman.

Living in a society which defines femaleness as gentle and maleness as aggressive caused me and a lot of other people a great deal of pain. I felt so locked in that I only felt good when I expressed certain parts of myself. I want to feel soft and be able to express all the different sides and levels of myself. Yet, when I expressed my aggressive side I sometimes felt ugly. Being aggressive is an ascribed male characteristic and I didn't feel feminine. (At some level I accepted the sex role definition of what is to be female and male in this society. Each of us has to some extent integrated these sex role stereotypes into our very being because we had been indoctrinated to do so.)

478

It would be much better for all of us to define ourselves as people from our insides — from our feelings — not by outside social definitions that we must force ourselves into. In that way all the parts of ourselves can emerge freely; we can be more whole. To do so we must learn to distinguish the different voices within us; those which are society's and those which represent our true feelings.

One of the reasons I had so much difficulty accepting my love for women was because my feelings were threatening to my femininity. I defined my feminity from the outside by sex role definitions and by choice of sex partner. I felt that liking women was masculine and that having a sexual partner that was a woman was masculine. It is not until I went inside to see how I felt that I began to define my own femininity, my own sense of being a woman. Femininity or masculinity is not determined by one's sexual partner.

Jackie suggests that we would be far better off not labeling the different parts of ourselves as female or male parts, but only as different characteristics of our total selves:

Receptive, soft, open, compassionate, passive, feeling (traditionally labeled Female).

Aggressive, strong, active, pushy, hard, driving, objective (traditionally labeled Male).

Androgynous — is the word used to connotate a person who has both "female" and "male" characteristics. A person who has all the characteristics or parts listed above. To me that person is a total person.

Ideally we should strive to be androgynous. To define ourselves in terms of being a total person rather than as a woman or a man. But in this time in our history I prefer my identity as a woman rather than as androgynous. I am not ready to define myself simply in terms of being a person because I feel that we as women have a great deal to contribute from our perspective of the world. And the characteristics that are labeled as female have been defined negatively. It is up to us to make sure that female elements not only are incorporated into the very fabric of our society but be given their place of importance too. Feelings particularly have been ignored in this "objective" society and have been discounted.

I'd be a woman now — I AM proud of my new identity.

I tried to understand why the women and men I interviewed who loved both women and men seemed to be more open about how they defined themselves. They did not limit themselves to strict sex role definitions. The men were more accepting of their gentle side; the women of their aggressive side. The men were exploring mothering their children; the women were invested in their work. People who are open to their sexual feelings for both men and women are more likely to be in touch with and accept the different parts of themselves society labels masculine and feminine.

Inner Strength

One time a friend that I liked very much hugged me so close that I got scared and pulled away from her. She got so close that my heart hurt.

Later in therapy I did a fantasy around my feelings of being scared when this friend got so close to me. During this period I was exploring feelings that I was hiding from myself. In a sense I was afraid to be close to myself and look directly at myself.

In my fantasy I saw my friend hugging me and coming so close that she put her hands right through me and pulled out a bloody baby. Her hands were all bloody; she was shocked and disgusted. I remember feeling surprised and upset when I had this fantasy. I felt it was grotesque. No wonder I was afraid to have anyone be close to me! No wonder I felt if some-one got too close to me when I was hurting I would hurt more if they tried to hug and comfort me.

My therapist suggested that I fantasize holding the baby to see what would happen. At first I was afraid to, but when I did the baby grew strong.

All that week I thought about finding a bloody baby inside me. At first I was devastated. I tried to nurture myself and (figuratively) the bloody baby too. I spent long hours walking in the woods and by the ocean.

I decided that I didn't want the "baby" to grow, that I wanted to keep it inside. I wanted it healthy and strong. But I wanted to keep it as a child. I wanted to keep the child part of myself.

I realized that the baby was bloody because I hadn't taken care of myself and nourished myself properly. I was so busy being a strong woman in the world that I didn't take care of my inner self.

By the time I arrived in California the strong woman part of myself was so disconnected from me that the professional woman (me) in the suede jumper scared me.

I realized that if I had a baby in me, a soft vulnerable spot, that strong women I admired had a child in them too. That made them less scary to me and in fact made me less scary to myself. The strong woman that I used to present to the world was hollow without the child, without the soft vulnerable part. I looked good but "I was the hollow tin soldier that glittered." I decided I always wanted to keep the childlike part of me. It made the other self, the strong woman, real and connected to me.

What a relief to find my soft spot! Being strong isn't so scarey now that I have the child in me. Now that I am connected to myself and have myself.

"We don't share each other on a
deeper level,
that is why there is so much loneliness."*
We don't share our soft sides.

Sometimes we scare and intimidate each other
because we don't share our soft parts.

---

* Anaïs Nin at a speech in San Francisco 1974

Six months after I left Topeka community health my relationships with Jessica and Alan resumed. Jessica and I maintained our relationship throughout but we began to see each other more after she broke up with the man she had been living with. Jessica, Alan and I no longer saw ourselves as in a triangle but as sustaining separate relationships to each other. With Jessica in Point Reyes, Alan working in Larkspur and myself writing in Berkeley, it seemed the competition and tensions between us had diminished.

One evening as I was about to go out with Alan I received a call from Tracy. I remember telling Tracy about my excitement over renewing these relationships. She responded:

"Comrade Falk, good luck in the sexual revolution!"

That evening I told Alan I was pleased with my new hair cut and that I felt softer and wanted to show my new softness." Alan said "Why are we so afraid to show our softness? My answer was that we both thought we were supposed to be strong." But later I realized that the answer was not that we both thought we were supposed to be strong, but lay in how we defined strength. Being a strong woman just wore me out. I was always doing an internal battle about being strong. I partially feared it, because for me being strong meant being alone. After making love with Alan that night my mind and feelings were just flowing. Suddenly I knew that being strong didn't have to be bad when I could be soft inside — being strong is not being alone. I have my insides to comfort me. I have myself.

Alan and I, like many people today, defined strong as being tough. What I realized is that my strength is my softness. I changed my thinking.

So what I have been trying to hide from myself is my softness. I feel it in my body now and I enjoy who I am. I enjoy this part of myself. My softness is my new strength.

I thought if I allowed myself to get strong and in touch with myself, I would be alone.

People sometimes experience disorientation when they meet a woman who is strong. Men not women are supposed to be strong. There is sometimes a feeling of admiration for the strong woman but also resentment and anger. How come she is strong and I am not? Sara told me she hated me and other women for being so assertive because she felt she couldn't be like that.

Being strong and fearing being without a man.
Another level of reality.

I talked once with Joan who runs women's groups about strength and my fears of being alone if I got stronger. She says women who are still wanting to be with men find there are not many men around who can deal with a strong woman. She tells the women in her groups that "If they do indeed develop themselves, they take a risk. They may not be able to have that relationship they wanted with a man."

484

Their choice is of course not developing their strengths — holding themselves back as women have done for centuries to please men. But then they may be miserable. Joan feels a women's only real choice is to go forward. She said "She wished men would begin to work on liberating themselves because women will be leaving them behind. There are so many more exciting women around today than men. It is the women who are doing things, trying new ways! It is wonderful!"

Strength

soft inside, hard outside or
soft outside, hard inside
soft inside, soft outside
hard inside, hard outside

Part of my journey in California has been to bring my soft-side outside. Back in Washington I felt hard on the outside. Often when I pushed for change I felt ugly and hard — mostly because I did not feel it was feminine to push or to be tenacious. I have learned to expand my definition of who I am and not allow the rigid definitions of what it is to be masculine and feminine in this society choke me. Or affect how I feel about myself.

It is almost as if I were embarrassed to be too feminine — sweet, gentle, pretty. I had to look striking and bold — attractive! Only just recently have I been able to let out my pretty side. It used to feel icky to me.

The model in our society for strength has been the masculine model. To be feminine was not positive. It has been my concern since the movement began that we need new models and new structures if we are going to make basic changes in this society.

To be masculine according to traditional sex roles is to be aggressive, hard-driving, competitive, decisive, certain, thick-skinned, in charge

We often use these characteristics to describe someone as strong.

To be feminine has meant to be soft, sensitive, receptive, compassionate, passive, uncertain, gentle.

These characteristics are often used to describe someone who is weak.

We talk about a person who is too sensitive, too soft, too passive, as weak. An administrator who is considered weak is often described by these adjectives. A man who allows his feelings to interfere with his decision-making is disparaged.

Efficiency instead of effectiveness is emphasized in our bureaucracies and in our industries. The administrator who can make quick objective decisions is much sought after. Many men can readily make complicated decisions affecting the lives of many people because they are so cut off from their feelings. There are many men who easily make decisions involving people, office space, job cuts, promotions, budgets, etc. Because to them they are just moving around bodies, space, and allocations. They are not necessarily the type of men that often come up with alternative job sharing plans or alternative innovations for the best use of space. They are made of the same fabric as those men who (being cut off from their feelings) can readily bomb Vietnam, thinking in terms of body counts not human lives.

Many women and men trying to succeed in a "man's world" have had to give up so much of their insides (soft-sides) by placing a strong, competent aggressive person on the out-side. Not realizing what this does to their insides. One friend of mine, Janet, who is 35, said that she feels some anger and some jealousy toward young women because the movement came so late for her. She is now trying to bring her soft side out. She spent so many years being a "strong woman in the world" that she hid her soft side from herself. Janet says "You'll find a whole bunch of warmth behind my hard exterior wall."

I have found that some people who are soft on the outside paradoxically are hard on the inside. My inside is soft, but my outside may seem harder. Some people, often men, are hard outside and hard inside. My goal is to bring my soft side out.

Women in the movement talk about searching for new models of strength. The male macho leadership role with its hierarchies will not do. I used this aggressive model at NIMH sometimes but it wore me out. I had a sense that though the "pushy way" to make changes worked, if I wanted the changes I made to be sustained over the years, another approach was also needed. Women now talk about the need to be assertive, to be aggressive, but emphasize the need to be receptive and open also. When women talk about new models of strength we often use such words as gentle, soft, sensitive, receptive, warm.

Julia told me about a women's group in which everyone wanted to be close to the leader and looked to her as the authority on women's issues. She is a very attractive dynamic woman who got her degree from Harvard. She is very aggressive and assertive. Many of the members of the group were very attracted to her and some wanted to be her lover. In one heavy session she said to the group "Why do you all want me? You want someone who is open and loving, and I am mostly very aggressive and closed."

The model in society for the person who is often sought after — the leader — is someone who is assertive and dynamic. And that person doesn't necessarily have the qualities to be a loving person, to be nurturing or giving. Certainly we have seen many dynamic strong men in society who are almost cripples when it comes to intimate relationships. It is hard to give up old models. We are all struggling to learn new ways. The women in this group were responding to this leader the way women have been programmed to respond to men in power positions, often giving up their power in an attempt to be close to the male leader. Certainly Jessica and I did this at Topeka. What women are trying to do is explore our own powers, to learn to erase hierarchies and to look to ourselves for answers rather than to someone outside ourselves. Often men who are in this hierarchial role are assumed to have the answer and know the best way to run things.

Women are learning to work together collectively, exploring, sharing power, and integrating work and life. Personal issues are not seen by us as separate from the work at hand. Nurturing and supporting each other, dealing with our feelings, is an integral part of our working process.

As we explore new models and new roles and learn to develop our strengths and powers we must be careful not to fall prey to the old ways. To present only our assertive sides and not our soft sides — our feelings, our uncertainties — will put us into the trap of the macho role that men have placed themselves in for years: establishing hierarchies and isolating ourselves from each other.

The society is over balanced in
Characteristics labeled male
We all need to develop the characteristics
Which have been labeled female.

We need individual change
Before we will be able to
Change the social
structures of this society
Basic change will come from within.

We need to get in touch
With our feelings and act
From them.

Models: Inside/Outside

I came to California looking for a new way of life, looking for a place where I belonged. I kept on reminding myself that I had learned things that others had not yet or I had dealt with things in myself that others had not, but nonetheless I kept looking for models. I didn't like the way my friends in D.C. had chosen to live their lives for myself, but I wasn't sure of my own alternatives. I thought in terms of integrating life and work, non-monogomous relationships, loving women, bisexuality. How was I going to fit all this into the suburbs of Washington, D.C.?

I kept looking for people who not only had tried these forms but who were happy living them.

It was not until I met a group of feminists in San Francisco that I felt I finally found people like me who were dealing with the same issues I was. These women helped me to affirm myself. My ways of being were understood and supported, but I was still looking outside myself to be sure that I was okay. I needed to take my inner journey and to do the work of teaching myself that I was okay.

I followed everyone's life with an overwhelming sense of curiosity. One of my friends once commented, "I get the feeling that you are watching, taking everything in, trying to make sense of everything, trying to see how it fits together." And she once commented on my wide-eyed enthusiasm for her life. "You must realize that my life is not all that wonderful. It certainly has its problems."

Later I learned that just because these women were non-monogomous and had women lovers didn't mean that they

490

had their lives worked out, or had a corner on the market for intimacy. Because they were open about their struggles, it did not mean they had resolved many of the conflicts in their own lives. Nor because they were active feminists did it mean there wouldn't be problems or competitiveness between them.

We have been conditioned to be isolated from and competitive with each other. It takes time to change. It was naive of me to be angry and expect no competition and gaming. But because we are not supposed to be competitive with each other it was sometimes more difficult to deal with such feelings openingly. There is so much pressure to do what is "right in terms of feminist principles" that it was sometimes hard to feel free to talk about ways we are not supposed to behave.

Not only had I looked for other women to be living the life structure I wanted to live but also I wanted them to be the type of person I wanted to be: gentle, soft, assertive, open, receptive. I once yelled to Jeanette about a woman that I admired being almost crippled emotionally in her relating to me. She said back, "Why do you need people to live the way you want to live *or* to be the way you want to be? You can develop your own way."

I feel this discussion is particularly important because I have seen other women angry at their women friends because they weren't the way they wanted them to be. "One more image down" is a way it is often expressed. "She is not how she appears or projects." When I did this I wasn't taking responsibility for being who I wanted to be without needing another person to be that way too.

491

It has taken me a long time to erase hierarchies, and take responsibility for myself instead of looking outward as we have been taught.

One day, my first year in California, I remember lying on the sand at Muir Beach talking to one of my friends I admired. I began to tell her how in therapy I had realized that I was always looking for someone to replace my mother, someone to teach me, someone to look up to.

My friend said: "Funny, because they don't come stronger than you. We all have different strengths; we are all strong and weak in different things." How long has it taken me to learn that I can give up looking for the parent figure, the heroine, the authority outside myself?

And I did learn that the woman I wanted to be was inside of me.

Exploring Redefining Strength

This society demands definiteness and permanence. It disparages uncertainty and change. But how can we explore if we have to be certain and absolute about everything?

I feel that acknowledging my uncertainty about issues is a strength. The ability to admit to myself and others that I have been unsure about my sexuality could help other people. If I have been raising questions surely others are too.

492

Crying

I began to see that my ability to cry and get in touch with my feelings was a strength. Crying helped me get more in touch with me.

At my mother's funeral I wanted to cry. That was a comfort to me, except that everyone tried to stop me from crying. Was my pain too great for them? Did it make them think of their pain? They preferred that I kept my feelings locked up inside. At least not let them see how I felt. That is the way our society is. Keep it under control. Keep yourself locked up. Don't allow your feelings.

Ellen tells me of an administrative meeting in community health in which one of the women cried. Later this woman told Ellen she felt badly because she cried. Ellen said "Why should you feel badly because you showed your feelings? I feel that is strong."

In an earlier meeting Ellen had become very angry at the way some men were dealing with administrative power — not supporting the work being done by the people who were actually dealing with the clients in the community.

At first she was embarrassed that she expressed so much anger but then she received support from the other women members of the administrative staff for expressing her feelings.

The women have banned together now and are not allowing the men in power to ignore the issues which they feel are important. And they are expressing themselves in a way they

493

feel is important and can be heard. They will no longer tolerate being placed in the role of hysterical women because they
express their feelings. They have brought into the open the
sexual relationships between the men and women on the staff
which affect decision-making and the way power is distributed there. The men protested that their meetings would
be more efficient if issues were kept objective, unemotional
and not personal. They say it is best not to integrate work and
life!

Anger and Strength

> Such an angry person I have become!
> But I feel more powerful and like myself more.
> My anger isn't the old kind, as
> when I would feel ugly.
> In fact now I feel more soft and lovely
> than I ever have in my life, not because
> of my anger but because of getting in
> touch with myself.
> My anger now is just coming out as I
> get more into my feelings — closer
> to myself. At the same time
> I have become closer to the women
> and men in my life.
> Anger and love go hand in hand.

The anger is powerful and I love it. Thomas laughs when I
tell him I am angry that Sam didn't call. It is so much better

than the whinney worry, panic, in which I gave away my power. And I hated myself and my self image. "Will he call? Do you think he is upset with me? Will he continue the project?" So much better to be grounded in my strength.

It is powerful to feel and be angry.

Think Well of Yourself

I feel more powerful
when I can give myself the
things I want, when I can
look at myself, see my strengths
and support myself.

We are taught to think negatively of ourselves. Women have had such negative self-images. It is hard to learn to compliment ourselves. I have started saying good things to myself, telling myself openly the things I like about myself. I am pleased with myself. Women are not encouraged to think well of themselves, let alone think they are powerful or competent.

Alice tells me about the women in her belly dancing class. Not one woman was satisfied with the way she was, with her body, with her hair. There was always something wrong. Women have been hard on themselves and have put themselves down.

My strength is recognizing my weakness and uncertainties and my weakness is not recognizing my strength.

Giving Yourself Comfort

I have found that being able to comfort myself makes me feel powerful. Finding that I have myself and can comfort myself is a strength.

I am writing the book that I wanted. That is a pleasure I can give myself. What I always wanted to see in a book I discovered was inside of me.

Being able to give yourself things you fantasized only having a man could give you:

—Pleasure

—Support for a year off to write a book.

I felt very powerful recently when I joined the local tennis club. It was something that I always wanted to have — a pleasure that I thought so enjoyable I would have to wait for a man to give it to me. I feel incredibly powerful that I can get such things for myself now.

Strength Is Asking For What You Want

I really admired that Melinda could ask for a hug or other things she needed. That was something difficult for me. I had always seen the asking or the need in myself as a weakness. That made it difficult for me to ask for or admit my needs. Melinda didn't see asking for what she wanted as a conflict with her strength, it was her strength.

I saw wanting a hug as a weakness because if I were strong I wouldn't need a hug.

Learning to ask for the things I want or need applies to all areas of my life. It is up to me to be in touch with what I need or want and put that information out to people I interact with. That way I take responsibility for my life. I do not expect someone to intuit my needs and I am less likely to find myself waiting for someone or something to happen to change my life.

At first I was afraid to ask for things I wanted or needed. I was embarrased or feared rejection. But by asking I have learned that I feel stronger, even when the other person says no. And often they do say yes. I feel freer because I am not waiting or guessing or hoping the other person will give me what I want. I can go to other people to find what I need. Try it!

Strength and Personal Power

I see my personal power so much clearer now that I am not working for NIMH. And now that I have taken time to be with myself. I was really scared to quit NIMH. I thought that I would be giving up so much of my power. I had no sense of my own personal power. I knew that people related to me a certain way because I was at NIMH and could influence the funding of money. Would they still be interested in me without the job? I was scared to be on my own to write. I had never worked outside of an institution and outside of a 9 to 5 structure. I was afraid I would feel again that I was floating free in the universe. I was afraid to give up the power I had been able to use at NIMH.

497

After I quit and worked on my own for a while I found that I felt good about myself. I felt attractive and strong and could feel that people were attracted to me for who I was not for where I worked. On one level I did not have a separate identity between my own power and the power I had because of my position.

The more I worked on my own the more I got in touch with my own power and my own skills. I saw myself more clearly. And with distance and time I was able to see more easily what I had accomplished.

My separation from there gave me an incredible sense of freedom and power. Leaving the institution did not decrease my power and strength as I had always feared and believed, it increased it. Finding I can survive without being within the structure of a large institution makes me feel more powerful. When and if I return to work in such an institution I will feel freer because I know I can survive without it.

ANGER TOWARDS MEN

IN THIS section I discuss and express my anger for the way men behaved when I acted outside of traditional female sex roles; when I wasn't waiting for men to take the lead; when I wasn't being quiet, uncertain or nurturing to them. Most of the examples I have drawn are from my work situations.

I have had difficulty determining the best way to present this section. Do I explain my anger, make reference to the fact that men truly have difficulties and are caught in their sex roles too? That there have been men who have been very supportive of me and other women? But the fact still remains that men control most of the power in this country. And the type of male behavior I describe in the following section is intolerable and must stop.

When I took my inner journey exploring my feelings toward myself and other women I also began to deal directly with my angry feelings toward men. I soon realized that I had been uncomfortable with my angry feelings because I felt they were unfeminine. The male dominated society has defined such feeling as "unladylike." To have angry feelings toward men is ugly! In fact men get you coming and going if you buy *their* definition of what it is to be female in this society.

You feel ugly when you are assertive because such behavior is "unfeminine" and men let you know it.

And then when you feel angry toward men because of the way they treat you when you are assertive, you feel ugly because your anger toward them is unfeminine!

I have learned it is powerful to feel angry and assert yourself.

It is wonderful to feel angry at men for the way they have mistreated you. The whinning quality suddenly disappears when you ask for something you want — or when you accuse your boss of treating you badly because you are a woman.

At first I didn't want to let myself know if I *had* angry feelings toward men because just having these angry feelings was very threatening to me. Hating men was wrong. Well, I suggest being angry at men for how we have been treated is very powerful and liberating. It beats feeling ugly and angry at yourself. It is very healthy to feel your angry feelings for people who have been holding you down.

I am not encouraging women to hate men, but to get in touch with the angry and sometimes hateful feelings that are

502

sometimes in them; feelings which women have often used against themselves. (It is difficult to express anger. Often when we are mistreated we don't trust our feelings and ask ourselves whether our own behavior is appropriate. We tend to feel that somehow we did something wrong. Thus, we internalize our anger and feel badly about ourselves.)

There is a point in one's journey at which being angry at men is healthy. The positive energy that is released from this experience I use toward myself, towards other women, and towards more self-positive interactions with men because I feel good about myself.

Going Beyond Traditional Sex Roles

Because most of us have been raised in this society according to traditional roles, when we behave in ways which are outside these roles we often hear negative voices within us criticizing our own behavior. Every day we are bombarded by the media, advertising and our institutions with what the "proper role" for a woman is supposed to be. Those of us who have gone beyond these roles have had to struggle with ourselves and with those who react negatively to our becoming whole human beings. Having the support of other women makes this struggle easier and rewarding.

The important thing I have learned is that a part of me accepted traditional sex role definitions. I know this at a different level than I have known it before. This knowledge has made me feel very powerful and has in a sense freed me.

In Washington, I didn't know clearly why I felt ugly when I was assertive. But when I reached California and met more women who were comfortable with their aggression, and began my inward journey, I realized that I felt ugly being assertive because I felt it wasn't feminine. Part of me felt that aggressive behavior was masculine. Why else would I feel ugly when I was assertive? Why else would each victory eat away a little bit more of my soul?

On the one hand I thought it was okay to be aggressive. I felt it was very important to be assertive and that more people should stand up for themselves and get what they want. And yet on the other I didn't realize that all along another part of me didn't agree with my own behavior. I call this part my negative voice, the voice that made me feel ugly inside when I acted aggressively. It is not surprising that I had this negative voice — that I felt this way. I and thousands of other women have been conditioned along traditional sex role definitions. Yet I was surprised to find that my negative voice was the same as that of my Washington women friends when they criticized me for being too pushy and assertive. I was angry at them in D.C. for not supporting me, and when I discovered I had the same voice in me I experienced anger towards myself.

What has happened to me now is that I have been able to quiet that societal voice inside that used to make me feel ugly when I asserted who I was. A new voice has risen in its place, a more positive voice. It is springing up in many women across the country. What is so powerful about discovering my negative voice is that I can recognize it, know where it comes from and silence it so that it no longer can undermine who I am.

504

Some of my friends say that they used to feel ugly, and still do, when they are assertive. It is most important to rid ourselves of the scripting, the male definition of what it is to be a woman in this society. All of us have this negative voice to some degree. We must re-program ourselves to lose it. Society, our parents, our schools, all our institutions help teach us this voice; it will take each of us a lot of work to get rid of it. The support women give each other is essential. We are living in a society in which there is tremendous pressure to be a woman by traditional sex roles definitions. The responsibility to rid herself of this negative voice should not be placed on the individual woman. We cannot expect to change ourselves alone. We need each other's support.

A friend of mine suggests saying a mantra when one conducts business with hostile men and one's negative voice begins to speak. For instance, say over and over again silently:

> it is him, not me
> it is him, not me

Recognition

One of the places with men I struggled with my negative voice is around the issue of recognition. Men often try to invalidate a woman's behavior in a variety of ways when she steps outside traditional sex roles. One of the most painful and insidious methods is to deny women recognition for their work.

505

So many times when I worked as an assistant to a man I would have to struggle to be sure that my name was placed on my work. Dr. Tilbet would say "Miss Falk, you are too concerned with recognition. You know most work produced at NIMH and done by others is placed under the name of the director. Everyone is treated that way."

Each time I would complain to my friends I would be told "That is the way it is. The boss usually gets credit for the papers in his section. It isn't against you. How many times does a person write something and find the boss takes it for his credit?"

And often when I would ask for credit I would feel awkward — as if there were something wrong in my asking. Most men I knew were given credit for their work. Their bosses probably would never think of not giving them credit.

Women in this society most often get recognition for their work within traditional female roles and not for their professional work outside the home.

Recognition and Scripting

"Say over and over again: It is him, not me; it is him, not me. Stop saying that you are acting crazy because you are upset that the program chief took your name off an NIMH publication that you wrote a year ago. Stop saying it. If they tell you that recognition is not so important, that it doesn't matter, they can take *his* name off your paper and put your name back on." Inside/outside.

506

Thinking this way helps me get out of the defensive position and is a way of taking my own power. We have been made to feel that it is wrong to ask for credit for our work. Our need for recognition is often disparaged. "Miss Falk you need too much recognition. Miss Falk, you have written the word I too many times in your paper. Your ego is too involved." I took the I's out and felt guilty that I said I. I would have to disguise my work by saying that "the section" did such and such; giving credit to the nebulous bureaucracy. Do not be personal! Do not mention the many people who actually did the work!

And the fact that it was a woman's name that replaced my name, and my written introduction giving credit to the people who did the work, doesn't matter. It is still an example of the white heterosexual male dominated society with its super heroes and super organizations, in which one person is given recognition for what many have done, leaving people feeling powerless and ripped off. Today women's groups are trying to deal openly with the sharing of power and recognition. Many women are learning to work together collectively. And are exploring the creation of non-hierarchial structures in our society.

Throughout male history women have gone unrecognized. It is as if many of the strengths and talents of women never existed before. Creative and strong women have been erased from our history. Today J.J. Wilson and Karen Petersen have written a book about women artists who have never been recognized. Their exciting book is entitled *Women Artists Through Ten Centuries: Recognition and Reappraisal,* Harper and Row, 1975.

I spoke with J.J. about including several works of art by women artists of women loving women for this book. She explained to me why very few pictures existed. Women artists did not feel free to depict such feelings between women because this behavior was condemned. And if they did they were exhibited under disguised titles such as Charity and Justice.

Today with the support of the women's movement more and more women are being given recognition and power within our institutions. Women are also forming new and powerful structures outside the mainstream of society. We are discovering our own power, our women's power. This time is our Renaissance!

Male Behavior

I have drawn several examples from my past history of how men have behaved and how I felt when I asserted myself in my work and in my personal life. These examples when I first wrote them down were very painful to me. What is so pleasing to me now as I complete this book is that I find them no longer personally upsetting to me. I feel so much better and stronger. There is so much support from other women for all of us to assert who we are!

I present these examples because it has been especially supportive for me to share with other women work experiences and feelings we have all encountered, and still do from time to time. I had felt especially isolated in D.C. around my feelings for being an "aggressive" woman and the anger I felt sometimes from men when they responded to me when I asserted myself. By the time I reached California I couldn't take the way men saw me as threatening anymore and like anyone, I did not like being hated.

The feeling of being an assertive woman in D.C.

That painful space, when you are fighting for or talking very seriously about an issue you believe in — and men get angry and hostile, and start attacking you not so much for your ideas but for asserting them. And no, its not the fighting and assertiveness that leaves you so raw — that drains you. Or the men's hostile reactions against you (though indeed they are painful) — like dismissing what you are saying by commenting in the middle of a discussion: "Isn't Ruth cute with her round glasses." Because you could protect yourself from their hostilities if it weren't the fact that half the time you are also fighting yourself, convincing yourself that the way you are behaving is okay. When you finish, often when the battle is won, there is a little voice inside of you saying "you are ugly and awful and a creep for being aggressive and hard."

Once when I was upset because NIMH seemed to be dropping the youth program my boss said to me: "For god sakes take it easy. Just go get married. You are too invested in what you do." Gloria said that she felt what I was doing was wrong because it was killing me. She said: "There are some things that you do that you don't know what they do to you — slowburners. They eventually catch up with you." I guess that

509

one could say my battles with men were slow burners. At first I didn't realize how much they were taking out of me.

I do remember how fighting for my promotion really tore me up, having to write a thousand memos justifying my work for a desk audit. They said I didn't have the proper credentials, yet I knew men who got promoted doing the same level work I was doing who did not have credentials. And they would say, why do you need two rewards? . . . i.e., a scholarship and a promotion, when the man downstairs got both . . . but of course he was a man and he had a family.

I was treated as if there was something wrong with me because I was assertive and cared about my life's work. I wanted to be treated with respect and I cared about having an equal relationship.

Dr. Tilbet would say: "If you want an equal relationship why don't you get involved with a woman, that would be easier."

And Larry and I would fight over taking turns using the diaphram and the rubber. People would say I was silly, that was a small issue. I finally got sick of arguing and found it easier just to use my diaphram.

Male responsibility for birth control is not a small issue. Women usually have to put up with the inconvenience and expense of contraceptives. Every day women endanger their health and/or their lives by using such methods as the pill and forms of the I.U.D. Worse if these methods don't work it is the women who must deal with the emotional and physical stresses of being pregnant.

Men control most of the power and financial resources of

this country. They control birth control. They control research for effective contraceptives. Clearly a country as advanced as ours could develop more humane technology and more sensitive delivery of services in this area for both men and women.

Ask your lover how he feels about someone he loves risking her life using some contraceptives. Is he/or are you both aware of risks involved to your health? Ask him to explore his feelings about using contraceptive devices. What responsibility can he take on? I encourage all women to explore this area with their male lovers. It is crucial. (I have learned that the use of rubbers combined with foam is very effective. And rubbers have an added advantage as they are a protection against V.D.).

Power

Men had the power at NIMH and I had to go to them to get what I wanted and needed. Often many men were in power positions only because they were born male into this society. Some of them were incompetent and not as intelligent as I. It made me angry that I had to deal with them and that they constantly held me and other people back. I often felt soiled when I tried to get one of these men to support my work. Some of them were so disdainful of me and of other women. Had they not been in power I would have never associated with them.

Sometimes when I felt a policy or a specific project was badly in need of support I would become relentless. I would wear a man down. "We must do this program!" And when he finally said yes I despised myself — for hating him. Most men in power were into playing politics, and protecting their jobs. So often those in power, though some may have the best of intentions, often wind up using most of their energy to maintain the system they are in rather than in innovating or improving it. Such is the nature of systems and bureaucracies.

I remember once walking with two friends at lunchtime under the tall redwoods in Larkspur. I suddenly screamed "God damn it!" They were both shocked at my unexpected anger and cursing. I had just come from one of those meetings with one of those obstructive men with whom I had to hold back my power so that I would not threaten him. He didn't like the project we were working on because it was not his idea. He thought of as many excuses as he could for what was wrong with it. To get his financial support I would have had to show him how important his criticisms were and that some of the ideas for the project were in fact his. This administrator was the same man who told me that he would run me off the staff of community health if I said one more word at administration meetings. I explained that I was surprised he felt that way. I was taking a more quiet role than usual because I was tired from NIMH and since I was new and I particularly needed to listen. Then he complained that it bothered him that he didn't know what I was doing. He said he felt I didn't say enough and he felt left out. I couldn't win!

What angers me is that to deal with him and other men like him, I and other women have had to hold back our power. Being who I am was too threatening to him. I felt if I came on too strongly, and did not humor or flatter him, I could not get the money or support necessary to institute the program. I no longer can stand having to hold back my power because who I am is threatening to men.

Personal Power, Male Power and Sex

I asked Jessica why the men at work didn't seem to be as angered or as threatened by her. She said that she didn't deal as directly with them as I had. She said it was easier for her to deal with the other men and get what she wanted because she was sleeping with the boss and when things went wrong she could always "run to daddy."

Julia said the way she handled men at work, got what she wanted and avoided their anger was to be seductive with them, not direct. She said other women she knew found it easier just to withdraw from dealing with any conflicts with men.

At a Conference on Bisexuality once I met professional women doing research in the field. I learned that these women had been pressured by male government staff members to sleep with them in exchange for getting their research projects funded.

One of these women chose not to sleep with the man and in fact did not get funded while one of her colleagues who chose to sleep with the same man did. Another woman I met had been propositioned but her government suitor was nicer. He still tried to help her get funds even though she had turned him down.

You suspect that these things go on. I had always heard of them from the other side. Everyone thought when my work

513

went well that I was sleeping with my boss. Or when I got a promotion that I was sleeping with the man in personnel who processed my claim. Right. A woman could only be doing well because she slept with a male colleague.

In Larkspur when a good story was printed about community health in one of the local papers, the man responsible for getting the story in the paper showed the article written by a woman to the administrator who was pleased and asked the man "how many times he had to fuck her?" I told them both they were sexist and disgusting. They pooh-poohed me.

The vanity of their belief that a woman in a power position would do something for them because they slept with her is beyond my comprehension.

I talked to Emma once about why men think a woman is sleeping with her boss when she does well at work. She said men think a woman is not good enough to make it on her own. She said secondly they are jealous that they can't or don't have the option of sleeping with their bosses to get what they want.

Men seem to think that only if a woman has sex with them can she get ahead. Never do they assume she can do it under her own power. It is true that the way this society is structured today, most of the power is in the hands of men and often women derive their power from the men they hitch up with. Women married to powerful men are often viewed in terms of their husband's power.

Often it is too threatening for men to see a woman in terms of her own power. Men who have been defining them-

514

selves through traditional sex roles must see themselves as stronger than women. Seeing a woman as stronger and more powerful than they are is threatening to their very identity. The idea that a woman is sleeping with her boss is a more pleasant and unthreatening way to define her power; i.e., that her power is male-power by another man. It is not her personal power.

For men to see a woman in terms of her own power they may have to look at themselves perhaps not in terms of the social power positions they have (often because they are men) but in terms of their own personal power. Their power is many times based on abusing other people's power and not really on themselves — on a personal sense of power.

Men often have no sense of their personal power. Their power is often based on sex roles and the power positions they hold. But then again, most *people* don't have a sense of their personal power. Neither did I. I got lost behind my NIMH credential. Most people lose their sense of personal power in the institutions where they work. Few feel they are doing what they want to do; most feel powerless. And those who do have power have no sense of personal power, only power they have because of their position.

I thought I could choose never to work with the type of men I encountered in large institutions. To a great extent I have been able to remove myself from the situations I described by writing at home. I also have learned to get into my own power and into women's power. But sexism is in the very fabric of our culture, a part of its institutions. There is no way I can completely remove myself from this arena. Nor

515

should I when millions of women work within institutions and must deal with sexism every day.

We are all learning a variety of ways to deal with men's power. What I want to learn to do is protect myself and other women so I am not drained from the type of male behavior I encountered at NIMH. I refuse to have my energy ripped off by men. Women working with the support of other women are making important inroads in our institutions. As we come into power postition ourselves we will have continuing dealings with sexism and the type of male behavior by men that I described. Let these men beware, let them start working to change themselves. Their behavior will no longer be tolerated. I repeat their behavior has become OBSOLETE.

Loving Women/Stronger Sense of Self

For years I didn't think that relating to a woman was as desirable as relating to a man. I thought the best thing to have was a man. That is what society taught. I remember screaming angrily with tears at Dr. Tilbet "Well, would you want your daughter to make love to another woman?" "I want a man, I want to be married."

What is frightening about women loving women? Why is it so frightening? Why are we taught it is wrong to be lovers with other women?

What frightens the patriarchial society about women loving is that it will change the entire power structure when women begin to feel much stronger about themselves. The issue is not so much women making love to each other. The real issue is women loving and respecting each other and themselves; and not giving away their power or allowing their power to be taken away.

By going after men, by waiting for men, by feeling that men are more important than women — we give away our own power. By putting men first, before ourselves and other women, we deny our power and the important ways we see the world. We need to be in touch with our own magic and our own visions.

Men have been invested in keeping women apart, in dividing us so that we focus on them. They want us to continue to give them all our power and to keep us out of our own power.

Jessica: ". . . when I think of the shit we were going through with Alan and when I think of the richness you and I shared, but yet, there was still the distance, I really felt he created a distance in some ways, even though we were really together, and we really were friends, there was always a three-way tension thing. And the *energy* that you put in to him and that *I* put into him! And I put energy into us but I don't think I put in as much as I put into him, but I got more out of us. Think of what I could have gotten if I really put all that energy into us, oh god!"

Learning to love other women is learning to love yourself. Since I have become closer to other women I feel a much stronger sense of myself. The women that I have interviewed and other women who I have spoken with who love women feel this same way. We feel a greater sense of ourselves in terms of our own sexuality, our strengths and our powers.

Dr. Tilbet used to tell me if I worked out my feelings for women it would be easier to get closer to a man. "If you get closer to women you will get closer to men." What Dr. Tilbet didn't and couldn't tell me is that by getting closer to women I would get closer to myself and know and like myself better — get into my own power.

What is true is.

If I get closer to a woman
I will get closer to women
I will become stronger
I had hoped if I worked out my feelings for women
I would get closer to a man: power
But I got closer to myself and have my own power and can
give myself the things I want.

WORK

Looking Back

In D.C. I viewed my life along one dimension

My life was trying to maintain a balance and an easing of tensions between those two aspects of my life. I divided my world into work and relationships and struggled to have both. My primary focus was both on a long term personal relationship and on my work — not on me, on connecting with myself, or pleasuring myself. Such concepts did not exist for me in D.C. There was almost a complete omission of myself and of nature and its abounding pleasures and comforts.

During that period I was very diffuse. I had no center. My world view of life — work and relationships — was very narrow. I call this period Stage I in my development.

It was almost as if during that period that I did not see my personal relationships for the sake of pleasure. They were for meeting my needs — making me content so I could do my work undistracted. My personal relationships were a way of trying to ameliorate my work frustrations.

In California now I do not feel diffuse. I have a center, a core and am connected to myself. My work view is much wider. This is Stage II.

I have:

1. myself
2. my living situation
3. my intimate relationships
4. nature
5. my horse
6. my work
7. pleasure

It is not that these other things
weren't in my life in D.C.
I just did not put much emphasis
on them or count them. I was going
too fast to see beyond my narrow vision.

Stage I—Work and Relationships

I had various feelings and fantasies about work and relationships:

I was afraid if I got close to someone I would not be able to work — that they would take up my work time. My fantasy was if I had lots of primary lovers across the country (away from me) I could get my work done.

On the one hand I felt I needed relationships to fulfill my needs so I could be content enough to get my work done. On the other hand I felt relationships would interfere with my work. I was in a constant bind — feeling I needed the relationships to make me happy but feeling the relationships would intrude on my work. I had no sense that I could be happy without being in a relationship.

Having lovers but having them live far away seemed to be my perfect fantasy solution. I recall at Tracy's dinner we talked about the advantages of having lovers from out of town.

The emphasis of my conflict changed over time.

In college I told myself if I had "the relationship" I could easily get my work done.

In D.C. I feared if I had a relationship with a man I couldn't get my work done.

1. Because of the demands men made on my time
2. And because of the emotional roller coaster I experienced in my relationships with men.

Intimacy, Space and Work

That was the rub for me. I was afraid if I got in an intimate relationship particularly with a man I would lose my space, my work space, completely. That was the threat. I wake up knowing that I was going to work this morning after sleeping through the night alone, waking up occasionally in the first hour of sleep to write down my thoughts. I knew that I would do my work because there were no other factors which would affect me. I am in control of my life.

Now if Alan were here I would be thinking "is he going to stay and play today? I have work to do but I guess I would want to play with him. After all, what is life about?" But if we played I would be conscious of "giving up" my work time. And if he didn't ask me to play, then perhaps I would ask him what he was doing and try to persuade him to stay and play at least for breakfast. "After all, what is life about?"

So this morning I got up and made the cream of wheat I had been fantasizing about for the last two hours of sleep. I made it for Colette and I. After apologizing for its uncreamy texture, I presented it to Colette and then sat around the kitchen kibbitzing a little with her and Rhoda before I began my work.

Now this was probably no more time than I would have spent had I been with Alan. But I did not feel conflicted at all. I felt in control of how I spent my time. Had I been with Alan I could have stopped playing with him at any moment and begun my work just as I did with Rhoda and Colette but I would not have felt as free. I would say to myself relationships come first rather than I come first. I would continue playing with him and then of course I'd feel that tension.

In California I have found I experience this tension a little with men and women that I like very much but much less so than I ever have, now that I've learned to structure my own space. I have more of a sense of me. I ask myself what I want to do and try to do it. If I want to be with myself or my work I do that. My base is me. Obviously seeing my life in broader terms than a tug of war between my work and my relationships is a wonderful release.

Women have been raised in such a way that we often feel we have to choose between work and family. This is an ancient issue. And that the family relationships and nurturing of others comes first. We have not been encouraged to go off from the family and do our work. We have been taught that to do so is selfish.

I realize that I now feel it is okay for me to say me first, my work first. In Washington I always felt my friendships came first before my work — that I would fit my work in later. If a friend called with a problem I would immediately drop my work. But then I felt perhaps I liked my friends too much.

I can see how I got myself into such a situation. Being with friends I loved made me happy. I am not saying now that I don't need relationships or if my friends need or want to be with me that myself or my work always comes first. But not believing that relationships *should* be first frees me. I can choose more easily what I want to do.

When the women's movement began I worried that women in their striving to achieve to become independent people would become not unlike men in their work — being

527

unfeeling and putting their work before relationships.

What I am talking about is not so much a matter of work before relationships but taking care of me first. Heterosexual relationships are now changing, with women becoming more their own person. Women are not going to sacrifice themselves or their work for the sake of a relationship. Women are no longer going to do all the work to maintain a relationship. Both partners will need to share nurturing and supportive roles.

Women are exploring integrating work and relationships. Today my life is not built so that my work and my relationships are separate. More and more there is less of a dichotomy between my close friends and the people I work with. I have integrated my life and my work more successfully than I did even at Topeka. My close friends are people I work with. The issue of work vs. relationships, work first, becomes almost a non-question when both the working processes and the friendships are an integral part of each other.

In D.C. I just did not see that I could have both intimacy and work at the same time. It always had to be one or the other, never both.

When I was working at the poverty program I remember that when I wasn't asked to be the boss' special assistant I thought: "Oh well, I have this man and Joyce (the woman who got the position) is miserable with her social life." And when I was at NIMH it was either that things were great at work and bad at home (Larry and I weren't getting along) or they were great at home (feeling good with Larry and my friends) and bad at work. During those awful periods at work I would say: "Oh well, it is just a job to give me money so that I can do what I want — travel, ski, go out.

Work/Play

My work is very important to me. I like to be thoroughly involved and excited about what I am doing. I like other people to be excited and committed about whatever they do. What is wonderful is seeing so many women excited about their work and their play!

The women I have met in California do a work/play trip that differs greatly from the 9-5 career I was trying to get away from in D.C. They are on more creative trips, and work and play a great deal. They focus specifically on trying to improve or learn a new skill but are not career oriented in the sense I was in D.C.

Often women work independently or in small groups. Not working in bureaucracies allows more flexibility. Other women who are more into traditional professions i.e., lawyers are working for themselves. What is exciting for me is that working with other women I have come closer to learning to break down my boundaries between work and play.

As I am learning to integrate my work and my play the distinctions between them are beginning to diminish. I was talking to a woman yesterday who is a carpenter about work and play. She said when she works with a group of women on a building project it is all play to her. She said it turns into work when she feels a time pressure — a deadline. I thought about that and my own work and agreed.

Writing is a pleasure for me when I don't feel pressure about it. In the early stages of writing this book I would get up mid-morning, have a quiet breakfast on the back porch in the sun and then begin work about 11:00. I would write until I was tired and then go play with friends or swim. I was very happy and feeling very open; as my feelings just flowed from me. As time pressure mounted for the book's completion my writing became less like play and more work. And my life became less play and more work.

Having Myself

When I began thinking about work my emphasis was on being able to have a long term relationship and my work. Now my main focus is myself, to be happy with myself, to pleasure myself and to enjoy my fuller world. (Stage II)

I remember one day while writing I suddenly realized that as long as I have myself life will be fine, that things will be okay, that I'll make it. I never felt that way before. I've come a long way since beginning my journey. It was no longer "If I'm not in a good relationship soon I'll kill myself" as I dramatically screamed in Dr. Tilbet's ears. Knowing I have myself is wonderful, a new revelation and a new way for me to look at the world.

PLEASURE

I HAVE talked about pleasure in the core issue alone. But I feel it should be emphasized as a separate issue. I have not begun to explore this area as much as I would like, yet I feel it is key in our lives.

We all know and have been taught to plan for time to do our work. But we haven't been taught to plan for pleasure and play in our lives. I try to keep time for play, ride my horse or play tennis as I plan my work. Play is just as important to me as my work and I am learning not to "fit it in between my work" but have it an integral part of my life.

There is so much guilt in our society about feeling good. We can more easily experience pain than pleasure. We are scared to feel the intensity of our pleasure because we fear the pain of losing the good feelings. So we hold ourselves back from the pleasure. I know that I have been very much that way and have written more about the pain in my life than the pleasure here.

I am particularly interested in exploring pleasure because I was so work-oriented in D.C. I want to be sure that my life is more balanced in terms of pleasure.

I have learned that it is okay for me to enjoy myself. I feel really good just walking outside and feeling relaxed, and feeling that it is okay that I am not working all the time.

The key to finding more pleasure is slowing down enough to enjoy my feelings.

It is so sensuous for me to watch
the shadows on the grass
move from the trees above.

Integrating Your Child and Your Adult

When I turned 30 I felt like I was hitting my head against a wall. Somehow when you turned 30, that magical age, you were supposed to be an adult. That adult world I knew did not fit me. I like to play a lot. When I'm 70 I'll probably still be throwing snowballs, buying ice cream cones, gobbling up frosting with my fingers and rolling down sand hills, if I can.

In our society one minute you are, child and the next you are an adult. In the 50's everything was compartmentalized. Boys had one way to be and girls another; children were one way, adults another. In the hippie rebellion of the 60's, people began to recognize all their parts. The strict sex role limits between girl and boys began to blur, as well as those between children and adults. For a while many started to look alike —

a 13-year old wore jeans and long hair and so did his dad. I don't want the traditional cultural definitions of child and adult to cut me off from part of myself as I once allowed traditional sex roles to do. To reach a magical "age" of adulthood and to drop the child part of myself is to suppress a very important part of life. I always want to play.

I told a friend, a colleague from work in Washington, that I was now tap dancing and she responded "Whatever for?" When I told her I was in two performances she responded "You've been in California too long."

My friend could understand if I were taking a course, or studying, or going to a lecture — but something like tap dancing that wasn't goal oriented seemed absurd to her.

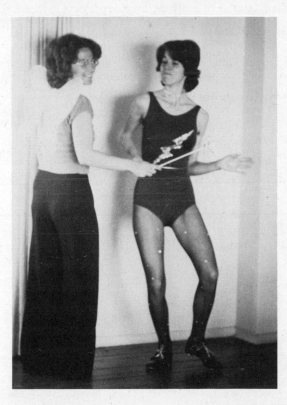

In California I have been able to be more in touch with the play side of myself. I played in Washington but I wasn't as in touch with the child part of myself. I skiied and played tennis but that is not the same. Riding my horse, tap dancing, dressing up in costumes, role playing, reaches into a different part of myself I hadn't been in touch with for a long time. I feel freer, younger and my energy flows more easily. I am more in touch with fun fantasies which make me feel deeper and richer. In my next writings I want to reach into this part of myself further. The other day I had a fantasy about my grandmother. I was up in the hills of Marin riding Shadow and my grandmother, who was a 70 year old woman, came out of the sky and asked if she could ride Shadow. She hopped on him and rode off in a trail of dust. She told me she had been riding Shadow late in the evenings in Point Reyes. I asked Jessica if she had seen an old lady on horse-back lately and she said no. I told this story because the idea of my grandmother on horse-back I found amusing.

I have shared
my childhood
with men

Now I share
my new childhood
with women

Pleasure and Guilt

I once said to myself: "If I work in the morning then it is okay to play in the afternoon." But I don't want to have to work for it to be okay to play.

I told myself it was okay to join the tennis club because I deserved it. Do I have to deserve it? Can't I just have the pleasure without justifying it by work?

I saw Jack the other day. He said "It was such a beautiful day today. I felt guilty working."

I guess we can drive ourselves crazy.

Vacations are for Making Love

I flashed back to a time I was traveling in Africa with Mandy. We were together in Morocco at a small hotel with swimming pool, linen tablecloths and the Moroccan breezes not unlike California weather with its cool clean air. We ate asparagus with hollandaise sauce in a silver dish — my most favorite vegetable ever. And over linen tablecloths and silver dishes I said to Mandy I felt I could never drop out or be a hippie in California. I liked fine things too much. Mandy said she herself would never ever consider being a hippie. The two men who were waiting on us at poolside brought us wine as we sat waiting for lunch to be served.

Then in our room after sitting in the sun, we were lying on twin beds napping and talking about the people who were staying in the room next door. As we watched they seemed to

539

be very much in love. And Mandy said: "What else are vacations for but eating good food and making love?"

Collective Pleasure

Jean said jokingly to me the other night that I would never make it in the revolution because I was so much into pleasure and luxury. I responded that I thought pleasure was very important to everyone. I am figuring out ways I can get such pleasures collectively. Just because the revolution is supposed to redistribute wealth, does it mean that we have to get rid of pleasure and live asceticly? Why can't we learn to develop ways that everyone can afford the important pleasures of life?

I think the revolution should be pleasure.

Somehow people feel if we change society we have to give up pleasure — that we need to deny ourselves. I think the need to be indulgent, pleasure oneself, is essential to the soul. When I give myself permission to experience pleasure and to play I feel a release of energy. I feel play and the creative life are part of each other. When I play my creative life blossoms.

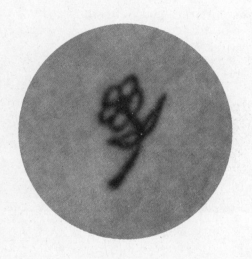

Acknowledgements

Many people have given me the support and energy to write this book, and some of their energy flows through it.

Ann Perry typed most of the interview transcripts. She gave me a great deal of personal support, believing in the book when what existed were only the raw interviews.

Anne Kent Rush helped me during the early stages of this book. Her support was very important to me personally and helped me believe that my book idea in reality could be a book. Conversations we had and her advice on the process of writing a book of this kind were very helpful.

Jackie Weiss was my woman reader and together we began to learn what the function of a reader is. We learned as writer and reader to work together and we are still learning as the book nears completion. Jackie helped me in so many ways it would be hard to enumerate all of them. She was a listener, a teacher, a friend, a sounding board and at times an editor. We argued, cried, laughed, screamed, and learned together about ourselves and feminism. There is a picture of the two of us working together on page 520 in the section on work. Jackie helped me survive through the process of putting this book together.

Diane Fabric, Barbara Szudy, Sally Goodwin, Joy Schulterbrandt, Thomas Linney and Victoria Kristin read my manuscript and gave me feedback and a good deal of themselves.

I want to thank Imogen Cunningham for the use of her photographs on pages 362 and 413.

Erika Asher took the photographs for this book on pages 111, 118, 190, 420-421, 462, 541, 550.

Carole Clem, Washington D.C., on pages 60, 117, 466, 472.

Marion N. Fay on pages 305, 472 (two pictures).

Debbie Guyol on page 426.

Thomas Linney on pages 537, 542.

Wendy Moser on page 520.

The Women's Cavalry picture on page 420 grew out of a conversation I had with Anne Kent Rush on horseback riding pictures and romanticism.

I want to thank each of these women for the help and energy they gave to the book and to me personally.

The photograph on page 184 of Big Sur I took myself the first time I went there, eight years ago. Other pictures came from friends and family albums.

544

The picture on page 540 is a wall hanging entitled "Liberation" by Colette (Box 187, Talmage, Ca. 94581) and the picture on page 532 is a painting by Diana Coomans entitled "In the Gynaeceum" (1885) taken from Sparrow's *Women Painters of the World*, London, 1905.

I asked J. J. Wilson and Karen Petersen to suggest art work by women of women loving to include in the book. The works above were among two of their suggestions.

Penny Smith did most of the typing for the original manuscript. Nanette Pike, Pamela Martell, Linda Reid, Niki Gilbert and Sally Goodwin also did some typing.

Conversations I had with Chellis Glendinning, Anica Vesel Mander, Stephanie Mills, Julie Philips, Lillian Rubin and Molly Wilcox were also very helpful to me with specific sections of this book.

I want to thank Barbara Szudy, Marianne Moore and Nanette Pike for living with me, listening to me and for the specific support each of them gave me. I want to thank Nanette particularly for her listening and nurturing.

I also want to thank Chellis Glendenning for teaching me about herbal teas which helped me to relax and sleep; Thomas Linney who showed me a level of commitment that I had never known before (his help and love were very important to me particularly at the end of the writing process); and Diane Fabric who wrote the preface gave me a lot of love and support as the book reached completion. Don Gerrard, my publisher and editor, and I struggled from the beginning to the very end of this journey. I want to thank him for those times he was there for me and gave me his personal energy. When I was overwhelmed by the large quantity of material he taught me to work on things one at a time.

And I want to thank the women in the interviews who shared so much of themselves.

You can write to me c/o Point Reyes Stars, 976 Creston Road, Berkeley, California 94708. Please enclose a self-addressed stamped envelope.

546

Booklist

Reading writings by women has always been a way for me to get in touch with my feelings. Here is a partial list of some of the books I enjoyed reading as I immersed myself in the lives and writings of other women. I have also included some exciting books which have been published in the last year and a half.

Sidney Abbott and Barbara Love: *Sappho Was a Right-On Woman*, Stein and Day, 1973.

Anais Nin: *The Diary of Anais Nin*, The Swallow Press and Harcourt, Brace and World.

Elizabeth Avakian: *To Deliver Me of My Dreams*, A Thesis submitted to Sonoma State College, Sonoma, California.

The Boston Women's Health Collective: *Our Bodies Ourselves*, Simon and Schuster, 1971.

Rita Mae Brown: *Rubyfruit Jungle*, Daughters, Inc., 1973.

Phyllis, Chesler: *Women and Madness*, Avon, 1972.

Judy Chicago: *Through The Flower*, Doubleday, 1975.

Helen Diner: *Mothers and Amazons – The First Feminine History of Culture*, Anchor, 1965.

Diane Fabric: *Poems, Pacific Sun, Point Reyes Light;* unpublished book of poems.

M. Esther Harding: *Women's Mysteries – Ancient and Modern*, Bantam, 1971.

Lillian Hellman: *Pentimento*, Little Brown, 1973.

Unfinished Women, Bantam, 1969.

Jane Howard: *A Different Woman*, E. P. Dutton, 1973.

Jane van Lawick-Goodall: *In the Shadow of Man*, Dell, 1971.

Violette Leduc: *La Bartarde*, Panther, 1964.

Doris Lessing: *The Golden Notebook*, Bantam, 1962.

Anica Vesel Mander and Anne Kent Rush: *Feminism as Therapy*, Random House/Bookworks, 1974.

Del Martin and Phyllis Lyon: *Lesbian Women*, Bantam, 1972.

Isabel Miller: *Patience and Sarah*, McGraw-Hill, 1969.

Kate Millet: *The Prostitution Papers*, Avon, 1973.

Flying, Knopf, 1974.

Jan Morris: *Conundrum*, Harcourt, Brace, Jovanovich, 1974.

Yoko Ono: *Grapefruit*, Simon and Schuster, 1964.

Karen Peterson and J. J. Wilson: *Women Artists Through Ten Centuries, Recognition and Reappraisal*, Harper and Row, 1975.

Anne Kent Rush: *Getting Clear*, Random House/Bookworks, 1973.

Vita Sackville-West and Harold Nicolson: *Portrait of a Marriage*, Atheneum, 1973.

Gertrude Stein: *Qued*, Liveright, 1950.

Virginia Woolf: A Biography, by Quentin Bell, Harcourt, Brace, Jovanovich, 1972.

The horse is a symbol
of female independence;
of our physical relationship
to the world,
"the mother within us"
intuitive wisdom
and our magic.

It is a symbol of the cyclic movement of the world of phenomena and pertains to the unconscious.

Horse symbolism in the form of pairs of horses represents
death and rebirth.

550